To Want to Learn

To Want to Learn:
Insights and Provocations for Engaged Learning

Jackson Kytle

First published 2004 by
PALGRAVE MACMILLAN™
175 Fifth Avenue, New York, N.Y. 10010 and
Houndmills, Basingstoke, Hampshire, England RG21 6XS.
Companies and representatives throughout the world.

PALGRAVE MACMILLAN is the global academic imprint of the Palgrave
Macmillan division of St. Martin's Press, LLC and of Palgrave Macmillan Ltd.
Macmillan® is a registered trademark in the United States, United Kingdom and
other countries. Palgrave is a registered trademark in the European Union and
other countries.

ISBN1–0439-6333–9 hardback

Library of Congress Catalog-In-Publication Data Available from the Library of
Congress

A catalogue record for this book is available from the British Library.

Design by Autobookcomp.

First edition: May 2004
10 9 8 7 6 5 4 3 2 1

Printed in the United States of America.

For Tari, Josi, and Ethan

Contents

Acknowledgements

I want to honor the contributions of colleagues without whom this project would have remained forever on the shelf of good ideas. Among those who inspired me while the project unfolded are: Professors Al Erdynast, Alan Guskin, Richard Hathaway, Jim Malarkey, Sherry Nicholson, Verbena Pastore, the late Ken Smith, and John Turner. Judith Block McLaughlin helped prepare me to be a college president and during a welcome sabbatical gave me a small office at the Harvard Graduate School of Education, where this work began. Dalton Oliver was generous in every conceivable way when I was with Vermont College, as has been my colleague Elizabeth Dickey at The New School. I have had wonderful teachers like Richard Christie, Paul Cubeta, Morton Deutsch, Fred Hutchins, Charles Kadushin, Stanley Schachter, and Leo Srole. Their influence on my thinking is on every page.

Some colleagues provided material support or read portions at different stages and contributed valuable suggestions: Professors Tom Abshire, Bill Hirst, Kathleen Kesson, Melvin Miller, Andy Schmookler, Roben Torosyan, and Eric Zencey, and President Richard Schneider of Norwich University. Allen Jones has helped me with my website. I am especially grateful to Arthur Chickering, my colleague for too brief a time at Vermont College, for his ideas and for his personal example as an engaged scholar. My assistant, Aimee Silverman, provided countless hours of proofing and research, and one day I know she will write her own book. So will my son, Ethan Kytle, who helped with several chapters. I thought of him often while framing my arguments to new teachers. In the book's earliest stage Brian Ellerbeck was the very model of a developmental editor. My editor at Palgrave Macmillan, Amanda Johnson, provided generous support and advice. Jen Simington read the final manuscript carefully and every page benefited from her work. I am responsible for any problems that remain.

Prologue

And the faculty of voluntarily bringing back a wandering attention,
over and over again, is the very root of judgment, character, and will.
No one is compos sui if he have it not. An education which should
improve this faculty would be the education par excellence.

—*William James*[1]

Of all the problems in living we humans must confront, that of self-motivation is the most important and the least understood. We move toward goals we want, sometimes motivated to self-sacrifice by religious fervor or political purpose. We move away from threats and things we fear or dislike, sometimes for reasons that prove short sighted. Rapid, unpredictable changes in attention span and consciousness run us ragged all day long, but we adapt and learn to cope. We keep moving through the life-world with a peculiar momentum.

What motivates the countless small acts and endless changes of direction that mark each day of existence? What motivates people to heroic acts? Why do certain actions seem to involve us fully whereas others bring only boredom? How do we understand goals and purposes in motivated acts ranging from studying to pass a course to performing religious devotion to enacting savage terrorism? Most challenging of all is the nature of human consciousness when it comes to human choices and actions, large and small. Pulled this way and that by misunderstood forces, we are only rarely aware of our motives. How does motivation work? What does it mean for education? These immense questions are the subject of this book and I will use its opening pages to suggest the range of topics we will study, discuss why educators should study them, and preview important insights as they connect to my own life and career in education.

Motivation is an important academic topic in psychology and has been studied in interesting ways in side literatures like behavioral physiology and social philosophy. In addition, staying motivated is a topic that is intimate and personal to an extent unusual in social and philosophic studies. Staying motivated in the face of distraction and fatigue is a daily challenge for individuals who must make lives for themselves in a problematic world of ambiguous choice. Different types of purposes drive the organism toward rewards and away from threat. Setting aside instinctual motives, the mechanics of approach and avoidance are not automatic—rather, conscious, sustained effort is required to build, and rebuild, motivation every day. And motivation has rhythms not always understood. One may enjoy a string of motivated days that seem effortless, only to find it necessary, suddenly and inexplicably, to have to rebuild the whole effort.

Learning, another problem in living, is the book's second focus. Learning is the species' most important survival mechanism. If I am good at learning, it is possible for me to adapt to nearly any circumstance, however dire. If I do not know how to learn, or am unmotivated to do so, survival is compromised. At the very least, quality of life suffers because challenges at work and school are not well used in one important respect—I do not learn from my mistakes.

Good reasons exist to consider motivation and learning together, to put them in the same phrase, as in the book's title, To Want to Learn. Most higher-order learning is motivated learning. If a learner is unmotivated, learning is boring or painful, and inefficient on both counts. Authorities resort to extrinsic rewards and punishments like grades to motivate learning rather than look for intrinsic rewards experienced by learners, such as the joy of learning.

While we will think about motivation and learning in broad terms, two forms—psychological involvement and social engagement—will get special attention. The latter term, engagement, suffers from multiple definitions, from a commitment to marry, to a course of action or belief, to rules of engagement that regulate combat. Still, most definitions imply some form or degree of deep, personal commitment, which is rooted in the original French word, engagement, an intense commitment to a political or religious cause.[2]

A Continental definition of engagement connotes moral and political motives not captured by popular American conceptions of involvement or flow, terms that refer to one person's internal psychological state at a point in time. On the pages ahead we will learn that psychological involvement has many interesting facets, but I am more interested in social engagement as a learned character trait. If a human life is to mean anything, there must be a deeper concept of *civic* involvement to benefit others and society, not just to gratify personal needs. As existentialist philosopher Maxine Greene reminds us, the citizens of Oran in Albert Camus's existentialist novel *The Plague* do not know how to respond to the spreading threat.[3] Most try to escape into diversions whereas Camus's protagonist, Dr. Rieux, sees it as his duty to stay conscious of the epidemic, to do what he can to help.

For our purposes, psychological involvement is defined as a hypothetical state of motivation characterized by sustained, purposive attention and accompanied by elevated mood. Depending on the purposes chosen and the ethic they carry forward, transitory moments of psychological involvement can, in time, be integrated into complex life activities like building a family or a business, eventually forming a hypothetical character trait, social engagement. Psychological involvement refers to a temporary state whereas social engagement refers to a learned character trait that extends in time.[4] As a temporary psychological state, involvement does not happen often or easily. As a learned, psychological character trait, social engagement takes hard work, patience, and self-focusing developed over many years. Even then, daily maintenance is required to keep the life-project moving ahead.

Both involvement and engagement can be learned, which is the goal for educators. Learning settings can be built to cultivate both attributes, and later I suggest ten considerations for creating engaging schools. In fact, among the most important outcomes of an education are the management of one's psychological involvement and social engagement. For most people, self-motivation is not easy. The harder project, by far, is to cultivate social engagement as a personality trait, a durable disposition extended in time and applied to different behavioral settings, ultimately leading to a life-project of achievement, contributions to community and society, and a high quality of life.

Involvement can be defined in opposition to what it is not: It is neither boredom nor an aimless roaming from one activity to the next. Being purposive, it is different from the half-conscious drifting that marks the times when we humans move in and out of a day's activities with no special intensity or satisfaction. By way of contrast, social engagement is closer to what Maxine Greene asks of us: to be awake in the world.[5] The state of intense focus, in its purest form, is not frequent, even though a person can learn how to produce learning settings that give rise to it. In an engaged life, many daily activities, but not all, will require intense concentration and be experienced as productive, pleasant moments.

I write for educators, broadly defined, who are responsible for learning settings, just as broadly defined. The term "educator" will cover many roles in education and the human services, including teachers in secondary and higher education, school and guidance counselors, as well as academic administrators. While my examples come from higher education, where I work, the best ideas should be useful for secondary education as well as the fast-developing fields of corporate education and adult education. We need not stop here because, after all, everyone is, or will be, an educator sometime in life, whether as parent, supervisor, coach, or community volunteer. Similarly, the terms "school" and "college" are used in the general sense of organized places and times for learning. I do not have in mind a student of a particular age or type of education; rather, I am trying to address any intentional, organized program for learning and assess how well that setting is organized to increase motivation and the possibility of learning.

Good reasons exist to think broadly about many types of educators and diverse learning settings as well as how both role and setting are changing. The frames by which educators understand education in all its many forms and venues—our mental models—are changing, as if we find ourselves in an old house whose rooms have functions we no longer quite recognize. After all, learning is increasingly spread across a lifetime and not confined, as it was once, to formal instruction early in life at high school and, for the lucky few, college. The old constraints of time, place, access, and modality by which one became a learned person and good citizen no longer hold, and the vocabulary is changing. What we mean by old words like "student," "teacher," "classroom," and "lab" have been challenged by advances in experiential education and new communications technology such as the Internet. At the same time, schools and colleges will continue as centers of focused learning, at least at certain points in life.[6] In that regard, the terms "learning community," "school," and "college" are used interchangeably to suggest that the motivation principles we seek apply to freestanding educational institutions and decentralized units inside large institutions.

I want the book to be useful to idealistic educators of every stripe working to create better learning settings, whether developing new schools and colleges or new programs to involve students within existing schools. Because the text goes well beyond enumerating motivational techniques—sources give that help—it offers educators a rich context for their own professional development as public intellectuals who have a responsibility outside college, school, and the workplace.[7]

Most of all, I hope students beginning long careers find useful ideas. In truth, I have written a book I could have used earlier in life. I hope its puzzles and dilemmas, insights and provocations, prepare better educators. As I say this, I want to introduce another theme, the need to think about the terms we use to understand education as we use them. As asked of teachers and counselors, let's expand the notion of learner, setting higher goals than graduating from school or earning a high GPA. That is, my book is written to students who, by earning a degree, are working to improve their lives, whether they would phrase it that way or not. Adults taking a course at night are closer than young people to the sense of personal transformation buried in that neutered word, "education." They say they want "to get a better job," or, being lonely, "to find new friends." Both statements express the unconscious motive of life change—to become a better person, to have a better life.

About education, I am a hopeless romantic. Critiques of education by the likes of John Dewey, Maxine Greene, Theodore Sizer, Henry Giroux, Deborah Meier, Matthias Finger, and Edmund O'Sullivan are well known, and in the pages ahead we will have opportunities to listen to their ideas. It may not help to ask more of a social institution so beleaguered. To raise the stakes feels like piling on. Still, let us ask how well the modern academy, second in importance only to the family as a character-forming institution, promotes optimal development of the whole person. Now we have a challenge!

Finally, I hope my book will appeal to public intellectuals, school board members, and parents involved in educational reform. When I speak in public about living an engaged life, the idea has broad appeal with adult audiences. Self-motivation, one's effectiveness as a lifelong learner and teacher, and quality of psychological experience—all become fascinating topics that are hardly academic.

So I will ask my readers to think about many theories and perspectives from several disciplines and intellectual traditions not always coordinated: psychological, physiological, and philosophic. While the language is as free of jargon as I can manage, challenging topics are ahead. I hope the best parts inspire personal and professional development. Reading the book should help educators become aware of their own motives and psychological processes, helping them search for learning and work situations that are satisfying. In a few places, I build new theory and invite readers to take the best ideas and use them. Teachers and counselors need better practice and better theory, two things that are not as separate as they might appear.

Uncertainty is a defining characteristic of modernity, and this holds true for economic predictions as well as our ways of knowing. Knowledge—how it is created, and its truth validity—is falsified in so many ways. Theory is not built with the same organization with which it is published, which will not surprise an active scholar or artist. The creative process is no different from the way Mary Catherine Bateson argues that character, like the pastry baklava, is built over a period of time by "folding-in" many pieces and disparate ideas.[8] The path is not straight but iterative.

The content of this book, for instance, is not an accurate representation of the meandering process that produced it. I want my readers to have this idea in mind from the beginning and to understand why learning process is so important for progressive educators. Not just an epistemological footnote, we educators introduce students to the creative process, broadly defined. We might help them understand one thing at least: The final products of any period of thinking in human civilization do not reflect the creative process so important to research and art.

Academic texts in psychology and philosophy are needlessly intimidating because only the polished final product shows. As students confront a new field of study, they may feel like they have wandered into a European garden of imposing marble statues, but they lack any sense of how the figures were produced. So well I remember reading in graduate school the high theory and experiments of social psychology, which felt alien. I thought, "Why does anyone write this stuff when so many important needs exist in the world?" Flesh-and-blood human beings, the carvers, are invisible. The elegance of the finished carvings misleads the learner as to the years they took to make, all the questions and blind alleys, not to mention the personal struggle, intruding egotism, and bouts of lost confidence. The final product, a journal article packed with abstractions, is just that—a highly distilled, final representation of a far more interesting process. Hidden is the wandering, idiosyncratic process by which a researcher works through intellectual puzzles not new to human affairs.

Making a life for oneself is not just an academic question. In a way, topics like motivation and learning require us to put aside the scholar's mask, which hides a human being. My work is both public and personal, and each effort informs the other. Although rarely obvious, a book, like all creative projects, carries forward a subtext about the author's life, especially that life's unresolved questions and recurring puzzles. Readers are forced to be archaeologists who search the found structure in their hands—this book— for clues about the writer, looking for touches of humanity with which to identify. But earnest readers are soon frustrated because the personal narrative is hidden by academic convention, especially those of the neopositivist, social sciences that struggle with murky boundaries among objective fact, formal theory, and personal experience.

Why is the personal voice so suspect in modern intellectual discourse, at least in the social sciences? Like the marking on a college term paper, the "I" is crossed out in scholarly discourse, which reduces the validity and reach of many arguments. Yes, early student writing has an excessive focus on self— and that passionate voice needs tempering. But education has gone too far by banishing the personal voice, which then must struggle to find itself. Indeed, as powerful as disciplinary inquiry can be, one symptom of the tyranny of scientific reductionism in intellectual circles is the loss of the personal. With regard to doing research and writing a book, an informed subjectivity seems preferable to the impossible goal of an impersonal objectivity.

Think about this example, a seminar I gave at the Harvard Graduate School of Education. As the course unfolded, I found myself comparing that seminar to my class given the year before at Goddard College, a much different academic culture. For the Harvard group, I asked for a final paper that integrated concepts from the course—on college leadership—with the student's personal and professional lives (a Goddard-style paper). As for formal scholarship, the papers were superior. No worries, here, about proofing and quality of writing! To a fault, these were polished students whose personal voices were unsteady, thin. Students felt uncomfortable writing about their experience, their hopes and fears. The papers read as academic exercises.

The topics they chose were careful and a bit lifeless. Perfect class exercises were submitted to earn a high grade and better GPA, but to find the real person behind the mask of good student was not easy. The best students learn to work the system but remain hidden as human beings. Letting themselves be treated as objects in school, they find it hard to become subjects outside school. The distancing they use to cope with school becomes a personal style of polite disengagement in society.

With topics like motivation and learning, especially, a personal voice is inevitable and quite necessary. I hope that personal examples and asides will not be a distraction but will connect readers to my argument. The point is not my life and how I have used it. Rather, I care most about the puzzles and dilemmas found when studying human motivation and learning, and my experience and reflections might help frame better questions.

My interest in motivation comes out of personal experiences as a student and a teacher in twenty years of higher education. To relate a few of them will suggest why the topic so motivates me. I certainly did not have my life sorted out for many years and do not now suggest that this "sorting out" is easy, or done to a particular schedule, or all that durable. None of this stuff about finding meaning in life comes easy. The knowledge needed from philosophy and psychology is challenging to acquire. The hectoring tone that finds its way into my text has been hard to control, and I do not know its sources. Perhaps the insistence for these topics I feel today is some mix of personal regret that I did not learn certain things earlier in life, the unrecognized importance of the topics for schools and society, and my attempts to use language to grab the reader's wandering attention.

Until I was thirty or so, I was an indifferent student caught up in popular culture. My focus in life gradually evolved by fits and starts much later than the authorities—parents, teachers, and coaches—wanted. A late bloomer, I could focus on projects outside school like building a hot rod, and it was not hard to apply myself to learning a sport. But school was more promise than performance. Career, involvement in the community, and personal relationships—all just rambled on without much steering by the driver. Usually busy, I was not committed to any sphere.

When as an educator I think about such moments, these bridges in life or forks in the road, I think we do not understand how they are approached, or the dynamics by which a person finds the courage to go in a new direction. In time, I put together the start of career, began to focus, and the pieces began to come together. But nearly thirty years later, I am aware—painfully and constantly—of how tenuous the progress is and struck by how much resolve it takes to keep the life-project moving ahead.

As a graduate student in social psychology at Columbia in 1968, I saw how the social protests of the day engaged students, giving a sense of power and purpose in life, if only for the moment. These powerful experiences stood in stark contrast to anonymous student life inside a large, urban institution. Classroom experience lacked immediacy and relevance. Like other lonely students trying to find their way inside a massive institution, I found it difficult to stay motivated, to respond to the demands made by teachers as a semester's grind unfolded. Not so outside Columbia's iron gates, where a community rent strike was intensely involving, or outside a lecture hall, where I could hear a student protest march forming on the corner of Amsterdam Avenue and 120th Street. While I learned advanced theory and methods at Columbia that I did not fully appreciate until later, only a few of my professors focused on anything other than the course's academic content. No attention was given to the process of learning in class, or to quality of advising, as if only academic theory mattered in a young man's education.

At Columbia I felt the seductive power of group identity when my partner and I became involved with an anarchist student group inspired by the Situationist movement.[9] We saw the group begin with innocent motives and evolve to make cultlike demands of its members, forcing my partner and I to decide to leave. From that experience as well as a class project a colleague and I did, an observational study of communes in New England, I became fascinated with small religious and political groups, an interest that continues to this day. I was intrigued by how intense groups make believers feel less self-conscious and uncomfortable as lone individuals in modern times. But as I discuss later, psychological peace inside a true-belief group has a price.

An indifferent student became a lifelong educator. Other career choices came open, but the endless idealism of education and helping other people kept me from following other paths. My struggle to become a serious student—to find my self, literally—and my emerging interest in motivation and learning led to work as a teacher, administrator, and trustee for colleges like Antioch, Goddard, Sterling, Vermont College, and to my current work for The New School in New York City. Without being aware of my motives at the time, I chose these schools because they offered more involved learning and democratic idealism than I had seen in my education at Middlebury College, a conventional place where the focus is academic content and discipline-based study. I was attracted to the ideas of co-op and experiential education at Antioch University and Sterling College, and to student-centered learning and holistic education at Goddard College and Vermont College.

We are addressing problems of living even though to frame it this way makes a social scientist uneasy. For a teacher, is there a more important topic, either personally or professionally? If we educators do not have this knowledge and cannot guide others to lifelong learning, who will do that work? Our questions are hardly new, but that does not reduce either their appeal or importance.

One caveat is necessary in an era when group identity has been made more important than species identity and those shared dilemmas that define the human condition. The advantages of my education, gender, ethnicity, and social class set the context for how I matured, to be sure. But everyone wakes up each day having to assert order, trying at the same time to understand what happened yesterday as they plan tomorrow. Canadian educator Edmund O'Sullivan frames the challenge:

> There is a day for every one of us in our existence where we become conscious and aware that we just *are*. We did not ask to be here, we did not choose to be here, we are just here. Some of us come into the world with the full use and potency of all of our senses, others do not. Some of us are born into affluence and plenty, others into poverty and want. We all come into existence with varieties of skin colour, different genders and different ethnicities.... For all of our variety and difference we share one thing in common. We are all recipients of the *gift of life*.[10]

Few easy paths through a school or life appear miraculously. Lives have to be built, plank by plank, floor by floor, and to underestimate the skills and the discipline required is easy. While objective conditions of poverty and prejudice reduce one's life chances, few people ever have the resources they need. While life chances are radically different if one wakes up to face a day in Sarajevo versus Scarsdale, human questions of direction and meaning in life are more alike than not, or so I want to believe.

Think again about learning as personal process, a familiar theme in progressive education. My quest to understand unresolved issues in my own life eventually led to a search for theory that explores attention and consciousness in learning, and the stages by which one may develop an engaged life. As the work intensified, readers gave advice and new leads. I kept reading and learned to appreciate enduring philosophical questions in a fresh, vivid way, quite unlike my experience with them when first encountered in college while preparing for an exam. The concepts had become my concepts, not abstract matters learned to please someone else, to pass a test, to earn a grade. As I wrote I was becoming an active learner.

Classic issues in social psychology, my academic discipline, resurfaced. I thought about the dynamic relationship between person and environment in new ways. I began using ideas from my reading project in lectures and group discussions, learning more and more from students and colleagues. Eventually, short papers were ready for conferences, which brought still more feedback from colleagues, leading to a book proposal, and so on in those iterative learning cycles of connection between adapting human beings and their evolving ideas.

As my reading project evolved, my thinking changed. I look differently at my own behavior and that of colleagues, friends, and students. For instance, if I thought of it at all, motivation seemed to be a binary construct, either all or none. What I understood about human attention and consciousness or awareness was, if anything, even less informed. Those mental models have changed and will change more as I complete the manuscript. Now I think in terms of gradients, interactions, and transitions among evanescent states of being that are so difficult to define. For example, the metaphor that now comes to mind when I think about human attention is this: Human beings are like sand sharks, moving endlessly through the water, one experience after the other, marked by dramatic shifts in purposefulness and concentration. Certain activities hold the fish's attention briefly, but it keeps moving. For human beings, our perpetually wandering minds seem drawn to events that are novel or complex. We tell jokes and play tricks to "get attention" (one's own and that of others) because humor plays directly to the imagination, as do spoken stories, great writing, the theater, and all forms of entertainment. Musicians use rubato, an unresolved chord, or a clever melody to get and hold listener attention. The restless mind, that sand shark, keeps roaming.

Now I think about reading in new ways. Consider how attention and motivation combine to affect learning when reading a book. An experienced writer learns to work within a narrow band of reader attention and knowledge. Push too hard, the reader is lost. Too little, the reader is bored. Offer up bad sentences, the content will matter little, and so on.

Not a day goes by that I do not think about some facet of motivation and learning even if the impression is as fleeting as an observation made of a street scene in Greenwich Village while walking to work. With rich topics like mine, my colleague Verbena Pastor would say, one falls in love. And the beloved is everywhere! While my personal experience is not the book's subject, wanting to understand motivation as well as improve my own life-project has motivated me, especially as the work reported here bogged down. I hope the cascade of ideas marched out for duty stimulates doubts and questions with which my readers will examine their experience, their emerging identity as educators, and the lives they are building for themselves out of the questions they, in turn, put before their minds.

Part I

To Want to Learn

[I]f teachers today are to initiate young people into an ethical existence, they themselves must attend more fully than they normally have to their own lives and its requirements; they have to break with the mechanical life, to overcome their own submergence in the habitual, even in what they conceive to be the virtuous, and ask the "why" with which learning and moral reasoning begin.

—Maxine Greene[1]

In modern society the voice of the individual seems reed thin, easily surrendered. Modernity brings fast pace and social change, all that noise and busyness noted by social critics. If one characteristic is defining, it is uncertainty—uncertainty about the future, uncertainty about one's proper role and prospects, and uncertainty about our ways of knowing the world and guiding actions in it. Demands are everywhere: An individual student or teacher making his or her way in life may be overwhelmed by all the institutions and their surrounding imperatives. Friendships, small groups, and the bureaucracies in which we work and live present their insistent demands and occasional support, which are often hard to tell apart.

Why should we care about the individual voice? A distinctive attribute of human beings is our capacity as meaning makers, and this book is written to students, teachers, counselors, and administrators who are making meaning of personal experience inside American schools and colleges. I start with individual existence to introduce the academic study of motivation and learning and will return often to the perspective of flesh-and-blood beings. Listen to the views on education and pedagogy in two recent conversations I had with educators at quite different points in their careers. The first was with a young colleague who is finishing his doctorate at a large public university and just beginning teaching. Responding to an offhand comment I had made about Fordist education and large classes, my junior colleague said many of his students like the anonymity of large lectures because they can hide. By saying "Fordist," I was thinking of all the ways that contemporary education is organized as a production system, producing commodities more than developing whole people.

Unmotivated for debate in class and unwilling to finish homework, the calculating students in his 120-person lecture class ask what they need to do to get a "B." Some are not embarrassed to argue over a "plus" or "minus" but are unmoved or unprepared to argue about theory or a particular lecture. Not many express intrinsic interest in the subject, American literature, a problem that my colleague blames on poor motivation. With some resentment, he and his fellow graduate teaching assistants think *they* carry most of the load—students do not do the reading for class, cannot write, and are mostly interested getting through academics so they can concentrate on the weekend's lively social calendar.

I asked whether he holds the university's traditional curriculum or earlier experiences in school responsible for unmotivated learners. If pressed, our young scholar concedes problems with high school education and, before that, family culture. But the animus is directed at students: "No," he said, "It's *their* fault. They're not serious!" Such a feeling, sliding toward cynicism, among teachers is not unusual. But it is sad to see it start so early because idealism about learning and human development—in a word, hope—is so important to becoming a good teacher.

A week later, it happens, I had another conversation with an experienced teacher at The New School who returned to teaching after a long career in academic administration. Talking about her freshman course on Jane Austen, my senior colleague worried aloud whether today's students ever read an entire book. She was excited about teaching; her students were charming, wrote well enough, and liked the debate in the small seminars that Lang College featured. While more image literate than older generations, even the best students skimmed to find the plot line, attending only to passages about which they might be asked or tested. I asked whether her students were using the library and she said, "I don't think so. They go to the web."

Today's students are good shoppers, a skill learned early. American students approach reading as smart consumers, reading "just enough, just in time" to let them balance homework against other activities, notably part-time work and parties. My colleague's students cut and paste what they need, she thinks, from convenient coursepacks and the web, seldom using the library for either its print or digital resources. Her faculty colleagues do not use the library as much as they once did except for personal research, if they are still doing research. Only the most conscientious teachers take students to a library orientation or integrate literary and research skills into the syllabus.

Rather than fault the unmotivated student or disappointed professor, continuing the cynical discourse of production teaching, we might challenge contemporary assumptions and mental models about learning and challenge the way we organize learning communities. Speaking to educators in our opening quotation, Maxine Greene asks the individual teacher to examine his or her own existence, to break with that life's mechanical momentum, to ask "why."

Taking a holistic approach to studying motivation and learning allows us to combine theory, self-reflection, philosophy, teaching, and stance in living. To pull these themes apart, or to force the conventional separation between academic theory and lived experience, would require several books, one per discipline. Rather, let's think "in between" the disciplines, so to speak, and take chances advancing a holistic argument. Theory development, personal change, and the transformation of social institutions like colleges and schools can and should be complementary even if they necessarily slow the conversation because so many layers are involved.[2]

So, our approach tries to be holistic and interdisciplinary, and I put this provisionally because both research goals are ideals where one can never be certain if a critical facet or two have been neglected. The next section describes the multiple perspectives around which the book is organized. My purpose is to expand the landscape for analysis, not reduce ambiguity by addressing a handful of specific problems within one discipline, its questions, methods, and one-dimensional reforms. A holistic approach requires two things: first, that we expand the perspectives via an interdisciplinary analysis, and second, that we improve expectations of what to ask from an education and a whole life. In chapter 1 we do this by thinking about the remarkable life of a Canadian pianist, the late Glenn Gould.

The terms "theory" and "perspective," used interchangeably, refer to a set of assumptions and a small number of loosely coordinated concepts that are useful in studying certain problems. Distrusting answers, philosophers say, "Make better questions!" This book, like most creative projects, has evolved by fits and starts, and certain questions in human affairs, such as, "To what extent can people control their actions?" have returned time and again. I think of these questions as enduring puzzles, unanswerable *koan,* that act as if they have lives of their own, moving in and out of consciousness and the text as I think about a part of an argument. Yes, that sounds dreamy and metaphysical, but it happens that way in one mind. Sometimes I think of them as having a physical presence with working parts, perhaps wooden toys to be looked at this way and that, or Japanese transformer toys to be manipulated endlessly.

After all, we are poking into problems of living that many scholars would find too unfocused to study. If studied, it is in academe's fringe literatures, namely, humanistic psychology, religious studies, progressive education, critical theory. Our intellectual puzzles operate at two levels: academic and general, directed at understanding society and human culture, and personal and particular, because each topic leads me to think about my actions and welfare. Some of these puzzles are:

> To what extent is human behavior determined by external situational factors or by internal dispositions? *Am I in control of my actions? How would I know?*

> What responsibility do individuals have for groups and the communities in which they live, work, and play? *What responsibility do I have for other people I encounter? Does it make a difference in deciding whether to act if I don't know them?*

> How do human beings function in relationships and social groups? *What is my role inside the groups in which I live, work, and play? How do I feel in groups?*

When do I act as a leader, when as a follower? Can I exist for long outside relationships and groups?

Why are moral standards important in human actions? *Do I know the* right *thing to do and when to act? Am I living an authentic life, being true to my principles? What* are *my principles and for which would I risk all?*

Is the possibility of a full, authentic life improved by thinking clearly and deeply about human existence and using better mental models? *Does my thinking about my experience make me more effective? Happier?*

What *is* human happiness? *Am I happy? Why am I mostly unhappy? Is that how other people feel? Should I do something different with my life?*

Ours is an idealistic project because the major constraints faced by contemporary American schools like scarce resources and tired pedagogy will not soon change. And that is a pragmatic, not fatalistic, assessment. At different stages in life, we all inhabit the roles of student, teacher, and counselor; but it is not realistic to expect radical change in education merely through changing these roles inside real institutions that resist change. Make no mistake, neither students nor teachers play powerful roles inside most schools. Somehow, educators have to survive, today, as lone individuals enacting our roles in the bureaucracy. Teachers and counselors may not control the levers of power, but we can think more creatively and fully about the whole enterprise. Thinking is one of few expandable resources over which teachers and counselors have control.

So, I want to orient the reader to perspectives that inform the whole, a whole formed of questions that have fascinated psychologists, educators, and philosophers for thousands of years. The inquiry is holistic, interdisciplinary, philosophical, phenomenological, and progressive, descriptors that I hope, by this book's end, will be clear to the reader, who will then take this form of inquiry to other topics.

Chapter 1

Educator as Idealist

I have one life and one chance to make it count for something. I'm free to choose what that something is, and the something I've chosen is my faith. Now my faith goes beyond theology and religion and requires considerable work and effort. My faith demands—this is not optional—my faith demands that I do whatever I can, wherever I can, whenever I can, for as long as I can, with whatever I have, to try to make a difference.

—*President Jimmy Carter*[1]

Of all the things demanded of us, we educators first must be idealists and optimists, packed with high purposes and full of hope for change. Higher education is where I have worked and is the source of many examples, but the general principles extend to other sectors. An education should, of course, do much more than just prepare one for a starting job, or a particular career. What counts most are the values one begins to live by as well as a certain striving to become a better person. That is the hardest work and the least explored by educators planning their courses, much less a school curriculum.[2]

Motivation is more than a technical intervention by an educator to encourage the student-as-object to do this or that thing better, and that theme will be repeated throughout this book. Methods have their place, but motivation for learning is best energized by passionate criticism of modern society, especially the fate of the individual in society, and by criticism of one's own aspirations and contribution to a better world. No contemporary educator should want to prescribe a set of political values, or a particular ethical system like Christianity or Buddhism. Yet, today's eclectic university curriculum driven by a requirement grid can leave students inarticulate about values and insecure in their criticisms of either themselves or society. One fears they graduate with a patina of enlightenment and the best of intentions but little churning to make a better world. The judgments I make can and should be challenged, but to step around a difficult terrain is almost always a mistake for an educator.

The Life-Project

Holism extends to how we understand and evaluate human existence. To ask about a whole life may sound odd, even faintly archaic, in a modern era that prefers reductionist terms like "a behavior" and psychological constructs like "self-esteem." But think about the whole of the life-project as we are constructing it, not just its segmented parts. Think of an entire life spanning eighty-five years, a life filled with hundreds of friends, different lovers, six schools, four careers with fifteen different jobs, and countless moments of heartache and achievement. Was this a whole life lived well?

Motivation is the engine for direction, persistence, and quality in the life-project. To suggest the type of choices in life people make, consider the life of a classical pianist, the late Glenn Gould, who went to uncommon lengths with regard to how he used his life.[3] As we think about the choices he made, let us reflect on the questions to which this book is directed: What is the best use of a life? To what purposes or beliefs do we commit? How do we sustain commitment in a busy, modern world full of distractions and ambiguous choices?

Gould was best known for his precise, elegant interpretations of Bach and Beethoven. But it is not his beautiful music that concerns us. Gould was also known for the eccentric lengths to which he went as an artist to prepare for a performance (playing from a shortened stool so that he could watch his hands on the keys, and soaking his hands in warm water before a concert). Gould gave great importance to achieving focused attention in his concerts and recordings, perhaps to the point of obsession, at least as judged by the rest of us whose drive for perfection in work and living is less intense.

The radical methods he chose for focusing attention did not stop with minor pre-performance rituals, which many artists and athletes adopt to focus the mind. In 1964, when he was at the peak of his performing career, Gould changed his work and living routine. He stopped his public performances, retiring to an apartment in Toronto. He worked at night, sleeping during the day. He sought total control over his performance, which was only possible, he believed, in the recording studio he had installed. Except for phone calls to friends, which he enjoyed, Gould chose to limit modernity's distractions, its endless busyness, what might be called the terror of daily living. Terror may be too strong a word, but to the committed artist, anything that distracts from a day's few creative moments—fleeting moments quickly lost—is to be feared.

Few people go to such lengths, of course, to be creative or productive. But everyone faces Gould's challenge: How can one focus a life and use it fully in a world of endless distraction? As remarkable as Gould's creative life was, especially the sharp focus he worked so hard to find, we might ask about the quality of his social contributions. Although fully involved in his music, Gould was not as involved with social and political issues as were, for example, activists like Dorothy Day, Mohandas Gandhi, or Martin Luther King, Jr., not to mention the many thousands of unknown soldiers in every social movement. While Gould was interested in animal welfare and the preservation of rural Canadian life, his engagement with social issues was secondary.

How does one weigh the value of these different life-projects, each one quite intense and disciplined? Not easily, and I am uncomfortable drawing sharp distinctions that would say that Gould's beautiful music is more or less important than King's self-sacrificing struggle on behalf of African Americans, in particular, and humanity, in general. Fine distinctions about the quality of the life-project are not possible. That is, while we want to ask about the quality of contributions to social advancement, to argue which contribution in what area of human creativity is better is not productive. Pluralistic, democratic society needs engaged artists and activists of all types, the more the better.

Artists face a special challenge because they do not enjoy the comfort structure, so to speak, of an office and its daily routine. They lack clear signposts of a career to assure themselves of progress. The insecurity and daily need for self-motivation are more difficult emotionally than what results from working inside an institution that has codified norms, procedures, and roles. Every day, the artist and those of us who work alone must build a temporary structure to live in.[4]

Contemporary existentialist philosopher and educator Maxine Greene, whose ideas anchor the next chapter and have so inspired my career, worries about giving into the routine, a repugnant word in her thinking. She warns about letting ourselves move half awake through a gray, humdrum existence and demands of us acts of imagination by which to challenge hidden assumptions. The hope is to break free of lives of habit and automatisms even though such imaginative acts contribute to unease.

To break the routine, Greene insists we ask: "Why?" But existential choices need not be as dramatic as her evocative language suggests. For most people, an engaged life is built of small acts of courage, as one of my students once put it. While people try to be self-reflective, what results is unfocused worrying. We enjoy personal hobbies and pursuits as creative pastimes even as there are occasional regrets about missed opportunities. Not so for Mr. Gould, who feared modernity's seductions, which he felt pulled an artist from his art.

An engaged life requires a dialectical tension between what *is* and what *ought* to be, between what one finds in life and what one *hopes* to find. This introduces a far more serious philosophical perspective than we discuss here. For the moment, it is enough to suggest that a degree of felt alienation in modernity is inevitable, even desirable, because the tension motivates acts to change things for the better, both for self and society. For most people, the subjective life-world is made of unending struggle, and a lonely one at that.[5]

The ideal engaged life *is* a social life, requiring commitment to a better world. Observers of different generations make this point. John Dewey argued that human development and learning must be defined within a social community, hopefully, a democratic community.[6] Writing about the civic mission of schools and colleges, contemporary political theorist Benjamin Barber sums it up:

> Learning communities, like all free communities, function only when their members conceive of themselves as empowered to participate fully in the

common activities that defined the community—in this case, learning and the pursuit of knowledge in the name of common living. Learning entails communication, communication is a function of community. The equation is simple enough: no community, no communication; no communication, no learning; no learning, no education; no education, no citizens; no citizens, no freedom; no freedom—then no culture, no democracy, no schools, no civilization.[7]

As individual beings we are accountable to one another for wasting a human life, our own or that of another person. The standard should be high; one should strive to construct a well-used life in service to others, not a thin project focused on personal needs, or a life lived for its possessions, which Paul Wachtel warned about in the *The Poverty of Affluence*.[8] An engaged life demands of us that we reject, or temper, a selfish stance of civic privatism, Jurgen Habermas's term for the retreat from civic life into possessions, family, and career.[9]

Consider the act of writing as it carries both individualist and social dimensions. Writing, especially creative writing, is usually depicted as a lonely, quite personal, activity. While true on one level, an individualist focus hides social exchanges so deeply a part of creative work. More often than we understand, creative work is an implicit, unconscious *group* project in which one person becomes the vehicle for advancing collective ideas. And the human group, as an intended audience, is involved in another way. Effective writers learn, after all, to use words and sentences to capture and hold the reader's attention, and do not allow the reader to be too comfortable or to anticipate too easily what is coming next.

Writers assume an audience and write to it. A writer, like most artists, does not tell the story in predictable fashion because the reader will soon anticipate what is coming next and lose interest. So, we have a band of learner attention within which writers learn to work in and around. If a writer does not understand his or her audience, the text may not be engaging in the first place, either too obscure or too banal. But if the story does not project authenticity and truth, or if it is rendered mechanically, reader attention is lost in other ways. So, good writers like good teachers are social communicators who aim to stay within narrow bands of attention and authenticity.[10]

For those whose basic needs are met, the ideal standard for a life-project looks to the degree of psychological differentiation developed, the purposes to which one's life is dedicated, and the personal sacrifices made for those purposes. The highest standard is neither survival nor getting by in the world, even though these are reasonable goals, given the life circumstances of many people, even in advanced, industrial countries. Human beings are, in their very nature, social creatures; and even though each exists alone with an insecure consciousness, that lonely burden is borne by an extended social community, beginning with the family and projected through countless social circles over a lifetime. Although we may *feel* alone, other people helped us mature in the past, help us cope with today's problems, and help us plan a better future. Given the certainty of physical decline and death, the date of which we do not know, we have an obligation to make the life-project intentional.

How does the life-project evolve? What are its building blocks? Psychologists have used different concepts to refer to the unconscious, loosely constructed models of cause and effect that people create to understand the world and act in it.[11] For the moment, think of a mental model as consisting of a set of assumptions about human nature and society (say, people are lazy and need strict controls on personal behavior) loosely connected to a few propositions about cause and effect in the life-world (if as a teacher I don't set strict limits in class, students will not learn).[12] The elements that form the pattern are neither explicit in one's thinking nor carefully formulated, although this may change when we begin to reflect on them. As human beings mature and strive to understand all the information in endlessly changing environments, we develop *mental models* of cause and effect that vary in terms of validity, articulation, integration among different facets, depth, and, most importantly, our awareness of them.[13] Mental models are elaborated upon, gradually and sometimes painfully, as individuals mature.

Mental models direct attention to certain facets of the information field rather than others. They carry rough attributions about cause and effect, usually too simple because most people do not routinely question the naïve realism by which they perceive the world, thinking that perception equals reality. Stereotypes about the poor or another race, packed with bad assumptions embedded in faulty logic, are commonplace.

Similarly, humans develop so-called naive theories of personality to explain interpersonal relations, naive theories of society to explain inter-group relations, and so on. Inchoate mental models combine to form a common-sense psychology, Fritz Heider argues, that people use to understand their subjective environment, to move about in the life-world, and to manage interpersonal relations. That psychology's assumptions and naive theories are not in awareness except if the situation asks the person to explain what he or she is doing, or to predict some event.

People gradually develop concepts about the life-world from experience with the family, other people, and different societal roles like being a student. With regard to formal education, a life activity for perhaps twenty years, educational psychologists Scott Paris and Richard Newman extend Heider's reasoning, asking about the *student theory of learning* that develops. As students learn about school, they construct implicit models of their skills and expectations for success and for the proper behavior asked of them in the classroom. They also come to school as children with learning experiences, good and bad, from home and community that set the frame for what happens at school. In time, some self-perceptions become enduring, as in "I am not a good math student," which may stimulate a self-fulfilling prophecy, iterations of low expectations resulting in low performance. Some assumptions of the "theory" are tested, others not. If students learn that the "good student" is passive in class, or compliant with school authorities, such a mental model will not serve them well later in constructing an engaged life.

Similarly, teachers, seen as the most experienced students in the human group, evolve a *teacher theory of learning*.[14] To stretch the notion, the "theory" will have modules about personality and social structure and will acknowledge, as we have, neurobiological mechanisms undergirding attention, mood, and motivation.

Mental models are not formal theory, but they can be elaborated and refined in that direction. Formal theory can begin in personal subjective experience and the crude contingencies we use to explain events and relationships. In that way, creating theory is not just the work of academics and intellectuals, says educator Frank Smith, but a formal extension of ordinary thinking.[15] To a degree, anyone who is alive is a practical theorist because "theories," with varying degrees of completeness and validity, are used everyday to manage life and guide behavior.[16] Finally, Theodore Marchese observes that these unconscious models are slow to change, which is important for educators to anticipate.[17]

Influenced by family and teachers, a directional element gradually enters these understandings in the form of ideas about self-development, which are partly integrated with one's emergent self-understanding. These early life plans lead people to make certain choices and to avoid others. People begin to work on improving parts of themselves, based on their understanding, if incomplete, of who they are and who they want to become. Even if first efforts are piecemeal, like trying to change a habit like nail-biting, the focus shifts from *being* to *becoming*, from who one *is* to an imagined person, a better person in comparison to ideals we have learned, a person we want to *become*.[18]

Human imagination performs a vital function by challenging inherited mental models and worldviews, thus opening up new vistas. A central aim of education, especially higher education, is to challenge traditional views of one's community of birth or social class. Students are asked to put distance between the received values and beliefs of their local communities in favor of a cosmopolitan and differentiated view. An essential part of developing an expanded worldview, in this regard, is learning to watch one's own mind at work, to be skeptical about its limitations and biases. Most recently, Maxine Greene called attention to the empty formalisms that give students a "view from Nowhere," arguing against the notion that one's thinking is not informed by other contexts such as gender, social class, and race.[19] Formal theories like those reviewed in the chapters ahead are, of course, considerably more refined than naïve theories of daily life, and there is no need to overwork Heider's idea. At the same time, I am asking educators to concern themselves explicitly with student and teacher theories of learning as they accompany, and hopefully help, the learning process. At the very least, society expects this of an educated person.

If we understand motivation and learning dynamics in ourselves, and as intellectual topics that we might teach, we are better prepared to help others address "first questions" in life. First questions are identified in three ways— first of all, they are fundamental questions about direction, values, and meaning in a life, and as such are the most important questions one can ask of oneself. Second, they are the first questions to be put to others and to the community institutions we create, serve, and want to improve. As teachers and counselors, we are supposed to be experts at motivated learning, quite apart from our academic disciplines. Third, they are first questions because, whether we face them or not, we wake up with them every day.

Beneath the surface of daily life, a silent stream of rumination runs in consciousness. If there were a way to eavesdrop on the world's internal monologues—billions of them in every language and culture—we would hear a internal refrain of ontological first questions: "Who am I?" "Where am I going?" "Will I get there?" "Is it worth the struggle?" "Why am I doing this?" And the refrain repeats. We would hear intensely personal questions people ask of themselves about life and purpose, crushing failures, and triumph over frustration, first questions that accompany busy lives, most of which are short and difficult. These silent, personal ruminations that accompany us through the life-world are closed loops of worrying about means and ends by which we think about our subjective experience of everyday life and all its changes, ups and downs. But worrying is not effective as a means to help solve conflicts from work and family life. While a certain degree of aimless consideration of a problem provides opportunity for insight, or may lead to the resolve to make a change, more often it is unproductive.

Becoming a Better Thinker, a Better Teacher

By this provocative title I mean to convey the spirit of Greene's injunction when she asks teachers to "break with the mechanical life, to overcome their own submergence in the habitual." She asks for daring acts of imagination.[20] Put simply, she asks teachers to *think* about what they are doing and to realize that thinking has several parts: to think about the craft as we learn and practice it, to construct motivating curricula, to build better theory about motivation and learning, and to think about our own lives and the mental models we construct. We move toward becoming a better person and a better teacher.

Teachers face inevitable compromises between what they know learners need and the real-life constraints of school as Fordist factory. They cannot adopt the easy Utopianism of critics like Ivan Illich, whose radical ideals do not account for real schools and the needs of people whose lives cannot wait for a social transformation.[21] Except for a few privileged schools, new and experienced teachers at all levels face demanding work. It should be otherwise, but funding will not soon be adequate to equip new science labs or reduce classes to manageable size. Idealistic prescriptions for progressive education are ludicrous if the concrete work conditions of teachers are not taken into account.

Most objective aspects of work are not under teacher control, except for the subjects to which one's attention and learning are directed. While external resources are limited, one critical resource controlled by teachers is expandable—understanding human motivation and learning. Unfortunately, the potential for learning and self-development does not translate into effective change within a school or college, as Seymour Sarason observes. Even if the teacher has a perfect analysis tied to an explicit agenda for reform, teachers are isolated inside the school culture, caught up with the demands of the bell and the school program as it is now organized. Not having a context for productive learning of their own, creating and sustaining a context for productive learning for students is problematic.[22]

Becoming a better thinker means paying at least some attention to building and evaluating formal theory. We turn now to the several ways that theory and theory building connect with becoming a teacher or counselor. I have already introduced the notion of student theories of learning in the context of the life-project and how it develops. The same idea applies to the role of teacher in the sense that mental models are formed and modified about learning, motivation, and, indeed, human nature. A faculty member's theory will have clusters of half-articulated assumptions about human development, group dynamics and learning, personality and social structure, curriculum and school design, and neurobiological mechanisms undergirding attention, mood, and motivation. Thinking of a teacher as a human group's most experienced learner, one hopes the theories will be more articulated and valid than those of students.

While it stretches the naïve theory conceit to argue that every teacher should construct an articulated model of motivation and learning, systematic reflection is reasonable to expect. After all, we teachers have to learn the craft as we go. Few natural teachers are born—most have to learn the art through experience and a meandering mix of theory and reflected practice. Developing teachers get much less supervision, for example, than psychotherapists learning their craft. After perfunctory student teaching, if one works in K-12, it is "sink or swim." To aid this learning, it makes sense to ask teachers to address their emerging theory of learning as they make themselves into Donald Schön's reflective practitioners.[23]

Most college teachers worry more about the *content* of what they teach, especially what matters in the discipline, than the *process* they use to motivate students and help them learn. There are exceptions, but many teachers act as if there are not significant, much less important, questions about pedagogy. They do not worry about pedagogy, either the effectiveness of traditional methods they inherited or their own teaching. Few, indeed, have an explicit theory of instruction that guides their own work. Their mental models for motivation and learning are implicit and inherited rather than explicit and examined. The mental models they carry are faculty centered. To appear to worry too much about the student experience in class or lab may seem soft because students are just assumed to be motivated, or not, and to learn, or not, what is laid out before them.

Apart from refining one's theory-in-practice, theory can be developed and learned. The possibility of better schools and improved learning in all human settings will follow from new and useful theory. Schools and colleges need new perspectives and lots of them. Imaginative theory building is the way to do this work, even if the resulting structure seems pallid compared to the phenomena one wants to describe or, better, change. Representations of the social psychological processes in a simple conversation, for example, will always seem insufficient because no abstraction ever captures a dynamic phenomenon, which is, strictly speaking, unknowable. Contemporary photographer Duane Michals expresses the postmodern stance: "To photograph reality is to photograph nothing." He adds, "I am a reflection photographing other reflections within a reflection."[24]

Whatever the problems, to build theory with which to work on seemingly intractable problems is a good thing. The word "theory" may, however, be off-putting to people who felt tortured with abstract theory in academic lectures. The word "theory" also has a poor connotation due, in part, to the American distrust of elites and intellectuals.[25] Theory sounds too hard, abstract, and difficult to master, like something one is tested for in school.

Notwithstanding American skepticism for theory and "that intellectual stuff," progressive teachers still reach for new perspectives by which to better understand motivation and learning. At the same time, I am more interested in reform and the practical application of theory than theory *qua* theory. All teachers will reject foolish ideas and use those that make sense. To integrate the public and the personal, or to mix the categories of theory and practice—both intentions express the essence of a holistic view of oneself in a fast-changing world.

If not theory, what do we have? The risk is mindless practice formed of habits rather than a reflective praxis that challenges conventional wisdom. Whatever the problems we face in building new theory, practical suggestions on increasing motivation in schools should come from theory and new philosophy, even if that theory is imperfect. The press of daily work inside a modern school makes it challenging for besieged practitioners to contemplate new initiatives or theory-guided change. Few teachers have the time or surplus energy; the pull is, if anything, toward incremental change—quick, inexpensive fixes to the existing production line.

Many educational bromides are not tied to a body of thought, and teachers without theory are vulnerable to fads. The cause of reform in education is not helped by one-dimensional ideas that come and go every year or two (ditto management theory). In fact, experienced secondary teachers grow numb to reform because of the relentless pace of partial solutions, one upon the other. Most reforms address only one facet of the deep problem, and the lack of a holistic vision for change dooms the intervention for a powerful reason: The dominant organizational culture of the school, embedded in a community culture, proves too strong. If not armed with theory with which to challenge and guide schools and colleges, educators are left alone with their personal experience, unexamined because of the press of Fordist work conditions in the modern academy. Awash in personal experience and hard work, leaning on personal, implicit biases that form the frame that carries that experience forward, teachers without theory are not in a position to lead. What can we change if we do not think differently about the entire intellectual superstructure of modern education into which we are thrown? Not very much, which partly explains the waves of school reform that teachers endure, imposed from above and outside the school.

The term "theory" as used in this book refers to a set of assumptions, concepts, and a few principles that will be used to examine a set of problems. Theory building is important in other ways. First, the discrepancy between espoused theories and theories-in-use is important in education and the human services, generally. Practitioners may assert they follow Theory A when a close study of what they are actually doing in the classroom is closer to Theory B. A contributing factor to this discrepancy is that, for many people, perhaps most, neither their espoused theory nor their theories-in-use are articulated. In the worst case, teachers are not conscious of what they are doing or why. They may be effective, but they are not likely to be able to say why, or to be able to pass their understanding and skills to students or other teachers.[26]

Secondly, theory building is important because the surfacing of implicit assumptions and refining mental models of motivation and learning are what teachers and counselors need most to improve practice. Not unlike daily life, personal practice is less examined than one might think—we just do it, going from one experience to the next like our ever-moving sand shark.

The aim of educational theory, given the complexity of the domain, is not to create precise tests of refined hypotheses. There are competing and complementary theories about human motivation and learning.[27] The goal is to create a framework of assumptions tied to a set of constructs used to address certain puzzles. We want to draw upon a theory's organizing and heuristic potentials, the extent to which the putative new perspective accounts for existing ideas and leads to new ones.

Teacher as Perspectivalist

For the problems we have in mind no single academic discipline offers sufficient insight. Philosopher Richard Rorty, borrowing from Nietzsche, describes the intellectual as a perspectivalist by which a time-bound and vocabulary-limited perspective is advanced, one that cannot know its own limits. Arguing against the possibility of knowing a pure object, Nietzsche said:

> There is only perspective seeing, only a perspective "knowing"; and the more affects we allow to speak about one thing, the more eyes, different eyes, we can

use to observe one thing, the more complete will our "concept" of this thing, our "objectivity," be.[28]

So, we will explore patterns among appearances rather than try to reach for a grand theory to capture a hidden reality.[29] To Rorty, a perspectivalist worries about assumptions and language, even risks appearing self-conscious. Adopting a self-critical view will, of course, slow the argument. Asides about epistemology and language are needed, but as-we-go reflection is an integral part of intellectual life. That is, competing and complementary perspectives are needed, many of them. To understand motivation, the perspectives reviewed are found in psychology, neurobiology, social philosophy, and existentialist philosophy, the latter two providing an ethical foundation.

Early in the research, I read social science perspectives on motivation and human potential. Psychological theories of peak experience, attention, and motivation put forth by David Bakan, Abraham Maslow, Mihaly Csikszentmihalyi, Ellen Langer, William Kahn, and Raymond Wlodkowski offer reasonable, if incomplete, views of the causes, correlatives, and consequences of involved attention. But it was soon apparent that motivation and human development cannot be studied as if only technical questions matter, or studied without consideration for ethics, especially the choice of purposes that guide behavior. Such topics are "how" questions, not "why" questions. To ask why such questions are worth studying, we turn to social thinkers as diverse as Friedrich Nietzsche, Maxine Greene, Charles Taylor, Edmund O'Sullivan, Jean-Paul Sartre, and Albert Camus. Psychological-technical insights, valuable as they are, must be set in a larger perspective, one that asks about truth, meaning, and justice, the deep dilemmas of the human condition.

The critical social and political theory movement, which began in the 1960s, raised much-needed critiques with regard to race, social class, and gender. But these relentless critiques also served, it seems, to reduce individual responsibility in the face of overpowering social determinisms and group identity, giving rise to a certain victim mentality. In contrast, existentialism focuses, first and foremost, on personal freedom and the absolute responsibility to construct an authentic existence, making conscious choices in a problematic world of poor alternatives. If this notion is plausible, it is time to revisit existentialist philosophy for what this perspective has to say about individual freedom and responsibility.

In an age where competing theories exist for every phenomenon, their number expanding every year, we must move quickly through difficult topics that have concerned generations of thinkers. It is tempting to simply name an age-old concern differently, thus to ignore earlier traditions or ideas. Several of the research programs reported later—namely, those on peak experience, flow, and mindfulness—do not always acknowledge earlier contributions. A false newness is created by such lapses—after all, the promise of "change" is seductive in consumerist society, with its billboard claims for "the new" and "the better." A new toothpaste, a new theory—

these become commodities to be marketed and consumed. Value is not assigned to the substance of the product, its heritage, or, in the case of theory, enduring, always messy, questions.

Becoming a Better Person, a Better Teacher

It is not easy to be a teacher. Once venerated in society, the role of teacher has become more demanding and less respected. And this troubling erosion is happening at a time when our fractured society depends, more than ever, on effective teachers, mentors, and counselors. Today's teaching work is less that of a respected craftsperson working with students known by name in learning settings of manageable size than that of a production manager moving batches of students through the factory with as much humanity as possible.

Such a description sounds exaggerated—one can recall examples where people have learned important things in the oddest places. Many small institutions create optimal learning settings where people know one another, and large institutions can create intentional, personal learning cultures within a smaller college or a department. But a long line of progressive educators, from John Dewey to Maxine Greene, Deborah Meier, Theodore Sizer, and Seymour Sarason all insist that students treated as individual, whole human beings will be better learners. Indeed, Sarason calls it the "big idea" to begin where the learner is, not where we *want* them to be.[30] To treat the learner as an individual human being, not a number, is nearly impossible inside the Fordist school that must contend with thousands of student objects.

Teaching and counseling, in the deepest sense, are moral activities. A teacher has the solemn responsibility, somehow, to become a model citizen, an exemplary, ethical intellectual who helps students construct their own adaptations to modernity. That is a high, almost impossible, standard. If not teachers, who will show the way? Maxine Greene asserts that the best teachers model a wide-awake stance in life, showing a deep interest in the world.[31] She applies to education social philosopher Alfred Schutz's conception of *wide-awakeness,* defined by him as "a plane of consciousness of highest tension originating in an attitude of full attention to life and its requirements."[32]

Greene's wide-awake teachers live as moral beings, not just teachers who deliver academic content. They ask "why" rather than accept the world as given. In turn, they ask their students to make awake, moral choices as they form an ethical existence of their own. In different terms, Parker Palmer makes the same point, asking about the soul of a teacher, "Who is the self that teaches?"[33] He calls for deep, authentic connections in teaching, not only to one's whole self, but to the subject matter and to one's students. Such rich connections are not simple in modern schools organized by a "structure of separations."[34]

The writer Virginia Woolf wrote about an ideal school in *Three Guineas,* and for her imagined school, Woolf sought good "livers."[35] In all these conceptions of the ideal, we ask teachers to integrate the public and the personal and to find a way to mix theory and practice. Please note that nothing has been said about writing a lesson plan, or how to lecture, by far the smaller, technical tasks. As Palmer has done, we ask about the qualities of teachers and counselors as *whole human beings and inspired citizens* after whom students want to model their own life-projects.

Having explored the idea of the life-project, let me change the focus to think broadly about the role of educator. In its purest sense, teaching is a calling, not a job, because a teacher works most closely with a student's spirit, its direction and vitality. Many teachers choose the profession because they were, themselves, enthusiastic learners and did well in school, almost from the start.

Others come to the profession, like I did, as students trying to find themselves. Like young psychologists who choose their profession, in part, to sort out personal problems, some teachers are curious about learning and motivation because they were not always good students. In the ideal case, teachers have an implicit, three-part agenda for change: They want to help students become motivated, they want to change schools so that more students are better engaged in learning, and, finally, they want to live more engaged lives themselves.

So, the choice of teaching as a profession is a way of working on one's own engagement with life—one's own life-project—while helping students find their projects, which is why this work is so ennobling. When one thinks about education, after all, we want to understand the dynamics of personal development and change more than the mastery of certain concepts and skills. In the best case, the learning process is mutually transforming and reciprocal. Indeed, one of the hidden rewards of teaching that sustains us is that we educators have such a high standard to emulate.

Even if individuals are not consciously trying to learn, the way educational settings are used is either educative or miseducative, in John Dewey's terms. If not learning in a progressive sense—that is, leading us to new experience, new reflection, and thus the possibility of new learning—individuals are unlearning already acquired skills, especially the complex skills of modern life. Physical skills like tennis and mental skills like chess or statistics erode quickly. Such skills take time to rebuild if one stays away from the game. Even if skills do not atrophy, time is wasted in which one could be learning something new rather than coasting on old skills.

John Dewey's progressive ideas about learning from experience figure prominently in the pages ahead, especially his powerful idea that the *process* of learning is more important to understand and master than on a body of academic *content,* a useful dichotomy. The focus in most schools and colleges seems to be on what is learned, the skills and knowledge to be acquired, rather than on the underlying thinking and feeling structures we want to transform. To contemporary philosopher Elizabeth Minnich, knowledge is necessarily transitive in modern society—it is the quality of thinking, feeling, and being that should concern us.[36]

We want to think in new ways about teaching and learning. Expert learners—teachers, mentors, trainers, counselors, and advisors—have a special role in society. All these roles have a common, if implicit, aim, namely, to help students manage the process of learning in addition to mastery of content. Effective teaching and mentoring require us to understand learning, attention and mood, and human motivation and its dynamics. If as teachers we understand these topics and ourselves as learners, we are prepared to help students become lifelong learners and engaged human beings.

Language Problems

We have a vocabulary problem. Abstract terms like "motivation," "learning," "attention," "mood," "involvement," and "consciousness" float by. The words "teacher," "student," "client," "learning," and "degree" sound stale, finding their way into every other sentence used by educators. As was said of Marxism, educators' words swarm like bats in a dark cave.[37]

A book written in postmodern culture, of course, must worry about language to the point of self-consciousness. An author's mind is all-too-aware of a world where no independent source, Richard Rorty reminds us, exists for truth claims.[38] In education and the human services, language problems abound. Not the smallest problem in education is the eduspeak used to describe learning and the school. Tired words point in the wrong direction, to the wrong solutions. The problem is not vagueness, which is understandable, but worse—the words have been reified to the point that dynamic processes like learning are made into mere things identified as the smallest, least important, part of the larger concept.

The burden as we learn the profession or pass it on is to challenge the categories handed to us as given, asking Maxine Greene's "why," doing so in the spirit of Hannah Arendt's injunction to "think without banisters."[39] Better mental models, consciously chosen models, are needed. Consider these questions:

> Why has that most essential human activity, learning, come to mean passing an exam or course *in* school when, in fact, most human learning occurs *outside* school in play, family, and work?

> Why does learning seem easier and more enthusiastic *outside* school and college?

> Why does learning appear to us to be a special human activity, mostly done in school when we are young, when learning is *inseparable* from every single moment in the life-world?

Why is cognitive mastery of conceptual material treated as the most important
form of human learning? Why are the emotions, the body and its sensations,
not thought important in school?

Perhaps we think that an *education,* writ large, only happens in approved,
teacher-supervised classrooms and labs. By this restricted mental model,
however, one underestimates the extended web of learning situations, the
entire landscape of human learning over a lifetime, whose power and reach
far exceeds time spent in formal settings.[40] By focusing on the present
moment and one learning setting, like a literature course, we underestimate
that learning, in truth, mixes past experience and future plans with present
experience in iterative dialectics. The obsessive focus on cognitive development in school is mistaken. Unrecognized is this pivotal notion: The highly
evolved brain-mind-body is *continuously* adapting to its environs, which
means it is continuously learning about that environment, even if most of
that learning is neither conscious nor cognitive.

These are not just games about words. Professional understandings—for
example, of what a teacher is—carry forward sedimented understandings
about power inequalities in human relationships and daily life.[41] Categories
that appear simple, like student and teacher, are not helpful, because they
carry forward implications that a "student" does not know enough to teach,
which is wrong, and that a "teacher" is not, first and foremost, a master
student and does not learn from students. Also implied is that teaching and
learning are easily separated activities, which they are not, if one uses a
dialectical logic that looks at process and change (in contrast to the facile
dualisms of formal logic like student or teacher, cognitive or emotional,
theory or practice). So, the categories we use to describe an essential human
activity like learning must be challenged while being used.

A final example may help. One of the most slippery terms in American
education is *progressive.* To John Dewey, "progressive" speaks to the
progressive use of experience in learning. But in American culture, "progressive" also refers to liberal or left *political* thinking, which has tended to
compromise progressive educational theory put into practice. While I share
those political values, which will be apparent when we discuss modernity
and Fordist production in higher education, it is prudent to separate
progressive education from progressivism as political ideology.

Another language problem exists. Human motivation is one of psychology's black boxes—we think we know some of the inputs and guess at the
outputs, but its inner workings are obscure. The most important parts, like
human attention, are hard to define. How different facets of personality
interact, for example, is not understood. Indeed, the difficulty of studying
motivation as a hypothetical construct has led a life-long observer of
education like Alexander Astin to focus on involving *behavior,* setting aside
internal states and the phenomenology of involved experience.[42] Astin is
right about the challenges, but we need to study states of consciousness in
daily life, ranging from boredom to partial involvement to the most intense
concentration. Most certainly, we need to understand *changes* in attention

and mood as they affect psychological involvement, and to ask how purposes that motivate people are selected and sustained.

In addition to having to use stale words to describe professional work, adequate terms cannot be found to convey evanescent psychological experience such as a peak experience in learning, much less the subtle shifts between boredom and partial involvement and between partial involvement and full. The study of human consciousness, in particular, is plagued by the vocabulary problem, the near impossibility of finding words to describe mental states that are intersubjectively valid. Words fail us when the subject is internal psychological experience—thin words and clever sentences used after the lived experience, with some desperation if one is a writer, never convey the depth and subtle quality of lived experience. The immediacy, perceived authenticity, and uniqueness of personal experience are lost to the page.

But scholarly caution does not mean that inquiry need remain only with observed behavior, as Astin says, by far the easier level of analysis. Human motivation can be studied via the careful use of introspection. In this regard, I use a phenomenological approach to explore different psychological states of involvement, hoping that my reflection on personal experience will encourage my readers to reflect on *their* experience in learning.[43]

Having argued the case for a holistic view of human development, one defined by high standards for the life-project, now I want to explore the social expectations of the role of teacher, the way that role is changing, and the rewards and frustrations that follow. To be a teacher, mentor, or counselor brings many pressures. Teaching is also a lifelong profession, and to sustain personal motivation over a long career will be difficult. But if the properties of the role are understood, as well as the social forces bearing down on a teacher, we educators are in a better position to effect change.

Chapter 2

Gritty Reality

From grade school on, education is a fearful enterprise. As a student, I was in too many classrooms riddled with fear, the fear that leads many children, born with a love of learning, to hate the idea of school.

—*Parker Palmer*[1]

We have begun at the level of the individual and the human need to self-manage motivation, and will return often to a personal perspective. But the focus of our work is less on self-help than on the pressing needs we have as teachers and counselors who want to construct effective learning experiences. Motivation, while essential for individual well being, is a fundamental goal of social institutions like schools and businesses that need self-motivated, lifelong learners. Thus, the nature of psychological involvement in a task or activity, and the intensity and duration of that involvement, are important both for individuals who seek to better their lives and for the social institutions that need engaged learners, workers, and active citizens.

While problems in education abound, some students use school and college the way we hope they will: They use the opportunity to transform their lives. Something marvelous happens, which we may not recognize or understand at the time, and a passive student begins to *want* to learn. We may say, variously, they become "active learners" or they "take control" of their lives. Becoming self-focused—a concept elaborated later—may not happen how we want or, more likely, *when* we want. The first active learning may not be toward goals the authorities think worthy.

However started, an essential developmental process begins. Good things happen to students, sometimes under the worst circumstances. How does the process work? What elements are most important by which marginal students awaken, taking first steps toward becoming engaged learners? What kind of learning community is needed? Experienced educators know that the right kind of learning community can lead to dramatic changes in a short time, if the curriculum inspires new purposes and a better life-project. But we know less than we should about how the pieces of an involving college combine to motivate students.

Motivation Problems in Schools and Colleges

While some learners use a learning community well, the school experience for the majority is uneven, to put it gently. If students are unmotivated, we should worry, perhaps more so, about faculty and staff who feel isolated, trapped in production systems over which they have little control. Feeling unmotivated, if not defeated, not a few teachers wonder if they chose the wrong career. John Gatto, who retired after thirty years of teaching in New York City schools, writes about unmotivated students who say they are bored by their studies.[2] So, too, are listless teachers who complain about the administration and an oppressive schedule. If teachers are not motivated by their work, and not engaged fully in their lives outside school, what example can they provide for their students, who face the challenges of their generation?

Signs of stress in education are not hard to find. The state of higher learning, so to speak, is not healthy. At least five small colleges in rural Vermont, all with long histories, are in danger of closing because of declining enrollment. Another three, including the state's largest public university, have financial problems and demoralized faculties and face reorganization. Stress on school and college leaders is increasing. Turnover for college presidents has increased, which means significant turmoil inside institutions. Superintendents cannot find school principals because the work is so unrewarding and underpaid.

To ask more of schools and colleges, as I do, will make the situation worse because today's institutions are hardly organized to promote optimal motivation and learning. For many learners, perhaps most, survival is a better description than transformation. Motivation and learning do not come easily or often to the isolated learner. Many institutions live hand to mouth, lacking adequate resources for learning. I think of learners who face rural schools in New Hampshire without special education services, inner city high schools in Chicago that feature metal detectors and bullet-proof glass in front of the principal's office, ill-equipped colleges for Native Americans, massive public systems in New York State and California in which learners are easily lost. The idealized image one has of college, based on media stereotypes of a New England private school like Middlebury College, wonderful as it may be, is neither accurate nor helpful because the landscape of higher education is remarkably diverse with regard to both type and quality.[3]

Listen to adults returning to college. Many say they do not like "school," an indictment of the whole impersonal experience. They lack confidence as learners and report feeling discouraged, even damaged, by their education. Few speak with passion about great things learned in school, or the way their lives were transformed. Few students I know have fond memories and sound as if they knew Palmer's opening quote by heart. Perhaps they liked an individual teacher or coach, sat in classrooms for the requisite hours, passed enough tests to graduate. But they did not commit.

Here is a curious irony: Even if formal education failed them earlier in life and whatever their own lack of motivation at the time, adults are effective learners *outside* school. Some have been enthusiastic learners at work or in hobbies, although most do not give themselves credit for what they have accomplished outside the academy. What does it say about schools that people leave feeling ill served, lacking self-confidence? Why do they find it easier to learn outside the apparatus of school, as if people enjoy learning most outside the very institution given to promoting learning and human development? Something is wrong about the way we think about—how we imagine—school.

What do traditional-age college students say about their experience? A national survey of American student attitudes about college and learning conducted in 1999 suggests that a higher proportion of students is disengaged from academics than ever before.[4] Four in ten reported feeling frequently bored in class, up from 38 percent in 1998 and a low of 26 percent in 1966. Sixty-three percent of students, more than in any other year, say they came late to class frequently or occasionally, compared with 49 percent in 1966. Lack of involvement in academics is evident in study habits: Only 32 percent of freshman said they spent six or more hours a week studying, down from 44 percent in 1987.

Looking to social and political attitudes, first-year students reported low involvement with social issues in addition to formal learning. But students are somewhat more involved in local needs and causes: 48 percent tutored another student, 61 percent read the editorial page in the newspaper, 75 percent performed volunteer work, and 52 percent performed community service as part of a class. Another study of college students, by Arthur Levine and Jeanette Cureton, drawing on diverse databases, finds the same pattern: disengagement with academics and formal learning; less concern with social issues but involvement in local issues and organizations; and liberal social values. These students were career oriented, aggressive consumers.[5]

Two observations by Levine and Cureton rise above the rest with regard to quality of learning and quality of life. Today's students are "weak in basic skills and able to learn best in ways different from how their professors teach."[6] Also, students appear to learn best from personal experience and involvement rather than from the lecture and test drill of many colleges. More worrisome to a parent is the sad image hidden in attributes they ascribe to American college students: hardworking, tired, isolated, lonely, prone to compulsive abuse of alcohol and more psychologically damaged than previous generations.

Finally, we want to understand motivation because normal conditions for learning in modern society are seldom optimal with regard to rest, attention, and type of work and task. Most of the time, we first have to work to motivate ourselves because we are tired, distractions abound, the clock is running, the task is repetitive or useless. Even if motivation is high, consciousness and attention ebb and flow all day long, changing within an hour and within the task. (For example, think about the changes in attention and consciousness while reading the last few paragraphs, especially now that a point has been made of it.) For teachers, the point is: The major components of psychological involvement—attention, awareness, and mood—are highly variable, but few schools and colleges make this assumption explicit in the way we organize learning situations. A college schedule assumes, implicitly and incorrectly, that every hour of the day brings the same energy, mood, and attention for both students and teachers. For example, think about how different and hard the work is for both teacher and learner if it is a large class right after lunch, late afternoon, or at night.

The everyday challenge, then, is to motivate oneself in the face of a boring class or mindless busywork of limited appeal. Moreover, it is necessary to motivate oneself to a task that makes us anxious, such as writing a job application or confronting a superior at work. Human beings have to move themselves to act—and possibly learn—when tired, given chronic sleep deprivation, especially among students. Individuals only rarely control the conditions at work or school. That students and teachers in schools report they are bored or fatigued is especially troubling because it is these settings that provide the understanding and skills with which to construct a more complete existence and a better society. But it is possible, of course, to work and learn within the cultural, social, and physiological constraints placed upon us, thus to make a better life out of difficult circumstances.

Problems in American Education

Over the last forty years the nature of teaching has changed. As has happened elsewhere in American society, a consumer mentality has kicked open the door to a cloistered academy, bringing new language and controversial changes whose impact is not easy to assess. Today's students and parents, having paid handsomely for what they believe is a product or service, demand satisfaction. In a buyer's market, parents argue with admissions officers about tuition fees; they shop for financial aid packages at competing colleges. Students argue a grade when the course is over, quick to threaten suit if a demand for better service is not addressed. An ever-cautious dean asks a faculty member to "paper" the process of failing a difficult student to protect the college against litigation, half-suspecting the college will settle the suit eventually because the cost of defense is prohibitive.

Prior to the tumultuous 1960s, such challenges to a teacher's authority were unusual. Today schools, colleges, and faculties everywhere face new pressures to be accountable. Traditional authority has been delegitimated, in general, in all democratic institutions. External authorities such as state legislatures ask schools and colleges to be accountable for measurable results, not just offering a curriculum of good intentions. Under pressure from their publics, accreditation officers call for a "culture of evidence," a dramatic shift, which challenges the conventional assumption that curricular inputs like faculty credentials and size of library holdings are all one needs to know to assess academic quality.

While the call for *evidence* of learning is a fair one if put in the right context, the assessment movement poses yet another challenge to teacher authority. To the teacher, an external authority now holds him or her professionally accountable for student learning (rather than *students* being responsible themselves for their own performance). Teachers of literature, feeling put upon by their social science colleagues, are asked to write operational definitions of learning outcomes. In the worse case, boards and external committees intrude still further to specify standards and the coverage of content areas they favor.

External forces are everywhere: economic pressure to increase teaching load and class size, federal and state government mandates, tighter financial aid policies, and a litigious society, and possible suits by students, which bring lawyers and deans into faculty decisions about quality. In addition, the social movements of the 1960s introduced race, gender, sexual orientation, and social class as legitimate factors in choosing curricular content. We know much more about individual differences in learning styles, emotional intelligence, and learning disabilities, which complicates faculty work. And now, here comes the accountability movement endorsed by accreditation associations, responding to external threats from the state, in which once-respected faculty members are told that passing their course is no longer a valid measure of learning. Facing these many changes from outside and above, teachers and counselors are tempted to retreat, focusing on an academic paper or the details of a class. Feeling increasingly vulnerable, both professionally and psychologically, Parker Palmer says teachers and counselors disconnect from the pieces they cannot control.[7]

Most certainly, faculty members do not consider themselves service providers in consumer society. This is hardly the inspiring image that motivated them to earn advanced degrees. Teachers resent the changes, loss of status, disempowerment. Worse, many feel trapped inside their present institution. Teacher unions provide boundaries for institutional conflict about means and ends, to be sure. But absurd ideas come with some contracts, such as academic administrators not being allowed by contract to teach, or faculty members not discussing the curriculum openly because it will make them vulnerable to the Yeshiva case if they act as managers, not workers. Teaching assistants become organized in unions to reduce exploitation, and institutions balance tight budgets by hiring itinerant teachers, using that ugly word "adjunct," with only tenuous ties to the institution and to students. More generally, college civility is challenged by scarce resources and endless committee meetings, many poorly run. While this portrait of academic life may seem bleak, this was precisely the conversation at a meeting of New England senior academic administrators.[8]

Worse, no one knows how to break the cycles of misperception and distrust that weaken a school's learning culture. One senior observer of national issues in higher education, Alan Guskin, talks soberly about endemic demoralization, commenting on the obdurate conflict between faculty and administration in the institutions with which he consults.[9] Inexperienced leaders make mistakes, Guskin says, but are not forgiven; the faculty is suspicious and resentful; trustees feel external political pressure, which they pass to the campus. Stereotypes of shallow motives, always made of the other side, multiply. Teachers may be willing to challenge how education work is organized but do not have alternatives in mind to move from a culture of teaching to a culture of learning.[10]

Why would anyone want to work in such a place? The short answer is: "The work is so important!" The high ideals of education, while impossible to put into practice, are ennobling. The human spirit is resilient, and teachers and students find ways to survive difficult circumstances. And schools and colleges, imperfect as they are, are still the best means yet invented for testing the human spirit.

The political context of these social changes bearing down on American schools and colleges is worth a few more sentences. In so many ways, the political issues of the late 1960s haunt contemporary institutions, especially conversations inside.[11] Equal parts of social progress and political excess seem mixed together, not possible to sort out. The social dislocations of that era led, on the one hand, to resurgent democratic impulses expressed by individuals and groups. As individuals, modern citizens are more aware of their rights as stakeholders. They now are willing to speak up more than was the case in the sleepy America of the 1950s. Minorities are better protected, if imperfectly, where once their needs were invisible. On the other hand, well-organized protests by special interest groups—left and right, and many quite extreme—challenge social institutions at all levels and erode legitimate authority.

An anomic culture of distrust has crept into institutional life even as modern institutions have, arguably, become more democratic and respon- sive than the unchallenged hierarchies of the 1950s. Today authority of all types is suspect where once the authority of the teacher, the policeman, or a sitting president was unquestioned. Since World War II, the authority of individual faculty members, department chairs, deans, and presidents has been reduced. But who, then, will set the institutional agenda and drive the work? Who makes tough decisions to fail a lazy student, close a dated program, or remove an aggressive employee? Institutions drift when no one is in charge and interest groups inside, competing for resources, are in perpetual standoff. Under the name of shared governance, a reasonable idea, oversight committees watch the administration and other faculty members, and the faculty and the administration trade nasty stereotypes about motives and performance. Decision making within modern schools and colleges can be slow torture, and the grinding process and water cooler back-biting do not build trust.

Which value is more important: Including others in important decisions? Or the ability to move quickly even if participation is sacrificed? I have been a teacher and administrator several times over and in some combination both elements are needed. The democratic impulse toward inclusion is both powerful and positive because today, more people get involved, although inclusion slows decision making. Such changes in American culture and its fluid democratic institutions are not easy to assess. Perhaps we find ourselves as a people struggling to revise our understanding of postmodern authority and the need to manage all the work inside modern institutions as both skilled, loyal followers and compassionate, visionary leaders.

Finally, lest we forget, teachers are always in direct competition with other experiential providers. We teachers face a formidable competitor for learner attention and psychological experience: television. Perhaps television and the particular culture it carries accounts for the reading-focus problem as well as the increased media literacy. Political scientist Robert Putnam's research on the increasing isolation of people faults television viewing as a correlate of social disengagement, which we may suspect when evaluating our own habits.[12]

In 1950, Putnam reports only 10 percent of the American population had a television set whereas by 1959, 90 percent had one. In the 1990s, 75 percent of American households had more than one set, which encourages individual watching. Nielsen ratings for daily household viewing hours have increased steadily: 4.8 hours in 1955, 6 hours in 1975, 7.3 in 1995. Also, the way we use television as an object-tool—and do not use the book as object-tool—may generalize to other life activities. Students watch television today as channel surfers, less deliberate in watching a specific program, Putnam suggests, which may carry over to the way contemporary learners "sample" other parts of life.

All the important critiques of modern education connect, directly or indirectly, to failed motivation within the school. Whether the complaint is poor student performance, classroom disruptions, or passive citizenship after graduation, the root problem is unmotivated learners who do not "apply themselves," a phrase sent my way many times. The best facilities and richest curriculum will not automatically engage students, and besides, few schools and colleges are so equipped. Students survive the drill laid out for them, and many graduate, albeit with uneven skills and low self-confidence as learners.

Students pass exams or meet requirements of a major without having thought deeply about that major's values and questions, much less considered interdisciplinary study. While they may have learned most of what is asked of them by an older generation, at least enough to pass exams, they have quietly learned another set of skills, namely, how to beat the system with all the cynicism this implies. In this regard, it is not quite fair to say that students are unmotivated, because poor academic performance can be associated with highly motivated achievement in sports, dating and social life, and out-of-school work to earn spending money. The purposes expressed are just not those their parents, teachers, and coaches want them to have.

Complaints made about teachers and professors also point to failed motivation. An all-inclusive "they" do not work hard, care only about money and career, do not publish, cannot teach. The noble image of the self-sacrificing teacher of high moral standards has devolved to that of a lazy, self-interested liberal who belongs to a union that dominates a poorly run, costly, "soft" institution—and that nasty stereotype has been used by the press and politicians from left and right for their own gain.

Having worked with many educators, I know the stereotype to be false and pernicious. I know teachers and administrators who have cleaned school bathrooms before students arrive—others take on aggressive students whose families gave up years ago. I know administrators who, after denying a student appeal, have been assaulted (I myself was twice), and faculty members who have been physically threatened because they withheld credit.

Like all human institutions, schools and colleges are flawed. But the special energy behind the criticism reflects displaced anger from enormous social problems largely outside a school or college's control. To the contrary, most teachers see teaching as a *calling*—they work hard under difficult, sometimes dangerous, conditions. Except in better schools, teachers endure dirty, overcrowded facilities. An urban high school in New York City or Chicago looks more like a prison than a school imagined as a noble center of human potential. Teachers choose the calling because they hold idealistic, romantic views about human potential and the good of helping others. They stay in the profession—despite mass production elements they detest—because they want to help; and most teachers continue to care about their students long after graduation.

Criticisms of modern education are well known—schools and teachers are regularly flogged in public. Politicians from left and right weigh in on: the failure of schools to prepare students for work and citizenship; poor coverage of math and science; low academic standards, generally; behavior problems in class; the excesses of political correctness in liberal education; teachers unions, and so on. So-called free-market reform concepts like privatization, vouchers, and charter schools become popular even though they threaten the very foundation of public education, thanks to the foundation we owe to Horace Mann, America's greatest gift to the possibility of democracy. Few politicians have firsthand experience, of course, with the considerable contradictions of an urban high school, or those of a poor, rural college. But their opinions are no less passionate.

Elementary school principal Deborah Meier, in her 1983 book *A Nation at Risk,* critiques the idea of "educational crisis" trumpeted by the federal authorities. Theirs was a false alarm that led, Meier says, to the wrong solutions.[13] The crisis was supposed to be about dumb students, lazy teachers, uncaring mothers, and unaccountable schools that did not prepare students for the new world economy. The proposed cure would be standards-based reform, more and better tests, and, in the free-market spirit, private competition to give parents choice. The real crises, according to Meier, are weakened human relationships and the decline of community. America and the democratic experiment are threatened less by inefficient schools than by low voter turnout; the poor care that the elderly, infirm, and poor receive; growing income inequity; and high rates of incarceration of minorities. Of course, schools have problems, but Meier says "the heaviest burdens fall on the poor, the young, and people of color."[14]

The most searching critique of education I have read is by Edmund O'Sullivan and his colleagues of the Transformative Learning Centre at the University of Toronto. They do not pick at the small pieces. Rather, they challenge a deep, unconscious assumption: "The matrix of western culture, originating in modern European culture and transplanted all over the world, that considers human existence and, above all, human consciousness and spirit as independent from and above nature."[15] They challenge educators to understand the control and exploitation, both psychological and material, of "the third world majority" by the "first world minority," of women by men, of the poor by the rich. This international ideology of domination and exploitation, sometimes disguised as "development," not only harms other peoples and indigenous cultures but limits those of us in the first world and our search for meaning, community, and a sense of place. These patriarchal and imperialist assumptions are spread by schools and colleges, become fixtures of the larger culture, and force upon all people three forms of learning: the "dynamics of denial, despair and grief."[16]

Theirs is a deeply idealistic critique of modernity, its global systems for economic control, and the global market consciousness that increases individualism and despair. An ecofeminist analysis provokes us to understand the mind and human consciousness as it is influenced by social forces bearing down on the individual, especially women and the poor, who have little control of the future. That modern, secular man has lost touch with personal feelings, spirituality, and nature is worth hearing. I am less sanguine than they about the totalistic nature of their critique and the possibility of sufficient change, given all the dislocations and inequality.

This is not the place to catalogue ideas for building involving schools and colleges, which is the purpose of chapters 6 and 7. It will, however, be important to briefly describe the major problems teachers face, pulling small points together. Having described the teacher's role, I want to characterize the work conditions teachers encounter. In the final analysis, the possibility of high quality learning environments must balance the most important variables: school mission, clarity of purpose, size, pedagogy and resources. Changing one variable, even an important one like class size, will not usually be sufficient to greatly improve quality.

Problem of Expanded Mission

Schools, especially poor, public institutions and struggling colleges, are asked to cope with a wide range of student needs and difficult personal problems, such as substance abuse, eating disorders, and aggression.[17] In economically depressed areas, schools and colleges have become de facto social service agencies because of personal problems brought to the classroom. (I have worked with college students on personal issues that twenty years ago would have been discussed only during psychotherapy.) Many schools find they must offer family and counseling services, which has stretched the traditional mission of education and diminished financial resources, leading to higher costs. Many faculty members and earnest administrators are not prepared for the range of physical and psychological needs brought to school by learners, and, indeed, some question why they should be asked to help in such ways.

Teachers should not be blamed for not fixing problems of unformed character or poor motivation that society drops at the school and college door. Most student needs seen by schools are pass-along problems—they are brought largely unresolved to college from overburdened secondary schools, which must cope with the pass-along problems of families, which often reflect economic problems of communities. At each level, one does what one can, but sometimes the accumulated damage is too severe. Some students do well, going beyond the circumstances of their birth. But many more do not use the opportunity fully because the positive aspects of school culture, seen as a counterculture, are not as powerful as we think in comparison to the potent peer group and the culture of the home community, its values and norms. Even so, we celebrate the near-miraculous instances when a student wakes up and takes charge of his or her learning.

Problem of Unclear Purposes

What should we expect of college as an intentional learning community? Seymour Sarason summarizes extensive research on school culture by posing two challenges to educators: "What is the overarching purpose of school, a purpose which if not realized makes the attainment of other purposes unlikely, if not impossible? What are the characteristics of contexts of productive learning?"[18] We will try to answer Sarason's challenges. For educators who have sat through months of institutional long-range planning, it is easy to be cynical about mission and vision statements as conveyors of values and purposes. The parsed words and packed paragraphs that survive an academic committee do not inspire.

As the institution's mission expands beyond that of an academy, its initial purposes blur, which makes decisions about allocations difficult. If the academic curriculum competes, in effect, with funding a campus daycare center, the ethical-political decision is challenging for most colleges.

Research evidence dating back to Theodore Newcomb's 1938 studies of Bennington College indicates that *clear, consistent institutional objectives* make significant contributions to student development.[19] In his landmark study of American colleges, however, the late Ernest Boyer found a pervasive absence of clear, consistent objectives, saying,

> during our study we found divisions on campus, conflicting priorities and competing interests that diminish the intellectual and social quality of the undergraduate experiences and restrict the capacity of the college effectively to serve its students. At most colleges and universities we visited, these special

points of tension appeared with such regularity and seemed so consistently to sap the vitality of the baccalaureate experience that we have made them the focus of this report.[20]

Boyer is concerned with educational purposes and desired outcomes of student learning and personal development. Most catalogs make vague, romantic statements. But seldom are these purposes taken seriously and seldom are they specific enough to drive decisions concerning institutional processes and practices.

Clear purposes and noble aspirations help build morale in a learning community—they spark hope. Colleges without high purposes do not motivate faculty and staff to shape visions of their own contribution to the learning culture.[21] Students who come to study with an older, wiser generation, in turn, do not find a vision for a better life and are not inspired, except in mechanical ways, to work on their emerging vision, their learning, their life-projects.

Problem of Human Scale

The problem of failed motivation in school can be traced directly to the lack of human scale in the design of modern schools and colleges, which are run more as production sites than as centers for optimal human development. The false ideal, according to Meier, is "school as ant colony," a smooth-running, efficient assembly of busy creatures rather than a messy, disorderly community where people of different generations get to know and help one another.[22] In the idea of "school as factory," student motivation is not helped by large lecture classes, perfunctory advising, a reliance on lectures for information transfer, and the multiple choice tests needed, then, to efficiently evaluate students in the large numbers to be processed. Meier is thinking of innovative elementary schools she led in New York City and Boston, but her critique applies to other levels: "Our schools have grown too distant, too big, too standardized, too uniform, too divorced from their communities, too alienating of young from old and old from young."[23] She calls for a "20–20 Vision" for American schools, or no more than twenty students in class and twenty teachers in a school.

Another progressive educator, Theodore Sizer, in *Horace's Compromise* captures the dilemmas and the tradeoffs faced by modern educators and all those who care about effective schools.[24] Teachers want to do more, and get more, out of their teaching. But the way the production line is organized, its scale, and the numbers to be processed overwhelm the teacher, forcing compromises in quality and authenticity. Overwhelmed by production imperatives, Horace, Sizer's fictional teacher, is wary of giving too many writing assignments even though he knows that critical thinking develops best through writing. Worse, a "conspiracy of the least" develops in which students promise to behave if teachers ask little or nothing of them. In the sequel, *Horace's Hope,* Sizer offers familiar examples of progressive educational practices, although he remains cautious about the prospects of widespread educational reform.[25]

So much time and good will are lost. Most teachers in high school and college face concrete work conditions that resemble an old-time production line more than craft work, that romantic notion of teaching that first motivated them to go to college and graduate school. Imagine a class of thirty students and a teacher, one of five classes she has to cover that day, totaling perhaps 150 students![26] The patterns of attention and participation are overwhelming because of the number of wandering minds in the room, including the teacher's. Students are tired, the professor is distracted by a struggle with a colleague, and a few students do not want to be there at all. Both teacher and students have a schedule to follow, and they somehow must focus their attention on the tasks and try to learn what they can. All parties feel trapped.

Poor motivation is the central, if unspoken, question in that room—and it is not just a problem of lazy students. Most of the day, the motivation of both teacher and student is worn down because they worry less about learning than getting through the day without making a mistake that slows the line. Meier and Sizer may be idealists and my characterization may be extreme. Of course, free space and quality learning can be created in the worst setting. But let no one defend the compromised values that force educators to put developing human beings in such large-scale settings in which students are then expected to become responsible, authentic learners and involved citizens.

Problem of Pedagogy

In even the worst situation, in the most depressing, dead-end school, teachers can do two things. They can challenge their own understanding of motivation and learning, and, using that knowledge, they can change their behavior. While personal transformation is neither simple nor easily achieved, the possibility of better praxis is one of the few variables under teacher control.

Two examples make the point. A college teacher at an Ivy League college has an introductory physics course of 300 students.[27] He thought he was being effective until he gave students an informal test that applied physics to daily life. Shocked by poor test results, the teacher revamped his teaching style. Now, lecture notes are distributed before class, and students come prepared to discuss a particular physics question. On arriving at class, they are asked to write down their answer to the question, and then defend their answer before classmates in small group discussions. Students who get the answer "right" are asked to teach those who got it "wrong." As a result of *active* learning, "engaging the students' brains," as the professor put it, learning increases. Before considering a second example, please note two things. First, the teacher asked what students were really learning and collected data (a test). Second, this teacher chose to *change* his mental model of teaching and his behavior to meet the expressed needs of students. He did not lecture longer, or use better overheads. He changed method.

An unadaptive response is told by Arthur Chickering. A team of evaluators went, it seems, to a number of colleges to assess teaching behavior and quality of learning. Arriving at one school, two of the team made arrangements to visit a scheduled class. At the appointed time and place, Chickering and his colleague learned that the class had one student, and were astonished then to sit through a lecture. Our inflexible pedagogue pressed on with what he knew best when he could have adapted his method to a changed environment.

So, teachers can choose pedagogical methods to increase student involvement and they can choose to promote authentic involvement where students invest themselves as whole persons in the work. Readers who stay with the narrative will appreciate that classrooms and labs are social theaters where the most interesting dynamics are nearly invisible. In fact, most participants in a social group are involved fully only for isolated moments as group attention ebbs and flows continuously. When the mood of the group shifts because the topic is changed, attention will be more uniform, as when a student suddenly challenges the instructor with a smart question. But the few minutes of lively class discussion that follow will gradually dissipate as students begin to distance themselves until the next moment of focused attention. The normal situation is seldom one of full attention.

Understanding the variability of group attention and mood, experienced teachers work hard to focus group attention by using anecdotes, jokes, and examples. The teacher will be dramatic by varying voice, tonality, gesture, and posture, addressing people with eye contact and moving about the room-as-stage. Experienced public speakers employ audiovisual aides like multimedia presentations and laser pointers. Charismatic speakers can emotionally move an entire audience.

Teachers remember the silent, powerful moments when it all comes together and the group is suddenly transported to a higher level. Moments of involved attention in the group are among the most powerful in life, and educators who want to be effective need to understand the causes and consequences, and how to focus learner attention in their choice of topics and methods. The safe assumption, however, is that teachers, reading the surface behavior of compliant, nodding heads, typically overstate the level and consistency of student attention and learning.

Problem of Public Will

Education always has problems, and waves of reform roll in and out. Today not a few recipes for reinventing American schools and colleges are heard, new schemes that "break the mold," to use the inflated language of reformers. Rhetorical flourishes should make us skeptical because schools are defined small cultures embedded in a larger cultures. Nothing about human culture changes easily or quickly! The first constraint placed upon schools and colleges is the marriage of unrealistic expectations to inadequate resources. Modern society asks a great deal of its schools and colleges, especially given the problems of the community and the family that are carried forward with children as they pass anonymously through "the education system" from elementary school to college.

We ask much but seem unwilling to fund education at the level of military investments. Having said this, adequate financing alone is not the only issue. Experienced educators know that the right educational ideas have to be funded to the right level, but that systemic reform will, nevertheless, be expensive. Most American schools and colleges are not wealthy places and Benjamin Barber makes the telling point that teachers are not paid at the level of, say, accountants or lawyers, a sad comment on contemporary social values.[28]

One does not have to be a pacifist to call attention to the relative magnitude of America's national investments in education versus defense. Educational leaders at all levels have failed to build a consensus to invest in schools to the extent that the nation invests in modern weapons technology, as stark as that contrast might seem. Consider just two of the weapon systems used in the first Gulf War. Two hundred and eighty-eight Cruise missiles were fired at a cost of about $750,000 each. That is a total of $216 million. Seven F-16s were lost at a cost of $20 million each, or $140 million. How many schools could have been rebuilt with that sum? To make the point another way, American military bases I have visited have more amenities than do New York City public schools. Rather than bash teachers, where is the national will to name this problem correctly and to act?

Failure of public will is the most glaring problem of all. Calls for reform have been described by Lewis Lapham as "a matter of pious ritual" because little of substance follows collective hand ringing. Periodic outpourings of concern are ceremonial because we think of education as "a means of indoctrination and a way of teaching people to know their place." Lapham's bitter opinion is hardly new.[29]

In every state in America, students somewhere will study today in dirty, unsafe, ill-equipped schools and colleges. Any administrator knows the burden of bone-dry budgets on academic quality. Not having enough books, suspending pay raises, sitting in lousy chairs, not having modern computers and lab gear, and packing students like sardines in large classes that are barely under control—not one of these factors predicts quality. While many suburban schools are supported adequately, urban and rural institutions are not. While adequate investment, alone, does not assure quality, as conservative commentators are quick to note, most citizens do not understand the extent to which financial values supplant educational values in discussions about contemporary education. The topic of the day, every day, is the budget, not academic quality or special attention to gifted or needy students.

Chapter 3

Perspectives on Engaged Living

We always live at the time we live and not at some other time, and only by extracting at each present time the full meaning of each present experience are we prepared for doing the same thing in the future.

—*John Dewey*[1]

Whether it is Karl Marx writing about the alienation of workers from meaningful labor or the American psychologist Carol Dweck writing about social-cognitive motivation, the general phenomenon of human engagement with life has fascinated minds of every age.[2] Like many ideas in social philosophy and the social sciences, involvement with life has been explored under different names, always incompletely and often without recognizing earlier contributions.

Not citing earlier work is not just a professional lapse but a sign of a larger problem, a certain individualism in our understanding of society, reflected also in social theory and educational theory and practice. Not locating one's work in intellectual history underestimates what has been a long conversation between artists and intellectuals of every civilization throughout recorded history. Each generation, it seems, discovers the topic anew, inventing new terms. While the constructs pertaining to problems in living are not identical, many are correlated to the extent that is difficult to disentangle them empirically: anxiety, depression, happiness, locus of control, field independence, ego control, burnout, intrinsic motivation, and older concepts like alienation, morale, and will, not to mention religious experiences in confession, religious conversion, and assorted mystical states.

We cannot possibly cover all these personality dimensions. Two important areas would add to our understanding of psychological involvement. Large and separate sociological literatures on alienation and anomie, although considered out of date (prematurely, reflecting the trendiness of social theory), would add insight to how we see macro social and cultural forces that influence human development. Extensive psychiatric literatures can be found on anxiety, depression, defense mechanisms, and character and ego development.

Even with limits, a rich literature exists with regard to attention, motivation, and peak experience in learning. With each perspective or theory, the focus will be concepts used to describe moments of short-term psychological involvement and those of enduring social engagement, and the mechanisms with which people self-manage mood and attention. I am fascinated by the nature of temporary psychological states, accessible by introspection, that play a special role in motivation and learning. Character traits paralleling basic theory such as Abraham Maslow's self-actualized personality and Mihaly Csikszentmihalyi's autotelic personality are noted but not discussed.

Several theories ahead are not standard fare for educators. Reading William James or existentialism might be considered passé whereas Csikszentmihalyi's notion of flow and Ellen Langer's concept of mindfulness are "psychology." Many of my examples, too, are not from the academic classroom or lab. But to understand human motivation, we educators need to explore the broad landscape of mood and consciousness as found in learning situations of all types, in and out of school. If we know more about such moments, especially the transitions between psychological states for their motivational effects and the interaction between the emotions and reason, we will design better learning situations.

William James and the Varieties of Religious Experience

William James was the leading American philosopher of his day, and most of his work was published between 1890 and 1910, the year of his death. James should be read for many reasons, not the least of which is that his writing from a much different age holds up so well. His lectures and texts on psychology, philosophy, and religion were popular and influential, and today his work is still relevant and inspirational. James was a remarkable writer who supports arguments with lucid examples and careful introspection about the nature of attention and psychological experience. All forms of human experience interested this holistic thinker. In particular, he was fascinated by mental consciousness and the stream of thought that people try to manage. Individual identity and the nature of the self, James thought, came from trying to manage consciousness, which is why I was initially drawn to his work.

William James is not the first to have studied peak experience or intense religious states, but his work is systematic in its treatment of different states of consciousness, and we start here.[3] Developed out of his lectures to the University of Edinburgh in 1901–02, James wrote a classic text on Western and Eastern religious experience. His religious perspective and concern for the proof of God may seem archaic in today's secular age, but James's analysis of religious experience is relevant to engagement theory because, it turns out, the psychological dynamics are comparable.

Faith-states, to James, can be separated from psychological experience and underlying biological dynamics. Even the most intense forms, those of a sudden religious conversion, are special cases of ordinary human experience, he argues. Most accounts of religious conversion reported by James begin with protracted and intense personal despair or melancholy preceding the conversion. During the conversion and afterward, a sense of relief from despair arises, if not rapture. James writes about the characteristics of the conversion experience, what he called "states of assurance": the loss of "all worry" leading to peace, "solemn joy," and the "willingness to be"; the perception of new meaning and insights; and a sense of newness and cleanness that "beautifies every object."[4]

The language of religious conversion is one of spiritual rebirth, regeneration, renewal, receiving God's grace, being inspired, being reborn, or "twice-borne" ("born again" in modern terms). To have this transcendent, emotional experience is to be *religious* (though the secular mind will not interpret it that way, especially if it mistakes religion for the rituals of a formal church). To James at least, the term "religious" referred, first and foremost, to a peak experience, not the formal rituals that attract adherents or stimulate the mood state. (The distinction between participation in church rituals and the emotional experience one has is a topic to which we will return at several points.)

The affective experience is intense. After it, James says, people are likely to remain identified with the religion in which they experience it. (In contemporary social psychological terms such as Langer might use, we would say that people remain attached to the frames used to interpret and label powerful experience.) James describes two dynamics that are essential in producing the faith-states of mind: first, the calming result of focusing one's attention, and second, the sense of peace that follows "surrender" to a higher authority (sacred or secular, I would add). Of such a personal surrender, James says " the chief wonder of it [the conversion] is that it so often comes about, not by doing, but by simply relaxing and throwing the burden down."[5] Both dynamics—focusing and surrendering—lead to feelings of "solemn joy."

James explores a range of religious experiences that focus attention, like prayer, the Catholic rite of confession, and forms of ascetic mortification, a few quite extreme to we moderns. The highly personal, anguished reports in James's catalogue of religious experience written by figures prior to 1900 define a religious landscape with its specialized vocabulary and phenomena just as the psychoanalytic vocabulary of the 1950s and 60s defined a psychological landscape. So, the labels and interpretations vary with the era and its dominant institutions. But underlying human needs, problems, and potential remain the same.

John Dewey's Progressive Philosophy

On close reading, John Dewey is a complex figure with more nuance to his thinking about education than is apparent in rhetorical flourishes by progressive partisans, or his conservative detractors, especially in the heated arguments being waged, once again, about quality and direction in American education. In the 1920s Dewey developed a philosophy that influenced many thousands of teachers then and inspired the second wave of educational reform during the 1960s and 70s. Although he was out of favor after that, scholars like Maxine Greene, Stephen Rockefeller, Richard Rorty, and Louis Menand, among others, are demonstrating renewed interest.[6]

On the anniversary of Dewey's birthday in 1997, Maxine Greene lauded the father of progressive education for a "spirit of hope and generosity."[7] Describing Dewey's work as a philosophy of possibility, Greene praised him for raising expectations for American schools as he did in 1938 with the classic *Experience and Education,* a thin, densely packed volume that teachers might usefully reread once a year for its thoughtfulness about human experience in learning. Just as Greene would, in turn, ask of her audience sixty years later, Dewey wanted to challenge traditional educational forms, asking teachers to imagine new possibilities for both students and schools. He focused on learning as process, asking teachers to look at dynamics in the interpretation of human experience, especially the need for students to be active meaning-makers in their unfolding lives.

Dewey's ideas about education are important for understanding motivation and engaged learning because he argues, implicitly but effectively, that the progressive school stimulates more motivation in students than does the traditional school. A prolific author, Dewey's lifelong interests in democracy, learning from experience, and reform in education—chiefly elementary and secondary schools—along with his respect for the scientific method are woven throughout his work. Our interest is in Dewey's theory of learning from experience and his hope for "an intelligent theory of education."[8]

Educators recall Dewey for his insistence that teachers value student experience in learning, and that aspect of his work is important. Two facets of his philosophy of education have, however, been underestimated: First, Dewey thinks like a social psychologist who situates the learner in overlapping social contexts where both person and environment are weighted equally, not unlike Kurt Lewin's field theory decades later. Like Lewin, when Dewey thinks about learning, he sees reciprocal, transforming exchanges between person and environment.[9]

Second, Dewey thinks like an experimentalist who wants to use the scientific method as the best means for rejecting hidebound and ideological customs in education, leading him to a call for educational experiments that challenge educational convention.[10] That is, Dewey as an educational philosopher was equal parts experiential educator, reformer, social psychologist, and experimentalist. (We could add political theorist and supporter of democracy, recalling that his views were formed in the political context of the Great Depression and the totalitarian movements in Europe that followed.) Each of these facets, and the subtle connections among perspectives, become important when contemplating the need for new theory.

Another reason exists to revisit Dewey's philosophy. Unlike William James before him, Dewey did not write about psychological states, or individual states of consciousness. Motivation was not a topic he addressed directly. Dewey was, however, deeply concerned with the individual student, his or her motivation and development. Dewey, after all, did ask the teacher to consider the lived experience of the individual student, here and now, rather than build a curriculum solely from past authorities. Paying little attention to describing individual psychological experience phenomenologically, certainly in comparison to James or Maslow, Dewey focused his progressive philosophy on two topics: the role of lived experience in learning, development, and education, and the way human experience is shaped in the school's social environment. To Dewey, individual human consciousness must not be separated from group forces and what he called the learning situation. For an educator, three questions are paramount when we assess Dewey's contribution: Which features of the school or college increase student motivation? What are the mechanisms by which to increase or limit motivation? And what are the limits of the progressive perspective?

After reviewing the structure of his theory, we turn to a depiction of the traditional school in contrast to the progressive school. While ostensibly opposed to "either-or" thinking, saying he did not want unfairly to criticize conventional education, Dewey's critique of traditional schooling is, nevertheless, relentless and penetrating. His ideas are still recognizable today in the criticism of progressive reformers like Theodore Sizer, Maxine Greene, Wendy Kohli, Deborah Meier, and Matthias Finger.

Two principles of experiential education are postulated: first, the principle of experiential continuum, and second, the principle of interaction.[11] (He describes the two as the longitudinal and lateral aspects.) The principle of the experiential continuum refers to the manner by which experiences are interconnected in two dimensions: *temporally* in terms of past, present, and anticipated experience, and *socially* in terms of the influence of social interaction. And it cannot be said too many times that experience, even deeply felt experience, is not educative—what matters most is the *quality* of reflection. Dewey cautions teachers, saying: "The belief that all genuine education comes about through experience does not mean that all experiences are genuinely or equally educative."[12]

What matters, Dewey argues, is the direction of that experience as it helps or hinders human development. So, "progressive" is defined by an experience that promotes *new* experience that is essential to *new* learning. Conversely, an experience is miseducative to the extent that it arrests the possibility of new experience, new reflection, and new learning, in the iterative cycles David Kolb captures so well.[13] Whether the experience puts the learner in a rut, or merely entertains because it is "interesting," it is miseducative because the possibility of progressive, new experience and new learning is reduced.

Dewey's conception of lived experience in human development is almost metaphysical: "Just as no man lives or dies to himself, so no experience lives and dies to itself. . . . every experience lives on in further experiences."[14] Giving his charge to teachers, he adds, "the central problem of an education based upon experience is to select the kind of experiences that live fruitfully and creatively in subsequent experiences."[15]

So, the value of a single experience by a learner is determined by its direction and quality, both broadly defined, assuming active reflection. But how, exactly, the dialectic between experience and reflection functions is left somewhat vague, both in terms of theory and with regard to concrete practices a teacher might use in the classroom or lab. So we ask: How *is* personal experience to be used? What *is* the role of theory, and how is it mixed with experience? What forms of supervision *are* effective? Answers to these questions are not simple, as the discussion in Part III suggests.

Dewey's argument is undeveloped in another respect, lacking as it does an explicit theory of human development. Growth or movement is not sufficient, he acknowledges, because experience and reflection might be used profitably by a burglar or corrupt politician (his examples). He is content to say that for these two examples, there are blocked opportunities for growth, presumably to becoming upstanding citizens in the community. The danger, Dewey asserts, is "to leave a person arrested on a low plane of development, in a way which limits capacity for growth."[16] As it stands, the argument does not include ethical criteria for evaluating individual choice, an essential topic in human motivation to which we return shortly in reviewing the contributions of American psychologists and Continental existentialist philosophers and writers. So, learners need ethical criteria for evaluating purposes chosen, or risk being lost in the slough of relativism where all rationales are equal.

Three pedagogic principles follow from Dewey's theory: First, students are invited into the design of learning situations as full, complicated human beings (with an emphasis on "being," not on them as student objects whose inner space is ignored). Second, encouraging students to integrate out-of-school, personal experience with their academic studies enriches learning. In addition to in-class experience, student experience and interests, generally, are respected and incorporated in academic studies, whether from work, home, or in the form of recollected learning. Third, students are invited to be active agents in the classroom and school governance even though this complicates a teacher's life. Although Dewey wrote about elementary and secondary schools, he believed in schools as laboratories for democracy— and this in the 1930s—even though doing so introduces the essential turmoil of democracy to an ordered, hierarchic place.

The intersection of these two ideas—the value of learning from experience for an active student and Dewey's deep respect for democracy—creates a profound tension in his philosophy of education between progressive learning process and progressive, left politics, a tension that has bedeviled progressive schools and colleges ever since.[17] In the first case, the teacher is eager to help students find their own interests and broaden their experience, which leads us from the classroom into the street, so to speak. In the second case, both students and teachers may be pressured to adopt specific political values and interest group platforms, which can have the effect of restricting new experiences, thus limiting development.

Human learning results from the mix of personal experience and reflection in social interactions and learning situations that can, and should, be diverse. Constructed and used well, learning situations are transformative in ways not anticipated by a mechanistic approach to learning because of the potent dialectics among different realms of experience. So Dewey posits a general principle of human development: The more diverse experience a person has, assuming emerging self-control and active reflection, the more learning is possible, which, in turn, strengthens character, leading to new purposes, better reflection, and so on in iterative cycles.

Perhaps we humans come, in time and with some sadness, to accept the realization that we exist alone as individuals but learn and live in a social community. Think about Dewey's second principle, that of interaction. Dewey's philosophy of experiential learning assumes that human development occurs in social interaction, both guided by and expanding what he termed "social intelligence."[18] He argues "all human experience is ultimately social: that it involves contact and communication."[19] Because this facet of Dewey's philosophy is less acknowledged than his other contributions, listen to his own words from *Art as Experience*:

> life goes on in an environment; not merely *in* it but because of it, through interaction with it. *No creature lives merely under its skin*. . . . At every moment, the living creature is exposed to dangers from its surroundings, and at every moment, it must draw upon something in its surroundings to satisfy its needs. The career and destiny of a living being are bound up with its interchanges with its environment, not externally but in the most intimate way.[20]

Experience links person and the proximal environment in dynamic iterations in which the view of self and the perceived environment are transformed in a progressive direction so that ever-new experiences and development are possible. Traditional education emphasizes objective, external factors when, in fact, we have to understand the interaction of objective conditions and how they are interpreted. Again, listen to Dewey: "Experience does not go on simply inside a person. . . . Every genuine experience has an active side which changes in some degree the objective conditions under which experiences are had."[21]

The interactions Dewey termed "situations" are defined by "transactions taking place between an individual and what, at the time, constitutes his environment."[22] The educator attends not only to what is done but to the way it is done in terms of choice of works and tone of voice, amounting to the "total *social* set-up of the situations in which a person is engaged."[23]

Traditional educators, Dewey asserts, give primacy to objective conditions such as the content to be learned, books read, or labs.[24] Progressive educators, Dewey hoped, give attention to internal factors including individual motivation and the active integration of the experience. Dewey's goal is the "future learning that springs from easy and ready contact and communication with others."[25] In all these ways, he points teachers and counselors to a close, creative relationship between how one constructs an engaged individual life of meaning and the web of social connections external to the self.

At the same time, Dewey frames an egalitarian view of the special roles of student and teacher, a relationship not captured in contemporary dichotomies of "student centered" versus "faculty centered." Because in progressive schools the possibility of learning is understood to begin with personal experience, the felt needs and experience of the learner are given more weight than in conventional schools—more weight, in fact, than those of the teacher, which sounds heretical. Although Dewey does not put it this way, both teacher and student are active, interpreting contributors to the learning situation.

Dewey's social psychological understanding of human development points to the ways in which student experience is interpreted in interaction with other students and with teachers. Ultimately, he argues for a process of "mutual accommodation and adaptation" between student and teacher.[26] The learning situation, for Dewey, should be regulated by a plan that is a "co-operative enterprise, not a dictation."[27] While teachers bring expertise and resources to learning—and they have a special responsibility to create effective learning situations—the student in a progressive school is given considerable authority, which can lead to immature choices of what to study and how to use time, at least initially. (For example, the first studies proposed by students unprepared for progressive education by their experience in conventional schools are too ambitious in scope and may, for example, depend more on self-help books than academic sources.) Teachers are present less as gate keepers who award or withhold credit than as co-architects, coaches, and mentors who share responsibility for the learning situation with their students.[28] Although Dewey's views about the student-teacher relationship sound modern, in part because of the long reach of his ideas in education, we are left without details about how the student-teacher relationship—that most essential human pairing—evolves, and how authority in the relationship develops and changes hands.

The progressive teacher's goal is to develop student self-control, which is judged more important than mastery of content. Dewey wants schools to produce students who have learned the capacity to act correctly in new situations rather than react to rote learning not easily applied to new situations. To Dewey, learning is not the result of great books, the culture of the past, and the teacher's authority and academic discipline. It is the unpredictable result of a fertile mix of process variables, namely, the *clarity* and *quality* of student purposes, learner experience and reflection, social interactions in the learning situation, and the school's democratic social arrangements.

Dewey's radical philosophy was meant to contradict the hidebound conventions of the traditional school that continue to the present. Listen to Dewey's language: The traditional school's subject matter consists of "bodies of information and of skills that have been worked out in the past." "Since the subject-matter as well as standards of proper conduct are handed down from the past, the attitude of pupils must, upon the whole, be one of docility, receptivity and obedience" "The traditional scheme is, in essence, one of imposition from above and from outside." Knowledge is taught as "a finished product, with little regard either to the ways in which it was originally built up or to changes that will surely occur in the future."[29]

Students are not empty vessels to be filled nor "lamps to be lighted" in the language of the Vermont educator, Royce "Tim" Pitkin, who reorganized Goddard College in 1938 to follow the progressive agenda then popular in American education.[30] The possibility of a progressive integration of experience into learning, one that advances the possibility of more learning, requires teachers to begin with the personal experience of the learner (begin with, that is, not necessarily end with or always focus on).

The concept of purpose is central to Dewey's implicit theory of motivation. Dewey distinguishes among three important terms: *impulses* and *desires,* which are transient and unrefined, and *purposes,* which emerge through active reflection. He seeks an active learner who gradually develops self-control over impulses, forging constructive purpose from immature desire. Desires are important as starting points and as raw motivation toward a goal, but they are not equivalent to purposes as motivating factors. But that is not to imply that helping students find their desires as a starting point for engaged learning is not important. The progressive educator worries, first, how to draw out reluctant students—to help them find their voices and imagination—before the second task of helping them move from transient desire to constructive purpose. Dewey puts it succinctly:

> There is, I think, no point in the philosophy of progressive education which is sounder than its emphasis upon the importance of the participation of the learner in the formation of the purposes which direct his activities in the learning process, just as there is no defect in traditional education greater than its failure to secure the active co-operation of the pupil in construction of the purposes involved in his studying.[31]

How self-control is developed in the learner is, perhaps, the major difference between the conventional approach to education and the perspective of the "progressive-experimentalist," a term Peter Hlebowitsh uses.[32] For the conventional teacher, self-control develops, presumably, from exposure to external authority in the form of teachers and text in a prescribed curriculum, whereas process variables like motivation and internalization are secondary to coverage of content. The progressive teacher, conversely, worries more about developing student self-control than academic content, focusing directly on the quality of student experience and motivation, and on building informed purposes.

So, the nature of learning, even in the confines of school, is a broad category for Dewey, one going well beyond a student's contact with one course or a specific teacher. To Dewey, learning occurs in dynamic situations that involve individuals and the whole range of felt experience, objects, and other people, including the teacher. As many teachers recognize, students often learn more from the whole experience of school than formal courses, what Dewey called "collateral learning." Students learn many things not covered in a lesson plan, such as the nature of authority, organizational skills, and ethics.[33]

Dewey explicitly rejects progressive educational theory when it becomes dogma, that is, when it is not willing to examine its own principles. A modern reader sees that Dewey understood the vulnerabilities of his theory and the school practices it inspired, even in the 1930s. Dewey issued three challenges, as appropriate today as in 1938:

> What does freedom mean and what are the conditions under which it can be realized?

> Just what is the role of the teacher and of books in promoting the educational development of the immature?

> How shall the young become acquainted with the past in such a way that the acquaintance is a potent agent in appreciation of the living present?[34]

Dewey knew about the excesses of progressive education of his day. He did not reject the importance of formal topics, books, or the intellectual content of the curriculum. On the contrary, all were valuable for providing experiences from which students might learn, if there was active reflection. What was important was the degree of learner involvement, not the prescribed curriculum as a timeless good.

While Dewey's ideals about learning, community, and democracy are appealing, his philosophy of education is not simple to put into practice or sustain, and the history of progressive schools and colleges is checkered.[35] Progressive schools and colleges have proved difficult to manage because of the centrifugal forces within, not the least of which is an unapologetic idealism about romantic categories like community and democracy, which gives the progressive school its distinctive, if turbulent, ethos. Idealistic concepts like community and democracy have, on the one hand, the power to motivate students and teachers, getting them involved in school planning and governance, which, on the other hand, complicates and slows down decision making and the routine business of a school. But if individualism is unchecked and governance boundaries to regulate intergroup conflict do not exist, Hlebowitsh warns, the possibility of real freedom is at risk because the response to anarchy may be authoritarianism: "Intelligent self-control and enlightened collective empowerment support the virtues of our democracy."[36]

Dewey's perspective is idealistic about human nature, particularly how willing individuals are to take responsibility for learning from experience, or how fast they can change—Hlebowitsh points to "romantic assumptions about the nature of the learner" made by progressive reformers of the 1960s.[37] Both questions challenge the progressive school, past and present, as Sizer suggests. Dewian philosophy *is* easily abused when progressive education is allowed to become permissive education, permissive to oneself, or to others, when the easier choice—the miseducative choice—is made out of fear or laziness. In less judgmental terms, the progressive teacher has, perhaps, less hard and fast categories with which to evaluate student progress. Student involvement is so important in the progressive school that it can overshadow actual performance, much less the progressive incorporation of passionate experience into new learning. It takes a well-prepared, disciplined teacher with a reasonable work load to handle the loose boundaries of the progressive school, more so than would be the case with the conventional school's fixed curriculum.[38]

Dewey understood all the ways in which a progressive curriculum is vulnerable: the mistake that all experience is genuinely and equally educative, that disconnected "interesting" experiences are necessarily educative, that external authority of teacher and text is suspect, that good motives make up for poor performance. Dewey would not approve of the excessive individualism of certain free schools in the late 1960s, or the abuse of democratic procedures by student interest groups in a progressive college like Goddard in the 1990s. Dewey would have rejected excesses in progressive education as a philosopher, and his teaching was reported to have been demanding (and conventional). Similarly, he also rejected the extremes in progressive political movements of his day. Instead, he asked teachers to value the "social and human center" within the school, and to create free, humane space in schools that was not crushed by schedules and bureaucracy. A certain turmoil was okay, but not chaos or anarchic drift.

Abraham Maslow's Theory of Peak Experience

The Progressive Era of the 1930s did not last, and progressive schools fell out of favor not long after World War II. Left-oriented social reform comes and goes in waves, perhaps, and it was not until the mid-1960s, thirty years later, that social change and democracy began to bubble again, only to boil over in the heyday of the counterculture.

Abraham Maslow stood apart from the excesses of the second wave of progressive reform. He sought a humanistic psychology, writing against two intellectual traditions of his day: the mechanistic learning theory that dominated psychology and what he considered the "negative" existentialism of Sartre (which we review in favorable terms shortly). He wrote about human potential and peak experiences, and how profoundly motivating such moments are.

Maslow's methods were interviews and questionnaires given to subjects who were asked to give the attributes of their most powerful experiences. Peak experiences are defined by a cluster of attributes reported: wholeness, an integrating experience, suspension of critical judgment, clear perception, loss of ego-centeredness, perception of beauty and goodness, sense of awe, a self that feels active and responsible, a feeling that the self is physically bigger, taller, and stronger, a feeling of gratitude, disorientation in time and space after the peak experience. People were left feeling intelligent, perceptive, witty, strong, graceful, self-confident, expressive, creative, and similar attributes.[39]

Taken altogether, such a list suggests that peak experiences are accompanied by elevated mood due to underlying physiological changes, a mood, which is then generalized to *all* dimensions of self-assessment and perception. Elsewhere, in a study of college students, Maslow reports two kinds of physical reactions to peak experience, which he declines to analyze, one of "high tension and excitement" and the other of "relaxation, peacefulness, quietness, the feeling of stillness." Either state is possible after "a beautiful sex experience, or esthetic experience or creative furor."[40]

Religious peak experiences share the positive attributes listed above and Maslow asserts that mystical experiences share a common essence. People report turning away from human concerns and suspending critical judgment. They perceive the world as an integrated, timeless and beautiful whole, and feel gratitude afterward for having had the transcendent experience. Like James's descriptions from a much different era, the religious experience for Maslow is one of "wonder, awe, reverence, humility, surrender, and even worship before the greatness of the experience."[41] In similar fashion, Maslow distinguishes between peak experiences and plateau experiences, the latter being serene and calm rather than emotional.[42]

Peak experiences, whether creative or mystical, about which James wrote, are acute identity experiences that express the "full-humanness" of the species. Maslow assumed, as did James, that this is a human capacity to which everyone has a right. Peak experiences should not be the special perks of an educated elite who have the time and money for massage and meditation.

Maslow also derived a description of a self-actualized personality from his research on peak experiences. The self-actualizing personality uses "Being-values" (similar to the list above) to orient one's life. While silent about how this ideal character was formed, Maslow's portrait influenced a generation of psychologists and teachers. With intellectual roots in psychoanalytic theory, he gradually expanded his ideas about peak experience to a larger project, a humanistic theory of personality based on the concept of the self-actualizing personality. Maslow was both a researcher and practicing psychotherapist who searched for a theory of personality that was, in his view, neither mechanistic (like behaviorist learning theory, popular in the 1960s) nor deficit oriented (like psychiatric models of pathology, past and present). His growth-oriented, humanistic psychology was intended as an alternative to behaviorist, need-reduction theories of motivation; to Freudian defense mechanisms that emphasized threat to the self and conscious and unconscious conflict avoidance; and to physiological, homeostatic mechanisms that cannot easily account for organismic growth.

In contrast to personality research that emphasized problems and psychopathology, Maslow studied psychologically healthy individuals. Even so, Maslow understands how deprivation reduces and delimits human motivation, because basic needs must be met first. He captured this idea in his notion of a hierarchy of needs, with biological needs at the base and spiritual needs on top.[43] Maslow, being a practicing therapist, also acknowledges the way neurotic defense mechanisms may not help a person cope with real conflict.

Maslow argued for a directional growth in self-actualization wherein personality expanded, wisdom increased, and character was developed. When people who are growth oriented are studied, he argued, the "coming to rest conception of motivation" is useless, because "growth is, *in itself,* a rewarding and exciting process."[44] This notion evolved to his concept of being-motivation versus deficiency-motivation.

Just as Maslow sought an innovative, positive approach to human development based on assets and human potential, he also sought a new, accepting approach to the way humans interact with their environment and the many objects and images they encounter. A theme in Maslow's theory is the value of an accepting stance of the ego toward objects in the world, including other people. In contrast to wanting to control others, or seek personal gratification in them, Maslow wanted perception that was "gentle, delicate, unintruding, undemanding, able to fit itself passively to the nature of things as water gently soaks into crevices."[45] In using such terms, Maslow urged a Taoist detachment of "Being-love" for the other person that had much in common with Eastern aesthetic and mystical traditions, which were less commonly recognized in his day than ours. Even though Maslow argued the advantages of "Being-cognition," he saw the limits of being too accepting in a problematic world. An accepting stance could lead to fatalism, indecisiveness, and reduced responsibility for others.[46]

Indeed, Maslow's search for an optimistic view of human nature led him to make assumptions that modern readers might find idealistic. He sought a humanistic perspective, one that emphasized human potential, in order to raise the sights of teachers, therapists, and researchers. Not one to define terms succinctly, Maslow reports that the self-actualizing person: has frequent peak experiences; achieves full humanity by living up to the highest standards; is focused on growth rather than deficiency; is being most authentic (the existentialist ideal); and is even godlike because the most perfect expression of ideals of selflessness, spiritual clarity, and the fusion of good, beauty, and justice are enacted.

Maslow assumes "a will to health" that may be undeveloped or repressed by subsequent experience.[47] If frustrated, physical sickness can result. To develop the potential for self-actualization and increased peak experience, he believes, is to become more fully human. Peak experiences are acute identity experiences in which people are closest to both who they are *and* what they can become.

As powerful as the transcendent peak experience may be, Maslow reported that true self-actualization as a personality trait is rare (he estimated it occurred in 1 percent of the adult population). Self-actualization does not mean a complete transcendence of human problems. Rather, it means moving from "neurotic pseudo-problems to the real, unavoidable, existential problems, inherent in the nature of man (even at his best) living in a particular kind of world."[48] Realistic guilt, worries, and existential anxiety continue to exist, partly because of imperfect human nature, and partly because of the world's challenges. Here Maslow assumes that growth motivation is a higher order motivation. It is "a hope, a yearning, a drive, a 'something' wished for but not achieved."[49] All people have such a wish but few develop it. Self-actualization as a personality trait must be learned over a lifetime. The implication for educators is that schools and colleges are sites for humanistic development.

To become self-actualized requires that we learn a world view, a demiphilosophy of life that expresses the human need to understand. Presumably, this work will go better if people have a guide, which other humanistic theories support. (Recall that Maslow was a practicing psychotherapist, his work informed by insights coming from his practice.)

Before considering Csikszentmihalyi's theory of flow, a contemporary perspective that extends Maslow's work, three limits in the theory should be noted. First, Maslow does not help us with an explanation about what it takes to move from deficiency to growth. Maslow's contribution was to open the topic, partly as counterpoint to the mechanistic, behaviorist theories of his day, and to describe the many positive attributes of peak experience and the larger construct of self-actualization. But he did, however, not leave us with a stage theory or an articulated model that could be used by people to construct a self-actualized life. Ever interested in human potential, Maslow describes what *could* be but provides no map for people to get there.

The second problem is one reason, perhaps, why his theory never advanced. All theories of human development face a core dilemma, one evident in the creative tension between accepting one's self as it is and acting to change one's self to what it should be. These are competing dynamics. To say that I must discover and accept myself, while also becoming someone different, is quite a challenge. Which motive is ascendant, when? Perhaps the way out of the problem is to argue that both dimensions—acceptance and transcendence—coexist, and both motives must be cultivated.

A third limit is common to most theories of human potential. Maslow wrote as if the tasks of the self-actualizing person are *intra*personal: that is, the discovery of self, the choice of which potentials to develop, the conscious construction of a life outlook. While Maslow acknowledged the importance of developing a life philosophy, his perspective seems uncomfortable with a self-actualizing person who must act, make real choices, in a world of deprivation and unending conflict.

Laudable in most respects, Maslow's humanism turns away from a social self that takes responsibility for others or the community. Without social and historical context, his is a soft humanism of personal well-being and individual potential. By his own admission, Maslow is uncomfortable with the existential dilemmas expressed in European intellectual circles, perspectives he termed "nay-saying," or pessimistic. Had he lived past 1968 to see the full expression of the youth movement—its idealism, social critique, *and* excesses—the social critique and personal ethics in self-actualization might have been articulated. To be worthy of the name, a humanistic psychology must somehow cope with the intrapsychic, the intrapersonal, and group and community development, all at the same time. While individual development follows different dynamics from those of community or group development, the strands are woven together. An excessive focus on the individual and stages of personal development lacks context. To existentialist Maxine Greene, discussed later in this chapter, lack of context makes humanistic psychology a "view from Nowhere."

Maslow's ideas are important for educators who want to understand human motivation. Whatever the type or degree, peak moments that are experienced as positive reinforce the activity that produces them, whether in church or school, or in interaction with others or during individual creative work. Such moments move us emotionally, although the peak moment is usually not in awareness. Consciously or not, we are motivated to pursue these activities in order to repeat the psychological experience. Leaders can create the circumstances for peak experiences and psychologically manipulate their followers, for ill or good. Peak experiences are possible in class discussion, during a lecture, or on the playing field. They are the result of individual creative work by students and faculty, though peak experiences often go unrecognized. If we knew more about such moments, especially the transitions between psychological states, we could design better learning situations.

Mihaly Csikszentmihalyi's Theory of Flow

Like Maslow a generation ago, contemporary psychologist Mihaly Csikszentmihalyi is interested in optimal human experience. While neither theorist focused on learning or the needs of schools and colleges, the ideas are important for understanding both the goals of education and learning as process. Csikszentmihalyi studies optimal experience in the moments when a person's body and mind is stretched to its limits in pursuit of a challenge, such as rock climbing or performing music. Concentration, which is the central mechanism, is total, and the characteristics of such moments resemble those of Maslow's peak experience: intense concentration, loss of self-consciousness, loss of time consciousness, and a certain effortless quality to the entire experience.[50]

Listen to Csikszentmihalyi's language: "Flow," his term, is "the process of total involvement with life."[51] At such exceptional moments, "heart, will, and mind" are joined together and people report a "sense of effortless action they feel in moments that stand out as the best in their lives." Csikszentmihalyi wants to help people develop the skills to find happiness in a world of scarcity and frustration so that they might "live in fullness, without waste of time and potential, expressing one's uniqueness, yet participating intimately in the complexity of the cosmos."[52]

Csikszentmihalyi's research began with a Maslow-like method in which several hundred people who had flow experiences were interviewed. Later, he created the Experience Sampling Method in which thousands of subjects in many cultures and occupations were equipped with electronic pagers or programmable watches, which were activated eight times a day at random intervals. Signals went off at random times within two-hour segments of the day, from early morning to late evening. When paged, study participants wrote down in a booklet they carried what they were doing, thinking, and who they were with, then rated their psychological experience at the moment on numerical scales assessing happiness, concentration, motivation, and self-esteem. In a week, each person filled out fifty-six pages, producing a detailed record of the day's activities and psychological experience.

Csikszentmihalyi's intention is to help people improve the *direct* control of consciousness and, thus, their lives. He makes this distinction: "We cannot expect anyone to help us live; we must discover how to do it by ourselves."[53] While this could be read to minimize the pivotal role of teachers, mentors, and friends, it comes close to the existentialist view that we are fundamentally alone in life, responsible for the choices made about how to live.

To take control of psychological experience people first must learn to control their *behavior*. Many parts of life cannot be changed or controlled, but we can try, at least, to control attention. Control of consciousness is the central mechanism—"the ability to focus attention at will, to be oblivious to distraction, to concentrate for as long as it takes to achieve a goal, and not longer."[54] Although the potential to improve psychological experience is present even in mundane activities like washing dishes or driving, most people never understand it is possible to focus their psychic experience in order to get the most from it.

Entropy is the natural state to which consciousness will return if not ordered by human actions and thought. Consider this description: "Without focus, consciousness is a state of chaos. The normal condition of the mind is one of informational disorder: random thoughts chase one another instead of lining up in logical causal sequences."[55] While people assume they control their minds, thinking is less orderly than it appears, because attention wanders easily if external stimuli are changed. When not structured by external activity, disconnected ideas intrude on consciousness, leading to uncomfortable feelings experienced as anxiety or boredom. Being alone, or having "nothing to do," are experienced as unpleasant. In such a state, it may take some minutes to reestablish a coherent line of thought. Evidence for this idea comes from stimulus deprivation studies in which people are deprived of external stimulation in a quiet room or suspended in a tank of warm water. (Consider, too, the "punishment" of solitary confinement.) Under such conditions, people grow uncomfortable and disoriented. Awash in uncontrolled fantasies, they lose track of their thoughts:

The mind needs ordered information to keep itself ordered. As long as it has clear goals and receives feedback, consciousness keeps humming along. This is why games, sports, and ceremonial rituals are some of the most satisfying activities—they keep attention ordered within narrow boundaries and clear rules.[56]

So, human culture both enriches life and provides a shield from entropic chaos by helping us concentrate attention and thought. Put in other terms, we humans create order daily for wandering minds, or are caught up with external events and lose control.

Two ways exist to avoid such feelings. First, distractible humans can impose order on the mind from "outside" by committing to an activity that provides structure to consciousness. The second method is far more difficult: to learn to concentrate when we so choose. In the first case, people have to learn to work around the limits of the mind-body by changing the stimulus conditions that shape consciousness (rather than trying to control a wandering mind). In the second case, internal discipline, a capacity that takes time to acquire, is not all or nothing. Few people are paragons of personal discipline—rather, internal focus must be constantly rebuilt, perhaps on a daily basis. Once learned, self-focusing is not a fixed attribute, a switch that is always ready to be turned on.

The psychological state of flow is most likely to occur in life activities when goals provide structure to the activity for which there is also timely feedback. Certain elements must be balanced, says Csikszentmihalyi: "When goals are clear, feedback relevant, and challenges and skills are in balance, attention becomes ordered and fully invested."[57] The conception is interesting even if the internal dynamics may not be as straightforward. If, for example, the goals are not high enough, or the skills required of the task not challenging, the psychological experience is less involving. Flow is not likely if the activity is neither challenging nor requires skill. However, when high challenge is matched to high skill, Csikszentmihalyi describes the experience: "There is no space in consciousness for distracting thoughts, irrelevant feelings. Self-consciousness disappears, yet one feels stronger than usual. The sense of time is distorted; hours seem to pass by in minutes."[58] When attention is focused on performance, distracting worries are fewer, and less attention goes to aches and pains.

So, quality of life depends on psychic investments made in nearly every imaginable activity, from washing the dishes to playing the piano to playing tennis. Csikszentmihalyi sums up his theory: "To control attention means to control experience, and therefore the quality of life."[59] Like James nearly a hundred years earlier, Csikszentmihalyi argues that life has unlimited possible investments every day. That is, if we humans learn to focus, the quality of the psychological experience improves independent of the nature of the activity. Whether doing housework or a repetitive chore at work, it is possible to invest psychic energy in the task, thereby enjoying the activity. (Buddhists call this being mindful.)

Contrast this involved experience with the experience of people, especially students, who report being bored much of the time when, in fact, they are surrounded by numerous investment objects. Why don't people use such moments fully? Consistent with his notion of life investments, given the normal state of entropy, Csikszentmihalyi acknowledges that interactions take energy, of which one has only so much. He neglects, however, the interaction between flow experience and what he calls "disposable activation energy," by which new energy can be created by positive experiences.[60]

Social interactions structure attention by introducing external demands. Interactions, even casual ones, bring goals and feedback. Csikszentmihalyi adds, "People are generally much happier and more motivated when with friends, regardless of what they are doing."[61] In modern technological societies, however, we are alone nearly a third of the day, and Csikszentmihalyi suggests that many people are not comfortable with this condition, preferring external structure to having to structure one's own time.

Flow appears most often in favorite activities like gardening or cooking, occurs in driving and talking, and at work. Notwithstanding deep ambivalence about work, an activity that consumes a third of the week, work provides a structure for activities. According to interviews of people reporting flow experiences, the intrinsic rewards of work are most likely found among those who have some freedom to control events, and where work and leisure are blended.

Flow is rare in passive leisure activities like watching television. In that regard, questions could be raised about the use of passive leisure like television to ward off negative feelings. Active leisure, which takes an initial investment of energy, has the only real chance to change mood; but it takes discipline to overcome the first resistance and start on the activity like jogging or writing a letter. While this makes intuitive sense, the theory still has a problem with intermediate stages that move toward the ideal flow state. What *are* the mechanisms? At one point, Csikszentmihalyi writes: "there are no gimmicks, no easy shortcuts. It takes a total commitment to a fully experienced life, one in which no opportunities are left unexplored and no potential undeveloped, to achieve excellence."[62] Few would challenge this injunction. But what are the stages by which one *learns* this life purpose and the habits of mind and body required to live it?

In its earliest formulations, flow theory was built around the assumption that individual happiness is, or should be, the central motive in human experience. The first chapter of Csikszentmihalyi's *Flow* is entitled "Happiness Revisited," in which he makes the case for getting control over one's life, and thus one's psychological experience and quality of life. Recently, Csikszentmihalyi's thinking has evolved to include consideration of social values underlying life purposes. The good life is defined by the "full involvement of flow, rather than happiness," by a "feeling that one belongs to something greater and more permanent than oneself," and by "an active responsibility for the rest of humankind, and for the world of which we are a part." Arguing that most world religions adopt similar values, he adds that the challenge for agnostics in modern times is to create new transcendent goals to give meaning to contemporary lives just as "earlier myths have helped our ancestors to make sense of their existence, relying on the images, metaphors, and facts known to them."[63]

Like Maslow before him, Csikszentmihalyi extended his theory of the characteristics of flow from a *temporary* psychological state to an *enduring* personality trait. He described the autotelic personality, which is comparable to Maslow's self-actualizing personality. Csikszentmihalyi argues that the autotelic personality (autotelic as in "self–goal setting") is developed out of family environments that have five attributes. They: 1.) support clear *expectations*; 2.) practice *centering*; 3.) encourage *choice*; 4.) demonstrate *commitment* to the person; and 5.) offer appropriate levels of *challenge*. Several steps encourage developing an autotelic self: setting goals; becoming immersed in an activity; paying attention to what one is doing; and learning to enjoy the immediate experience.[64] Still, the important question is how to construct, in Csikszentmihalyi's terms, a life of flow, which his theory only partially depicts.

Before moving on, I want to take stock of Maslow's and Csikszentmihalyi's theories of human potential and two problems that both share. The theories are flawed: First, they depend upon a false dichotomy, peak experience or not, flow or not. Second, this assumption leads the authors to underestimate the transitions between point A (lack of flow, not being in control, and so on) and point B (the full form of each attribute). What is missing in both Maslow's and Csikszentmihalyi's theories, as well as most personality constructs, are the intermediate stages between optimal experience, rare as it is, and the middle-range experiences of daily life, in or out of school. If we educators do not understand the middle range, we cannot possibly help students learn to self-manage transitions in personal motivation and attention.

No one would question the value of personal control, a centerpiece in every theory of human nature, or the value of peak experiences to enrich life and human culture. But a problem for both theories and most of popular psychology is how difficult it is, in truth, for people to take control of their lives and to maintain that personal discipline when tired or tempted. It is challenging enough to learn the concepts and skills necessary to be effective in school or business. Much more difficult for most people is to control impulses and change bad habits (think of how difficult it is to stop smoking, or not bite one's nails).

Ellen Langer's Theory of Mindfulness

Over more than ten years social psychologist Ellen Langer and her associates developed an imaginative series of social psychological experiments on the theory of mindfulness and the cognitive dynamics of attention. In choosing experimental methods to test her ideas, Langer's work goes well beyond Maslow's interviews and the sampling methods of Csikszentmihalyi. One dramatic line of experiments, for example, sought to increase mindfulness and longevity among the elderly in nursing homes, and the results supported her theory. Of interest to her was the mindless, automatic behavior of people doing things like washing the dishes or driving a car when attention is not focused. Her group also explored the problem of when preset ideas—premature cognitive commitments like stereotypes—limit the ability of people to make better choices, and, generally, to feel in control of their lives. Preconceptions that housework, for example, is arduous or mindsets about the nature of a particular task reduce involvement and diminish quality of work.

With regard to increasing motivation and learning, Langer notes that most human activities are intrinsically neither pleasant nor unpleasant. Rather, we invest those qualities in the experience in terms of the expectations and feelings attached to the activity. Like many observers of education, Langer agrees that "The fear of negative evaluation colors much of the school experience for most people."[65] Negative evaluation leads students to label themselves as "not good students" and to distance themselves from school and learning. To increase involvement in school, her experiments suggest a number of interventions. Asking students to make discriminations or draw distinctions in their work increases motivation.[66]

Mindful learning is increased by choosing tasks that increase relevance to individual students, an idea well known by progressive teachers. It is increased also by teaching students how to make the required material interesting to themselves, a point that progressive educators may miss because they give so much importance to student choice.[67] Finally, she comments on the "illusion of the correct answer," a fantasy so alive in American classrooms. (The correct question is far more educative.) In summary, to Langer, mindful learning emphasizes questions, the learning process, and developing self-control authority, whereas unmindful learning emphasizes answers, outcomes, and expert authority: "The theory of mindfulness insists that uncertainty and the experience of personal control are inseparable."[68]

Mindfulness or paying attention can be developed and taught. In other ways, people will sometimes persevere with the wrong solution to a problem, trying over and over to make it work. A mindful approach, according to Langer, will be flexible, create new categories while working, continue to be open to new information, and be aware of multiple perspectives. So, Langer suggests that cognitive reappraisal will help people reframe the situation, seeing new possibilities not obvious before, such as might happen during successful psychotherapy or school counseling.

Like Dewey before her, she focuses on process, not product, which is a limitation in results-oriented, American education. If the process involves choices students can make, Langer argues that they will feel more responsible for the results and be more mindful in the process. Like Maslow and Csikszentmihalyi before her, Langer observes that focused attention is experienced as pleasant and mindfulness is exhilarating. People find "a second wind" when attention returns.[69]

Langer's research suggests the characteristics of learning situations where students are more likely to be mindful: those that elicit personal choice and thus increase personal responsibility; those where the focus is the process of problem solving, not only the results; and where students are taught flexible, mindful approaches to problem solving.

As creative as Langer's experiments are, her theory lacks an explicit social or ethical context. Students should be mindful of what? Certainly, the choice of object or activity matters. Mindful *for* what? Surely, some purposes are more valuable than others. As useful as Langer's instrumental insights into human motivation are, the theory could be read as yet another theory of human potential that begins and ends with the individual. As was the case for James, Maslow, and Csikszentmihalyi before her, Langer's theory is context-less because surrounding contexts, which let us interpret individual behavior and development, are presumed or missing. The existentialists just ahead have much to offer on this account. But before we consider their ideas, another contemporary social psychologist, William Kahn, will expand the conversation. Kahn asks us to think about how we organize the workplace, especially the implicit messages sent to employees (and, extending his ideas to education, the implicit messages sent to students and teachers).

William Kahn's Theory of Presence in Work

Human beings spend most of their lives at work, but we know less than we should about how personal identity is shaped by social forces of the modern workplace. Kahn's theory of motivation in the workplace uses role theory and Tavistock theory to explain how people differentially invest themselves in work roles.[70] Using this framework, he explores the question of how people calibrate investment of self in different roles such as worker, parent, community leader, student, and teacher.

The theory of psychological presence at work places a humanistic value at the center of his theory: namely, the value of individuals using their full selves at work, of being fully there in one's work. Involved workers benefit the organization. But Kahn begins with the needs of the individual, which are usually treated as secondary to those of the organization in most organizational practice and theory. His interest in the individual and human development in the workplace is in contrast to the conventional view of worker-as-object, in which the corporation needs only certain skills performed, or a portion of the whole self used.[71] Traditional organizations emphasize command and control, not human development. What matters to the modern organization are chain of command, a strict division of labor, cost controls, and expectations that employees follow routines by which to assure efficient, high-quality products.

The dominant metaphor of worker (or student) as mechanism is both wrong and shortsighted. Rather than see the worker in Taylor-like terms— like "a water spigot," as Kahn puts it, that can be turned on or off—he asks for a holistic, humanistic view of how people draw upon all their resources and creativity while at work. When so engaged, workers are being authentic because self and work roles are synchronous. (Compare Kahn's notion of the authentic self to the existentialist view.) In turn, involved workers help create transforming relations at work *and* contribute to the organizational culture necessary to sustain transformed relationships.

In addition to role theory, Kahn draws from Tavistock theory, which applies psychoanalytic concepts to authority and human development inside groups and organizations. In particular, human beings are assumed to be fundamentally *ambivalent* about participation in intimate relations and social groups or movements. People may seek involvement because of the fear of being alone (or abandoned, once in a group). But they also fear being engulfed and losing their identity. (Fear of being overwhelmed is particularly threatening to individuals with weak ego boundaries.) Whether conscious or not of such ambivalence about belonging, people calibrate their investment carefully. Thus, the relationship between person and group is a *dynamic* one as individuals move to, and from, attachment and authenticity in their intimate relations and engagement at work.

Psychological presence or engagement at work does not come easily or quickly. Partly because of individual ambivalence about attachment, and partly because of organizational resistance to individualization, Kahn finds that people face slow, small steps toward presence and authenticity. Not unlike the painstaking progress of psychotherapy, change comes slowly because people experiment with new ways of being at work, gradually expanding their psychological defenses. To manage psychological investment in work takes effort and time to learn. Individuals learn to manage the psychological boundary with the organization and its culture, to not be too close or too distant.

Personal engagement, or a full investment of self-in-role, is most likely when three conditions are met: psychological meaningfulness, psychological safety, and psychological availability. The work and its component tasks must be perceived as meaningful, and the organization's norms must encourage the worker to a full investment of self. To fully invest oneself in any role is to risk being hurt, leading to feelings of vulnerability, which contributes to the sense of ambivalence about attachment to the group. Psychological availability refers to the extent to which a person has the physical and emotional energy to devote to a full investment. If a person is exhausted from difficulties in the community or stress at home, full investment, and hence engagement at work, is not likely. Please note that Kahn's definition of engagement is psychological more than social, in contrast to the distinction I have drawn between involvement and social engagement.

To create organizations that stimulate engagement by their workers and clients, Kahn suggests what supervisors (and teachers) should do to increase the possibility of worker (or student) engagement. Others things being equal, engagement is more likely when the supervisor: is attentive to the other; expresses a connection to the other and the shared work; integrates different parts of self in the relationship with the worker; and focuses on helping the other perform the assigned work. Important behavioral insights are proffered: The enabling supervisor will have these behaviors: physical presence in the form of being planted, and still; eye contact; nonverbal affirmation, like nodding the head; a full range of human emotion; a cognitive presence in the form of following the conversation and participating in dialogue; a fullness of speech (range, intonation); and recognition of the full self involved in the total work, not just a narrow skill.

What else can be done to increase investment of self-in-role, and thus engagement (as Kahn defines it)? Progressive educators will recognize the list: Involve the worker in the design of the job; encourage cross-training and other perspectives; minimize the degree of hierarchy and encourage participation; break down internal partitions by encouraging teams; emphasize positive reinforcement, not negative sanctions and guilt; use authority figures to both consciously and unconsciously model engagement and the full use of self in work for other colleagues; and avoid limiting roles, like the scapegoat, that stereotype complex individuals and limit their development.

Kahn acknowledges individual differences in psychological presence, making a crucial point: Psychological presence is *a set of expectations and behaviors that can be learned.* While some people seem to be naturally "present" at work—natural leaders, perhaps—skills like active listening and paying attention can be learned. For most people, then, self-in-role investment can also be learned, just as we have argued that many components of the engaged life can be learned.

Here is another insight from Kahn. While engagement behavior can be learned, the possibility of change toward greater psychological presence requires individual acts of courage. In complex institutional life, it is not always safe to be "present." Individuals have to make decisions to invest themselves, to trust, or to change their behavior. Organizations that encourage risk-taking will benefit from employees who increase self-in-role. Courage to invest more of self in role can be learned inside the organization or school. The behavior of authority figures or role models can be influential; if authority figures model presence, if they are seen by others as taking chances with their own self-in-role enactment, others in the organization are likely to act similarly.

As provocative as Kahn's humanistic theory is, it has its limits. Sustained psychological presence is exhausting because perceptual vigilance and personal effort are required. To maintain a high degree of interpersonal attention takes considerable energy, which suggests three problems. First, psychological presence is not possible to sustain, and it may, in fact, lead to burnout. Staff burnout, after all, is common to small, intensely personal, human service organizations where people invest themselves in their work. In such institutions, the organization becomes an extension of self. The staff may be engaged, which brings benefits to both the individual and the organization short term, but the degree of engagement cannot be sustained and individuals grow demoralized. Second, many work roles do not expect, or even allow for, full investment of self-in-role. (A hard-charging executive may not want a secretary to bring the full self to what is really a narrow job.) Third, institutions that do not help individuals develop realistic views of the organization's rationalized—even exploitative—needs may be letting employees in for serious disappointment.

In sum, Kahn's theory is dynamic, humanistic, and holistic because of the interweaving of individual development with relationships at work and development of the organization. He asks us, first, to focus on how roles are learned and enacted in an organization. Role theory gives us powerful ideas with which to study human and organizational behavior. To explain organizational behavior, we begin to think in terms of roles, norms and role sets, and organizational culture, not personalities, good and bad people. We envision the dynamic, developmental possibility in interpersonal interactions between workers and supervisors and, by extension, between students and teachers in schools as a type of organization. The role set of student and teacher is both learned *and* complementary—what those roles are, and how they are enacted by both parties determines the possibility of people feeling and acting engaged. So Kahn asks us, in effect, to consider *reciprocal development* when the organization's culture supports increased individual psychological engagement of self-in-role, which also increases organizational creativity and productivity.

Of the contemporary theorists we have considered, only Kahn surfaces the inherent conflict between individual and social interests, or includes a social critique, if thinly drawn. Dewey was quite aware of this dialectic in his thinking, but that elemental tension between person and society disappears in other theories. James, Maslow, Csikszentmihalyi, and Langer offer interesting ideas to improve quality of life. One reads in vain to find social context, much less direct criticism, of the social forces bearing down on the lonely individual, which leaves such treatments rather lifeless. To provide that context and one ethic with which to evaluate human purposes and motives, we turn to the Continental traditions of existentialism.

Maxine Greene, Existentialism, and a Life Made of Choices

I admire the unsentimental philosophy of existentialism and its exhortation that every person, having one short life, create a meaningful existence. The existentialist wants to believe that his or her philosophy faces up to modernity, rapid social change, and the pressures bearing down on the lone individual who must craft, somehow, an authentic existence out of the noise and modern busyness. While always having the possibility of psychic retreat, to withdraw and pull back from modern ambiguity, the engaged life is defined by the choices one makes—daily, monthly, yearly. Thus, we look to the ideas of existentialism and try to capture this special ethic. It is a view both sobering in its stark, cold assumptions about human existence and strangely uplifting, positing a resilient human spirit, one capable of creating meaning in the worst circumstances.

"Existentialism" refers to a group of philosophers and writers who, over a period of a hundred years, shared similar views, each writing about the loneliness of human existence, often by using a personal narrative. Three themes are commonplace: the individual facing modernity, the lack of rational understanding of the universe leading to feelings of dread or absurdity, and, in such a world, the importance of individual choice while constructing a life. The existentialist perspective dates to Continental heretical ideas in philosophy put forth, most notably, by Friedrich Nietzsche, writing in the last part of the nineteenth century. Martin Heidegger, Jean-Paul Sartre, and Albert Camus felt the general despair intellectuals felt, we assume, in the first half of the twentieth century, having witnessed two devastating world wars in twenty years. Nietzsche's stance as "outsider intellectual" was carried forward. Sartre, who gave the movement its name, was its leading theorist and Camus, its most influential writer.

To many readers, existentialism is an insistent voice for the besieged individual more than a body of intellectual work.[72] So much of the writing is personally evocative, as if the existentialist feels a special burden to speak out, somehow, for the lonely individual in an unforgiving world. Blaise Pascal captures that poignant sense of forever being alone in a well-known passage:

> When I consider the short duration of my life, swallowed up in the eternity before and after, the little space which I fill, and even can see, engulfed in infinite immensity of space of which I am ignorant, and which knows me not, I am frightened, and am astonished being here rather than there, why now rather than then.[73]

The existentialist tradition is not well organized as a body of thought. Indeed, its major thinkers would not like to be grouped together. Heidegger, for one, is said to have denied being an existentialist, much as Marx rejected being a Marxist. Camus did not like the label. Existentialism was never an intentional community, and the outsider loner Nietzsche would, in any case, not have joined such a movement. However, it is Nietzsche's intellectual stance in the world and the voice of everyman that he sometimes adopts that earn him this company.[74]

Something about the existential stance in life speaks to the human condition with great power and depth. The famous opening paragraph of Camus's *The Stranger* projects the existentialist tone in an unsettling, dispassionate discussion about the death of the narrator's mother, surely a traumatic moment for most people.[75] The existentialist perspective, more broadly, asks how people manage lives in a busy, impersonal, and difficult world where traditional justifications for personal sacrifice and discipline, once promulgated by church, state, and political party, no longer seem credible. If fundamental faiths—the engraved absolutes—are shaken, what justifies human existence? Why should one care, or even try, given the sacrifice required? On what foundation, indeed, can one build an authentic existence that is worth the effort? Not easy issues for any philosophy, these are an existentialist's insistent questions.

The ideas of existentialism are one response by intellectuals to the rapid development in Europe of a modern worldview. Over the last several hundred years, dramatic changes have occurred in how an individual existence is understood, not to mention changes in the belief systems used to explain the world and its rapid change. The Medieval period had been defined by a rigid feudal structure and hierarchy, captured by the Great Chain of Being, which set forth defined roles and responsibilities of the lowest entity to those of God. The dominant belief systems of the day, which people used to interpret their lives, were organized religions, which were gradually challenged by science, in general, and by secular political ideologies like Marxism, in particular.[76]

In the mid-1800s in France, today's social sciences like sociology and psychology began to evolve slowly, stimulated in part by Auguste Comte's criticism, among others, of the hegemony of the Catholic Church. Although cognizant of the integrating power of organized religion in society, Comte sought to separate values—in this case, religious ones—from the study and administration of society.

The impact of science, then and now, was to undermine a number of elemental faiths that made life easier for individuals to understand and accept. More broadly, Max Weber's concern was the increasing rationalization of life due to the rise of capitalism as an economic force that challenged traditional social forms in family, church, and community. The rationalization of life in response to economic forces served to disenchant the world, to push back the mystical and the poetic.[77] (In Part II, we discuss how the rise of fundamentalist religions, true-belief cults, and so-called New Age beliefs are attempts to re-enchant the world, to *restore* the mystical and the poetic.) By undercutting traditional and simple explanations for order and social change, people's worldview became modern and caused increased anxiety— disenchantment increased ambiguity about things that once were taken for granted.[78]

Intellectual provocations came from many directions. Nietzsche issued "God is dead," his famous challenge to institutional and philosophical legitimacy in religious Europe of the late 1800s. Sometimes misinterpreted— and dismissed too quickly—as a literal statement, Nietzsche's challenge was more serious than a petulant jibe at world religions. He questioned the very framework, religious or ideological, by which humans justify life choices.[79]

Expressing the same spirit, post–World War II French existentialists like Camus, Sartre, and Simone de Beauvoir argued that, outside of personal commitment, no higher authority exists to provide succor, direction, and meaning in life. The ideological passions of nationalism and socialism helped replace, in part, the faltering belief systems of conventional religion in the 1930s, at least among intellectuals. Both political ideologies were, however, exposed as flawed by the end of World War II. The internal contradictions of Communism, in particular, which had been supported by progressive intellectuals of the day, were also beginning to be exposed (although its full collapse as a belief system would wait upon changes begun during perestroika).

So, the good existentialist assumes—better, is forced reluctantly to assume—a fundamental tension, if not indifference, between individual needs and those of society. The large forces and institutions of mass society have different dynamics from those of the family, and individuals are naive to expect protection or special treatment. While this idea seems obvious to a modern intellectual, the insight comes as a surprise to people who dedicate their lives to serving a college only to be deeply hurt when the institution does not treat them fairly or "love them back." What is flawed, in part, is the childish projection of family dynamics onto those of large institutions whose nature it is to fit whole, feeling people into circumscribed roles. Institutions, even the smallest, are not families and can never be so (as if family dynamics do not themselves bring problems for individuals).

To the existentialist, everyone is alone in the world, start to finish. All are alone except for brief moments with friends and loved ones, or momentary passions. Not only this, a burden in itself, but all are alone in the face of life's problems, especially death. All will die, and most die alone, perhaps connected to life-support machines and drugged. My choice of language may seem provocative, but the feelings will be recognized by anyone who has spent time in a hospital, for example, dependent on a morphine pump after an accident, watching, as if under water, loved ones stop by for a visit. (Existential *angst,* a term for such fears, does not capture the poignancy when one is this alone.)

Maxine Greene reintroduced many thousands of readers to Camus's *The Plague,* set in the small coastal city of Oran in north Africa, which is suddenly subject to a mysterious pestilence from which no one is safe. First published in 1947 when Camus was thirty-three, Tony Judt says Camus's most popular novel is an allegory working at three levels: coping with pestilence, fascism and resistance to it in Vichy France, and, for our purposes, the dilemmas of human choice in a problematic world.[80] The fast-spreading disease paralyzes the city. Most citizens find it hard to think about the problem, or to act. But it is the dulled consciousness of Oran's citizens that Maxine Greene notices in Camus's powerful book.[81] The other plague that threatens the city—and modern civilization—is what Greene terms not being "awake in the world." Not only is there a denial of the fact that death is inevitable, but social problems like starvation that make us anxious, or feel guilty, are blocked from consciousness.

The forces that control the movement of stars, those that began life millions of years ago, and those that might inhibit the growth of cancerous cells inside us—all are serious questions that people find hard to think about, or stay with once called into consciousness. So, an ineluctable aloneness is made worse by ignorance and superstition about the world's nature, driven by an unconscious motive to not understand what is happening, or why (notwithstanding the rise of science).

Except for oh-so-brief moments, humans are alone for a lifetime without external direction. One must create one's own existence, daily, by making choices to serve others, to mark time, or to escape. Listen to Camus: "The truth is that I fight time and other people for each hour of my work, usually without winning. I'm not complaining. *My life is what I have made it,* and I am the first person responsible for the way and the pace at which I spent it."[82] The world we inherit—a world into which we feel *thrown*—is not necessarily pleasant, well-ordered, or rational. ("Thrownness" is an important concept in existentialist thought to which we will return.) The world is not necessarily anything but what one makes it. It is an "existential predicament," a term used by Charles Guignon and Dirk Pereboom to capture the pathos of the isolated individual tying to construct a life in the face of great odds.[83] The mysteries of the natural world—the origin of life, the nature of deep space, the functions of our own bodies—do not stimulate the curiosity we would expect. Rather, mysteries seem to overwhelm. The withdrawal by the public is not just from understanding but from political life and the possibility of acting to prevent injustice, to stop the plague of dulled consciousness.

Social critics add their voices. Jurgen Habermas warns about civic privatism in a depoliticized public realm where "political abstinence [is] combined with an orientation to career, leisure, and consumption."[84] Overwhelmed by the contradictions and pace of modernity, Christopher Lasch worries that the human spirit retreats to a minimal self that wants only to survive. Zygmunt Bauman argues that modernity has become "liquid" because fixed boundaries that once defined society and provided anchors for personal existence are gone. A society of strangers results, say Michael Ignatieff and Paul Wachtel, in which satisfaction of material needs does not satisfy needs for community and meaning in life. Freedom is reduced to the freedom to get ahead, or worse, to be left alone. The widespread adoption of television in American homes, Robert Putnam says, cuts deeply into civic participation and social interaction.[85]

To a radical anarchist like the late Guy Debord, true individuality is sacrificed as the person becomes a disengaged spectator, one content to watch the spectacle of modern life unfold.[86] The spectator lets himself be entertained, bemused by American presidential politics, perhaps. But an authentic individuality and sincerity are eroded. Worse, the citizen-spectator is aware, at least sometimes, of his or her own passivity and so colludes with external social forces, powerful as they may be, to create the alienation. One could, after all, choose to get involved at any moment.

I want to extend the argument. Not willing to face modernity, its uncertainty, layered social issues, and social change, the fragile human spirit finds comfort by controlling what it can, by escaping into small decisions of what to wear to work, to eat, or to buy. Suppose the suburban American family's recreation of the week, beyond the dull routines of school and work, is to visit the shopping mall, where the possibility of being recreated is tied more to consumption than to being a family.[87] What is missing, one fears, is a situated freedom of hope that acknowledges others and the needs of society. Listen to the edge in Greene's voice: "Stunned by hollow formulas, media-fabricated sentiments and cost-benefit terminologies, young and old alike find it hard to shape authentic expressions of hopes and ideals."[88]

Sartre argues that an authentic personal existence in such a world must be built out of challenges to that world's *facticity* (a concept he borrowed from Heidegger), its established facts and routines. Indeed, Sartre argues, a person is acting in bad faith if that facticity is not challenged, or if one routinely escapes into fantasies about reality. Sartre appears to have assumed that it is never possible to live fully authentically, in an ideal state, either because of sustained challenges to reality or our fantasies about it.[89]

We need to pause. Existentialists and social critics have raised issues about problems in living that are most challenging. As I suggested while opening the chapter, alienation, existential loneliness, falling from grace, dissociation, depression, anomia, and the like have been special topics of interest to artists and intellectuals in every age due, in part, to the nature of their stand-apart role in society. But what they write about is not just the special affliction of the estranged intellectual, the outsider who never quite fits. Rather, the psychological experience, albeit unnamed and largely unconscious, is part of everyone's lived experience.

What is missing in scholarly treatments is the phenomenology of alienation or existential thrownness, what it feels like to be thrown into an alien world set apart from one's immediate experience. Also missing are explanations of how this uncomfortable psychological experience motivates us to be nostalgic for childhood and its immediacy, eager for moments of fusion in school, work, or love, and vulnerable to belief systems that offer certainty in exchange for the heavy freedom to doubt and think.

Reflect, for a moment, on the felt experience of alienation, of finding oneself in awkward roles, with a web of social obligations and a work tempo that pushes us. We are concerned with the *phenomenology* of alienation or angst rather than with a philosophical category. There is, for most people, a palpable separation of the self from the given world one wakes up to and must now inhabit. For example, when I go to work on Mondays I feel like a stranger in an inherited world not of my choice, but I have to act in and upon it, nonetheless. For many people, going to work on Monday, that fixture of modernity and rationalized work, brings mixed feelings of relief and dread. The only course of action for that day is to act on that world, to make choices that are more authentic than those that just get us by.

Modern work demands calculated tradeoffs between the good and bad parts (and it requires instrumental calculations like tradeoff and efficiency).

Indeed, William Kahn would understand that the nature of modern work requires that we all treat part or all of ourselves as objects that we commit to alien activity. I like my job, although the foregoing may not sound like it. Ninety percent of the work is "administrivia." But if I take it on, I get to work on significant institutional problems for the remaining ten percent, which is a tradeoff I accept.

In a palpable way, the alienation is exactly this daily separation between the positive and negative facets of a job or a life. There are, after all, neither perfect institutions nor perfect jobs. As I experience the work week, the quality of existence is not constant and I often think of a crude ratio of good days to bad days. If the ratio stays above four good to three bad, it has been a good week. As I look around at my colleagues in different institutions and stages of life, few are completely happy with the work situations they have created. And yet, we choose the worlds, partly alien or not, and make as much creative space in them as we can for as long as we can. That is to say, although thrown into compromises of all sorts, an authentic existence is built of daily choices to push back the bad space and bad work, and to expand the good space and good work.

Camus makes the same point and shows us a way out of the existential predicament. Like his protagonist, Dr. Rieux, in *The Plague*, the way to fight the plague of dulled consciousness is by serving others. Prayer does no good, and modern science, little better. Waiting will not help. So, a meaningful, authentic life is defined, first, by facing the facts, not escaping the facts via fantasy, and second, by choosing to serve a higher good other than one's own survival. Rieux makes his choices "not out of heroic courage or careful reasoning but rather from a sort of necessary optimism."[90] Not much comfort, perhaps, but it is a start. Even so, existentialists offer no assurance of everlasting peace and happiness. The work in service is not done to gain admission to an afterlife, or a heavenly blessing, or the benediction of an earthly patriarch.[91] What counts are the daily choices to create meaning, here and now.

Existentialism's perspective is somber, indeed, which has limited its appeal. For one thing, while the existentialists might not warm to humanistic psychology, they also would miss the tonic effects of engagement in higher purposes. Human beings can be moved to higher purpose by the nature of the psychological experience in ways not captured by Camus.

Where is hope, much less happiness, in such a bleak landscape? Contemporary existentialist Maxine Greene finds hope by confronting the routine, the ok-everyday-world, all that appears complete or finished. In what follows, I include many quotes by her to convey the evocative language of a contemporary existentialist. Pointing to "lives lived mostly on habit," Greene challenges us to reject the "empty formalisms of the day." Such views project "the view from Nowhere," she argues, because no contexts are provided by which to evaluate those ideas and the choices made by the writer (what gets included and what is left out, like the Arabs that are not included in *The Plague*, even though the setting resembles Algeria, as she points out).

To understand society and our lives, we have "disembodied abstractions," knowledge without context as to who said it, where and why. *The Plague* opens with indifferent townspeople pursuing their habits. At first, Rieux fights the plague as his duty. Only later, Greene tells us, does he let his feelings emerge. The tone and language at the end is different—he has become engaged. Now he has a mission.[92]

The power of human imagination is central to Greene's thinking, particularly in her recent work. To the arts she assigns a special responsibility to stimulate the imagination, asking us to challenge, to look for hope and possibility in what *could* be, what *ought* to be, what is *not yet*. She insists we "look for openings." Adapting Virginia Woolf's metaphor, Greene asks that we educators liberate the imagination from "the cotton wool of habit, of mere routine, of automatism." In that regard, being able to imagine what might be, a critique of society—its facticity—is needed. What is striking in these representative quotes from her recent work—words from an existentialist!—is that warm optimism is coupled with the edgy anger she feels for the demeaning landscape that learners and schools face.[93]

Engaging the imagination makes that activity more than an exercise. In her 1997 lecture at the University of Vermont, Greene said that Dewey spoke to the value from participation in the world, seeing such involvement as an addition to, not subtraction from, one's life *and* society. (In the same spirit, progressive schools and colleges give credit for a wider range of life experience, past and present, than does the conventional school.) Reflecting on Dewey's contribution to progressive thought, Greene spoke about "the spirit of hope and generosity" in his work that constitutes a "philosophy of possibility." Both Dewey and Greene ask us to look at potentialities in the sense of her pregnant phrase, "what might be." Saying she is an existentialist, after all, she adds "I am what I am not yet."[94]

We return to profound existentialist questions of social hope and authenticity at the end of the book.

Part II

Brain, Mind, and Body

You're on your bike for the whole day, six and seven hours, in all kinds of weather and conditions, over cobblestones and gravel, in mud and wind and rain, and even hail, and you do not give in to pain. Everything hurts. Your back hurts, your feet hurt, your hands hurt, your neck hurts, your legs hurt, and of course, your butt hurts.

—Lance Armstrong on competitive cycling[1]

Stripped of academic terms, the study of motivation is the study of movement. People move toward a goal they find attractive, perhaps motivated by high purpose, or away from a noxious experience. On our best days, no task is too difficult and movement from activity to activity feels effortless. Feeling depressed some days, we hardly move at all because no goal seems worth it. And every day there is the hidden struggle against gravity, invisible forces pulling on the body that we only recognize when tired or sick.

Movement can be thought of as having two components: direction and energy. It is critical to understand the purposes that give direction to movement and the investment, sometimes considerable, of psychic and physical energy. To understand motivation, we want to understand human *purposes*, large and small, that move human beings to act as well as the *psychological processes* that stimulate movement in the first place and reinforce the behavior afterward. Also, the focus of the discussion will be goal-directed movement involving a series of actions as opposed to the incessant smaller movements of daily locomotion.

Consider the challenge of racing a bike in the Tour de France, which Lance Armstrong won five straight times beginning in 1999, thus joining an elite circle of only five persons. Extreme sports are punishing, near masochistic, expeditions, and Armstrong is not alone in his single-minded search for peak experience.[2] Such efforts are remarkable tests of human spirit, and the daring and self-sacrifice inspire. For educators, examples like his raise questions with which to study motivation in daily life, especially life in schools and colleges. These are less dramatic settings but no less important for the individual lives being formed.

Why do people take on such a challenge, what Armstrong calls the "sport of self-abuse?"[3] Arguably the world's most grueling sport, the 2,290-mile Tour de France is run in 23 stages, each lasting at least 6 hours. Some 200 competitors ride at speeds of 20–40 miles per hour, each rider losing 10–12 liters of fluid while burning 6,000 calories each day. What is it about the psychological experience of involvement and its underlying neurobiological mechanisms that attracts people to such purposes and sustains them in spite of intense deprivation and risk?

Armstrong's achievement is all the more remarkable because he won the grueling Tour for the first time after recovering from advanced testicular cancer that had metastasized to lungs and brain. What motivated him to take up such a sport, in the first place, and drove him to return to it against great odds? Of course, multiple explanations are needed for human actions. Armstrong is gifted with enormous lung capacity and the ability to quickly process lactic acid in his muscles (lactic acid produces fatigue). Having natural assets, he placed well in early competitions in swimming and triathlons, getting recognition and attention. Armstrong's mother, who raised the boy by herself, modeled an ethic of "nothing comes easy," encouraging a resilient spirit. Incidents in his life suggest, too, an egoistic, obsessive side, whether from nature or nurture, that helped him focus.

Other motives include camaraderie with teammates and competitors during the race, and the financial rewards he earned as a professional, even before winning biking's most prestigious race. Where some competitors may train for six months before the race, Armstrong and his team train eleven months. Bike racers fear hills because of the physical demands necessary to defeat gravity. After the cancer was in remission, Armstrong became more focused than ever, relentlessly climbing hills on his bike, preparing for the rugged *cols* of the Tour, where he wins the race by outclimbing his opponents.

Even in a brief sketch, multiple motives are obvious. Armstrong's achievements were possible because he possessed habits of mind and body learned over many years to support his riding. Those habits helped him win races and aided his fight against advanced cancer, allowing him to endure weeks of massive chemotherapy. For our purposes, three aspects are most important: First, Armstrong learned to be goal directed to the point of obsession, and this learned attribute helped him win races *and* fight cancer. More than most people, Armstrong pushed himself and his friends and family hard. Second, purposes chosen in life amount to little without habits like planning and perseverance, which are learned and refined over many years. Third, the demands of his sport produced the psychological experiences that are the subject of this book, especially changes in attention and mood, and that let him endure. Asked what he thinks about while riding, Armstrong provides clues: "I thought about cycling. *My mind didn't wander. I didn't daydream.* I thought about the techniques of the various stages. . . . I worried about the lead. I kept a close watch on my competitors, in case one of them tried a breakaway. *I stayed alert to what was around me, wary of a crash.*"[4]

What Armstrong describes is mindfulness or flow, a psychological state found in more prosaic examples than bike racing. What is common to the diverse examples we consider—examples from climbing, friendships, education, and public speaking—is that people participate in these activities because they seek the positive changes in attention and mood. That is, people choose certain activities to *change* their psychological experience, although that motive is not conscious, and they choose these activities to *repeat* the psychological experience.

Intense physical activities stimulate increases in neurotransmitters like dopamine and hormones like adrenaline and testosterone—these substances change a person's mental and emotional states during the activity and just afterward (different effects are lumped together and called a "runner's high"). Competitive cycling is demanding, making the brain-mind-body work hard, causing increases in neurotransmitters and hormones to cope with stress. For a dramatic purpose like racing a bike or a mundane choice like writing an essay, the act of focusing attention and complementary mood changes that result are common denominators for the pursuits that add pleasure, meaning, and depth to life.

Activities like bike racing, marathon running, and mountain climbing are odd pursuits—after all, participants do not describe most parts as enjoyable. Yet, time and again they punish body and mind for motives that are not straightforward. As we suggest shortly, high stress activities may lead to increased valuation of the activity due to what Elliot Aronson calls psychological self-justification.[5] Applying this theory to the Armstrong example, a self-observing racer, trying to interpret his behavior, unconsciously *increases* his attraction to the sport to justify why he is working so hard.

In Armstrong's life as well as in most of the examples ahead, three ideas stand out. First, human attention span as we experience it is highly variable and unpredictable as to duration and direction. Managing attention is a challenge and directly affects learning. Understanding this variability and how it affects human actions is essential for all educators. Second, most of the changes in attention, consciousness, and, to a lesser extent, mood occur outside human awareness. Most of the time, the human animal is not conscious in the moment either of the state it is experiencing (say, partial involvement) or how that state has changed from the one before (utter boredom). But if asked, most could report a change. After all, the brain-mind-body must cope with many channels of information from which those few patterns or anomalies that "catch our attention" are selected by unknown mechanisms. (In chapter 4 ahead, I describe the selection problem by which certain pieces of information are "selected.") At a few moments, attention is full and one is totally involved in a tennis game or the calm concentration of sewing. At other times, for example, one struggles mightily to stay awake while driving, an uncomfortable experience that most people have had. Even on an hourly and daily basis, the range of changes in attention and mood, which underlie the possibility of psychological involvement, is enormous and unrecognized.

The third focus is one of the book's leitmotifs: the rich, problematic interaction of the individual with social groups. Armstrong's remarkable achievements in bike racing and fighting cancer seem, at first, to be the result of individual heroism, Horatio Alger on two wheels, always a seductive theme in American culture. While Armstrong's own contribution is undeniable, Armstrong learned habits of mind and body from his family and in social groups, and cancer specialists helped him fight cancer. As for bike racing, cognoscenti know that individual efforts, especially in the mountains, are easily lost to the efficiency of the group peloton. Yes, Armstrong won the Tour de France, but he did so protected by a team that included remarkable riders in their own right who helped control breakaways and reduce wind resistance by riding in front of him. Winning requires remarkable effort by individuals working from and within groups with comparable skills and resolve.

To understand these phenomena makes me a better educator. If one thing is demanded of an educator, it is to know oneself as a learner, a very high standard. Being an educator means more than studying abstract principles about motivation and learning as if it were enough to survive a graduate course in learning theory. To put the question another way: How can we teachers use a pragmatic knowledge of psychological experience and underlying neurobiology to make better decisions, or, indeed, to live better lives? How do we stay motivated in school and work, both as learners and mentors?

Theory will be useful if abstract concepts purporting to explain motivation and learning are rooted in—and tested against—self-understanding as a learner and self-motivator. The mental models about motivation and learning teachers acquire, mostly without conscious reflection as the craft is learned, must be challenged. If more was known about dynamics and stages of attention, the knowledge could be used to make better mental models for educational practice. In less dramatic instances that define the school day and institutional life, generally, more could be known about the range of psychological experience and changes in attention and mood that accompany different levels of involvement.

Teachers and students alike move through the life-world without recognition of the immense variability of attention and mood. In colleges, professors use overheads or computer animation to capture the flagging attention of students. In most classrooms, for example, teachers act as if learner attention is all or nothing, saying "pay attention" to distracted students. Rather, let's assume that some day research will identify different types of attention. Perhaps the progressive teacher would say—"Please use floating attention to work on the project while you also enjoy being with your friends." And later in the class, the teacher might say, "Now I want you to use high focus attention because instructions to operate a laser band saw are important. Pay attention or lose a finger!" Conceiving of different states of attention, or the need to move among different states as we work and play, would make clear that learners do not pay full attention during most activities. (Full attention is rare and celebrated for this fact.) Rather, students need *flexible* modes of attention and consciousness, and the judgment to know how and when to deploy them.

Here is an extended example to support my case for understanding the neurobiology of learning. Suppose in middle age you want to study jazz piano. You know enough about the keyboard, having played classical music for years. Jazz harmony and rhythm, however, emphasize different aspects of music than does the classical repertoire, and it helps to learn diatonic theory or, for the blues, to learn the F7 scale. But learning to actually play "Take the A Train" by Billy Strayhorn requires patient practice in the form of breaking the song into small pieces, each played slowly until correct. To play it fast, forcing fingering mistakes, will not help. In this instance, the mental model being used (play to get the feeling regardless of error) is wrong. It is wrong, too, to try to play the whole piece through unless one is a skilled sight reader (that is, the wrong theory is "play the whole, however poorly").

Another theory is needed. The correct learning strategy is to treat the pattern-seeking mind-brain-body as a machine, playing one hand slowly until correctly done ten times, then the other, then combining both, one measure at a time, being sure to "burn" the correct sequence of notes into neural circuits. Under this theory, we force the pattern-seeking, brain-mind-body to learn the patterns we want it to recognize rather than create distracting, competing patterns full of wrong notes and errant tempi. It helps to repeat the pattern many times, several days in a row, in different settings, and looking at one's hands as one learns. The point is to burn in a differentiated neuronal network to carry the "memory," using as many connections to different senses and sources of information as possible. To race sloppily through a new song, which I am always tempted to do, or to work through mistakes as they are made, uses bad theory.

Theory in the form of cognitive learning is important, but not as important as one might think. If one adds to the building network concepts about the circle of fifths that is important in jazz, so much the better because the network will be made still stronger with cognitive links. But the task is to move information from short-term memory to long-term memory in the form of stronger, better-connected neuronal networks. And that takes correct practice, many hours of it.

The issues we take on are challenging, and to find the best language has not been easy. Getting the right words for the phenomenology of lived experience, peak or mundane, is tricky enough. But to also cover underlying neurobiology in the same text is even more of a stretch. Difficult or not, I argue that educators cannot understand the whole of motivation and learning without venturing into domains where existing mental models are incomplete or wrong. Here is a simplifying model I found myself using early on that turns out to be wrong. It is tempting to look for one physical location or organ to explain a critical human function (as if the brain "thinks," the heart, "feels.") Early in my reading, when thinking about human consciousness, I imagined a master control program called "switcher." The idea was silly, but I imagined a control room with banks of dials and screens. I was struggling, then as now, to think about human consciousness, to think about how the mind works, this most mysterious of all human capacities.

Engineer at console was the notion. Somehow, I thought, one entity must evaluate information from so many channels. Surely, some "thing" of a physical nature, chemical or electrical, had to choose which of the many competing purposes motivate the organism to eat, run away, or make love. But metaphors mislead, giving the impression that we understand more than we do. My homunculus engineer is, in fact, the wrong image, like most single-factor, one-organ explanations of human behavior. Indeed, a better idea is to conceive of the mind as coping with information streams within, and impinging upon, the brain-mind-body. As we consider shortly, neurobiologist Candace Pert says a systems construct undercuts the implicit idea that one entity, the brain, is the seat of human will.[6] She describes the large-scale organization of the information transduction network:

> Every one of the zones, or systems, of the network—the neural, the hormonal, the gastrointestinal, and the immune—is set up to communicate with one another, via peptides and messenger-specific peptide receptors. Every second, a massive information exchange is occurring in your body.[7]

All beings live in information streams. How we exist and develop is as dependent on the quality of information as a brook trout is on the quality of water. As a teacher I have tried many times to characterize the extreme information interdependence between organism and environment, never finding the right metaphor. Boundaries among the external world, the information-transducing system, and the mind, we shall see, are neither simple nor "crisp," as Daniel Dennett likes to put it.[8] Unlike the machinelike control room of the human power plant I first imagined, the nervous system is not constructed of media-neutral information channels. The neural path effects or transduces the signal at every juncture as it moves to and from brain centers.

Rather than imagine one control entity, think of a *distributed network system,* a system of systems that has evolved over millions of years. Supporting this theory, Dennett rejects the notion of a "nice clean edge" between body, mind, and brain, which is why some observers hyphenate the term.[9] Mind, consciousness, and learning are distributed in the body, both in peripheral neural networks as well as in brain functions. How we think about education should take into account the theory of distributed learning— distributed in the near environment *and* within the body.

Educators need to explore the unexamined, invisible world of neural and chemical events that accompany thinking, observed behavior, and emotional response. Humans only get sudden glimpses of underlying system activation. A skier may not, for example, be conscious of autonomic, involuntary reactions to cold until she feels her body shiver. Most people move through the day without awareness of the attention or mood states of the moment, or the constant changes, some quite rapid in the case of attention.

The problem of consciousness is arguably the most difficult one neuroscience must face. Think about the second term, "mind," in the brain-mind-body triad.[10] What do we mean by *mind* and its critical function, *consciousness?*[11] The most fascinating part of the triad—brain-*mind*-body—is the least understood.[12] Pert and others write about the psychological experience of mind, which is so ephemeral as to suggest, incorrectly, that it has no material nature. Rather, all thoughts have material consequences in the individualized adaptation of the human learning system. A leading neurology reference text by Eric Kandel and his associates says: "all mental processes are biological and any alteration in those processes is organic."[13] That is, thinking and feeling do not occur in metaphysical space beyond human understanding. Mental events like reading this sentence have material, physiological substrata, even if the events or dynamics cannot yet be described.

Philosophers and psychologists of nearly every era have said much more about the human mind. The debates can be intense, but we step around important issues to apply a theory of information transduction.[14] What we have discussed so far is enough to underscore one caution: *Nothing about brain-mind-body interactions is intuitively obvious.* If for no other reason, this is why such interactions have to be studied. For example, serotonin reuptake inhibition in the synaptic junction is not straightforward. But if we educators want to understand a hyperactive student or moody colleague, it helps to understand what happens "beneath the skin," as John Dewey put it in another context. Dennett's image of human being as biped information transducer, interpreting and responding to signals moving around the body between sensors and the mind-brain, is not a thing of beauty. But it is the best we have to explain the dynamic, functional relationship between the organism and its near environment.

So, we have interesting, hard work ahead in three parts. Practicing educators need a general overview of the most important *functional* relationships in motivation and learning—interested readers will find advanced sources on psychological interactions as well as neurobiological topics. Being an educator, I want to understand functional relationships linking person and environment, especially ideas that connect to two important generalizations: that learning is *ubiquitous,* hardly confined to school, and necessarily *individualized.* Chapter 4 reviews topics in the neurobiology of attention and mood. Ours will not be a technical discussion beyond a basic understanding of neuronal networks, the synaptic junction and its chemistry, brain structures, and the interaction of genes, behavior, and environment. A few details are included to suggest how these information systems have evolved. We will learn that the brain-mind-body's redundant learning systems help the species adapt to an indifferent, sometimes hostile, environment.

Chapter 5 addresses the experience of mindfulness (Ellen Langer), flow (Mihaly Csikszentmihalyi), and kindred psychological states. Of special interest are *intermediate* stages, which are not discussed by Abraham

Maslow, Langer, or Csikszentmihalyi. Numerous examples are cited because psychological experience, normally not in awareness, is difficult to capture with words. We need varied examples to think about our own experience of attention, mood and consciousness, and the subtle, dynamic operation of mind.

Chapter 4

Neurobiological Systems

The mystery of perception, at least for me, is not that our senses tell us so much about the world, but that they tell us so little. . . . Much of the world goes too fast to be seen or apprehended, much goes too slowly; much is too big, too small or too high-pitched or too dim or bright or off color.

—Jerome Bruner[1]

Educators, counselors, and human service workers are not well informed about the exquisite, highly evolved brain-mind-body systems underlying motivation and learning. Perhaps we acknowledge the effects of hormones and sex differences on behavior, joking about testosterone in exuberant males. Reference is made to "adrenaline rushes" from sky diving and "endorphin highs" from jogging. Topics like "left brain, right brain" or attention deficit appear for a time.[2] But an informed understanding is rare about topics so essential to educators, like the diurnal cycle and optimal rest, how neurotransmitters function, and the mechanics of attention and mood systems. Even psychologists, who take graduate courses in perception, learning, and behavioral physiology, may not draw upon this knowledge. After the odd graduate school course, unconnected to the rest of one's studies, few stay well informed.

An example will make the point. Writing the last sentence produces changes in short-term memory, and material changes occur on the surface of cells and in connections to neuronal networks. If I rework the sentence, play with its concepts in other contexts while jogging, the memory is more likely to pass from short to long-term storage elsewhere in the brain, where other cellular changes occur in neuronal networks. As I edit with a pencil, networks of motor neurons connect with the new learning. The point is: Coupling a learning task with other motor systems and their networks strengthens memory, which has implications for curricular design.

Nothing is simple or intuitive about the brain-mind-body and its information exchanges.[3] The scale and complexity of the information-cellular network are hard to fathom—Candace Pert calls us "trillion-celled creatures"[4] because a typical nerve cell, or neuron, has millions of receptors of different types on its surface. The scale of interior physiological events is staggering: The human brain has 10^{11} neurons and forms about 10^{14} connections; the average neuron has 1,000 synaptic connections and receives signals from 10,000; changes in electrical potential across nerve cell membranes involves 100 million ions per second passing in a single channel.[5]

As if the scale of events were not enough, studying neurobiology requires us to think *across* different levels of system integration: from molecular chemistry to the organization of neuronal networks to abstract systems that combine hundreds, perhaps thousands, of networks in support of an integrated response like running. Even a simple act like lifting a pencil requires effective integration of neural and motor systems, each consisting, in turn, of subsystems of neuronal pathways that conduct signals from muscle to the brain via changing electrical potentials in ion channels and neurotransmitters transducing the signal through synaptic junctions.

I start with this cascade of facts to suggest the limits of popular thinking about behavioral physiology. Partialist explanations of one organ, the "brain," or one transmitter, "dopamine," or one hormone, "testosterone," oversimplify the complexity, integration, and redundancy of adaptive information systems that Stephen Pinker reminds us have evolved over millions of years.[6] Consider this: Human beings share a common ancestor with chimpanzees and gorillas 4–10 million years ago, and a common ancestor with reptiles 300 million years ago. The vast scale of blocks of time this large stretches the mind as much as the complexity of the intricate nervous system, whose features humans share with most species.

While today's physiological concepts are tentative—there is much we do not understand—certain directions are emerging, lines of inquiry important for educators to follow as research questions and methods mature. At the very least, we might ask: What neurobiological mechanisms do our educational theories and methods assume? We want working concepts for three questions: What stimulates motivation? What mechanisms accompany motivated behavior (especially under adverse conditions)? And how is motivated behavior reinforced by its consequences?

What are the most important physiological dynamics and structures underlying the psychological experience of different levels of involvement? I have argued that human beings, at least, are motivated to pursue certain purposes and avoid others because of changes in psychological experience, especially those changes experienced as pleasant or aversive. Although not in awareness, the psychological consequences of acts reinforce the probability that we will want to repeat them either for the positive experience that results or possibly for the experience of moderate levels of change.

While we can define psychological states like a peak experience, or describe changes in states of involvement, much less is known about underlying physiological states and changes in those states, like increases in amine production because of central nervous system activation, the warm "high" from dopamine stimulated by strenuous physical exercise, or the dramatic, highly adaptive "rush" of adrenaline when an animal faces threat. That is, neurological and hormonal events are a separate level of analysis, which reflects, in turn, chemical-molecular events at critical junctures in the neurological path, especially the synaptic junction. As we shall learn, psychological experience reflects, presumably, parallel changes in neurological transmitters and how they accelerate or impede the passage of information.

As promising as the new research in neurobiology seems to be, other caveats are needed. To map neural and brain pathways, research has focused on simple conditioning experiments with simple organisms like the fruit fly, *Dropsophilia,* or the marine snail, *Aplysia californica.*[7] Also, neural structures and functions are inferred from people who have suffered lesions and major injuries like seizures and head trauma. From both lines of inquiry, inferences that may not always be warranted are made from complex behavior in normal subjects. Understanding of brain functions has also benefited from the development of brain mapping techniques like PET and MRI, which make it possible to see which brain areas and neuronal networks are active during a certain activity.

The first topics below address elementary mechanisms and basic nomenclature that are necessary before we review important functions of these highly evolved information systems.

The Nervous System

Before we can take on more involved topics like perceptual sets, we need a basic understanding of the structure of the neuronal pathway, the neuron, and the synaptic junction, the three most important parts of the distributed information system.[8] Even the most elementary action requires the integration of separate sensory, motor, and motivational paths upstream to the central nervous system. To understand human action, we need to know how neural pathways work, and Jerome Bruner captures the nervous system's great complexity:

> It comprises an array of processes far subtler than the physiologist can yet measure with even his finest electrochemical recordings. They signal from upstream in the cerebral cortex to downstream in the sensory and motor systems to tune or prepare the organism for what it needs in the environment and what it will encounter there. It is a system of a complexity that can accommodate the need to give special place to surprises, to the probability structure of the world as represented in 'models' that the brain stores, and to the requirements of acts-in-programs.[9]

Philosopher Daniel Dennett describes the human nervous system as an elaborate information network of connecting transducers, taking information from one medium and translating it to another. Each central nervous system neuron, spinal cord, or brain receives constant synaptic input from many other neurons.[10] In functional terms, the individual cell either fires or not, but processes up to the point of firing are not straightforward. As many as 10,000 different presynaptic endings may be found on a single motor neuron, some excitatory, some inhibitory. Different inputs can cancel each other out or potentiate the cell's response. All three parts of the nerve cell can be receptive or transmitting sites for synaptic contact: axon, cell body, and dendrites. Neuronal integration refers to the how the competing inputs are integrated in the postsynaptic neuron as the signal travels the neuronal network.

Composed of input nodes and effector, or output, nodes, the nervous system transduces signals like sound and temperature into neural signals via "trains of impulses in nerve fibers" throughout the entire body.[11] Electrochemical pulses travel the neural path, linked by synaptic junctions connecting neurons of different types, functioning like an "elongated battery" from fingertip to brain. Chemical differences inside and outside the nerve cell wall induce electric signals along the wall at varying speeds where the rate of signal transmission affects perception and the level of neural activation.

Throughout the body and its information networks, nerve cells are connected at millions of junctures, called "synapses," where microeffector/ microtransducer interactions take place. A wide diversity of transmitters, which number about one hundred, and synaptic mechanisms are found in the central and peripheral nervous system, which has been difficult to study because of the small size and great complexity of nerve cells. Electrical pulses at the synaptic junction stimulate the release of neurotransmitter molecules like serotonin and dopamine, which cross the gap, or cleft, by biochemical diffusion, then to be transduced into further electrical pulses as the signal moves along the network. Neurotransmitters like glutamate are all-purpose carriers whereas other neuromodulator molecules produce varied effects of their own when barriers to transmission are found at the junction's receptor side.[12]

Electrical and chemical synapses respond to patterns of excitation and inhibition. Electrical junctions, which are important for escape and defensive responses, provide *instantaneous,* synchronous communication with connected cells. Directly gated ion channels operate quickly and are used for responses that need speed, like the knee-jerk reflex. Chemical synapses, on the other hand, are slower acting by comparison and can simplify or modulate signals. Because it is more modifiable than electrical transmission, chemical transmission over the cleft becomes an important link in behavioral learning and medication.

Neurotransmitters like serotonin or acetylcholine act on channels, either directly or indirectly. A transmitting step (release of chemical messenger) is followed by a receiving step (transmitter binds to postsynaptic cell to allow transmission). An action potential is sent down the neuron's axon to the presynaptic cell, which releases a chemical transmitter to travel a small distance to the postsynaptic cell. Transmitters such as acetylcholine typically cause the opening or closing of ion channels on postsynaptic cell membrane of the synaptic cleft. The chemical process has one single action potential releasing thousands of transmitter molecules, allowing amplification from one neuron to another.

Recent research has focused on signal modulation due to second messengers acting on neuronal transmission.[13] Second messengers modulate the excitability of neurons and intensity of signal, which affects emotional states, mood, arousal, and certain simple forms of learning and memory. So neurological transmission is important for understanding mental and neurological dysfunctions like anxiety and depression. For example, overly rapid neuronal transmission stimulates hyperactive behavior. Psychoactive substances used to reduce hyperactivity, like serotonin reuptake inhibitors (SRIs), modulate the neurotransmitter, serotonin, in the synaptic cleft, effectively lowering the rate of signal transmission. Similarly, South American Indians use curare on arrows to paralyze animals they have shot. Curare blocks signal transmission at the junction by binding to acetylcholine receptors, preventing activation and slowing behavior.[14] Moreover, we want to think in terms of *continuous* individual differences in stimulus reactivity rather than a discrete syndrome like attention deficit disorder. Quality of signal transmission is important for quality of life.[15]

Prior to the 1970s, Pert observes that research focused on neurotransmitters in the synaptic junction or cleft, as they transmitted a simple "on/off" message along the system. Beginning with the 1980s, researchers began to include the peptides, which can act like neurotransmitters in the cleft. But peptides work differently as they move through the blood stream and cerebrospinal fluid, traveling long distances and causing changes as they "bump and bind" to receptors along their path.[16] Receptor cells are "scanners" that sense other information molecules or ligands that circulate through the extra cellular fluids in the cell membrane. The process by which the ligand connects with a receptor site is called "bumping," as if the ligand is trying to dock with a given receptor, which only receives ligands of a certain family type. When the message is passed, the receptor is changed dramatically, the effect being repeated more or less simultaneously in millions of receptor sites responding to millions of floating ligands.[17]

Information is carried by other systems within the body, and to understand we need a passing knowledge of how information is transduced at the molecular level. Pert's research career has focused on peptides and opiate receptors on the surface of cells in the body and brain, exploring changes at the receptor and cell level as they shape human emotional experience.[18] She says,

> Emotional states or moods are produced by the various neuropeptide ligands, and what we experience as an emotion or feeling is also a mechanism for activating a particular neuronal circuit—*simultaneously throughout the brain and body*—which generates a behavior involving the whole creature, with all the necessary physiological changes that behavior would require.[19]

Two assumptions are important in Pert's description: First, psychological experience is rooted in physiological changes at the molecular level, and second, it is the whole system, or integrated system of systems, that determines behavior more than any one system.

Neural Basis of Memory

The mind is not a digital camera. The images I think I see are not perfect, pixel-bright reflections of what is "out there" in "reality" because all human experience is interpreted experience. To navigate the world, people adopt a convenient fiction: that what one sees, smells, and hears is a literal, mirror reflection of reality, when this is never actually the case. The organism perceives wavelengths and attaches labels like "blue" and "green." Similarly, mental models underestimate the transformative nature of ongoing thinking and remembering as well as, finally, the nature of long-term changes in memory as new material gets added to existing memory.

What are the mechanisms or systems by which the brain-mind-body transduces information?[20] Three levels or systems are involved according to Eric Kandel, James Schwartz, and Thomas Jessell. First, *neuronal memory,* short and long term, is important. Information is stored that other systems require and search for. Second, some sort of *search-and-retrieval mechanism* is needed. Third, certain limited aspects come into human consciousness when people monitor learning and memory. Researchers do not know much about the latter two capabilities, but all three information-processing systems seem to involve *active construction*. Information is transformed at all stages: as it is processed as memory; as it is stored, searched, and retrieved; and as it is used by consciousness. Memory is transformed as it is acquired. Support for this theory comes from studies of people whose brain injuries have disrupted long-term memory. With such cases, post-trauma educated guesses are made with the information that does survive.[21]

Memory is more storytelling than perfect recall.[22] Recall is *an active construction in real time,* not the calling up of perfect, complete images. Being problem-solving animals, we work with incomplete, ambiguous information, trying to make sense of what we think we know, or what tasks we have before us. In that sense, Bruner reminds us that human behavior is more purposive, in general terms, than it might appear on the surface. How we experience the world psychologically—the immediacy and vivid quality of experience—may lead to the false impression that we "see" and "remember" cameralike images, photographic slides with perfect accuracy and permanence. But the phenomenological illusion of formed images deflects attention from the active, transformative quality of memory acquisition and recall.

A basic understanding of certain technical matters in memory is important before we turn to human perception and the use of memory in making sense of the world. A recurring theme in my argument has been the pivotal role of lived experience, both as it reflects and shapes psychological processes and, in the present context, as it reflects and shapes physiological mechanisms. The study of memory is an important topic in its own right because memory is how learning from person-environment transactions is stored for future use.

Researchers conceive of memory in stages, short term and long term. Short-term memory is limited to fewer than a dozen items—lacking rehearsal, it lasts only minutes. Short-term memory is stored in nerve cells that have other functions in the circuit. By processes not yet understood, certain information in short-term memory is transformed into long-term memory, stored elsewhere in the brain-body. Memory can be classified as implicit or explicit with regard to how it is stored and recalled. Implicit memory is unconscious, referring to motor and perceptual skills. Explicit memory, mediated by language, is conscious and records what we know about people, places, and things.[23] By virtue of connections to language and different sensory and motor systems, the memory is connected directly to the learning activity, *all* the sensory and motor systems used, and their neurons.[24] Kandel, Schwartz, and Jessell observe: "[S]torage of even a simple reflexive memory is not restricted to one site but is distributed to several sites within the neural circuit."[25] Disruptions or distortions in memory can occur where that memory is encoded as engrams in neural networks, or they can occur because of problems with the search-and-retrieval mechanism.[26]

One generalization is pivotal: *Memory and learning are distributed in all the sensory and motor systems used to acquire and process lived experience.* Such a concept of distributed problem solving challenges the dominance of, on the one hand, a disembodied brain and, on the other, the primacy of cognition as mental models for how people function. While brain locations, particularly the hippocampus and cerebellum, play important roles in both implicit and explicit memory, neuronal networks leading to these sites are vital and less appreciated for their contribution. Also, the nervous system may not have special memory neurons whose sole function it is to store information. Rather, complex tasks involve many body systems, and neuronal networks are modified at many places. The distribution of memory in the brain-mind-body is adaptive, as we can see, because some learning survives when a sector is damaged.[27]

How does learning alter the structure and function of nerve cells and neuronal connections? In general, the highly plastic nervous system and its critical synapses develop in three stages. In the first stage, genetic processes are prepotent when the animal is born. In early childhood, newly developed synapses are fine tuned, which requires activity in neurons, the results of environmental stimulation. If stimulation is lacking, so is development, another critical notion for educators, especially those who work in early childhood. The third stage, also dependent on external experience, is the regulation of the transient and long-term efficacy of synapses. In sum, the organism's adaptation depends upon appropriate neuronal activity caused by environmental stimuli. But such theory is preliminary because researchers do not agree on whether the brain has the capacity to generate *new* neuronal networks in response to stimulation or whether it stores information in pre-existing networks established early in life.

In still another way, then, we see the intimate, dynamic relationship between human development and the stimulus properties of the near environment.

The human nervous system, whose general features are shared with most species, is never static. It responds to—indeed, requires—external stimulation from environmental actions. The organism acts on the environment, changing its stimulus properties, leading to new learning and more articulated memory. For educators and counselors, optimal human development demands that we make the brain-mind-body do its work because cellular mechanisms in learning are activity dependent. We return to curricular implications later.

What happens to neuronal networks not in use? Networks grow stronger and more articulated with use, which accounts for the well-documented effects that practice has on learning. But what happens when circuits are not used? To address the question, we need to back up. First, we know that competition exists among different axons that stimulate the same target cell. Research with simple animals suggests that long-term habituation leads to pruning of synaptic junctions by as much as 30 percent. Neuronal networks are in constant competition for body resources—some pathways grow stronger with use, others weaken.[28] We also know programmed neuronal death occurs, especially during embryonic development. Thus, growth and maturation of neurons depends upon gene expression, in general, and upon neuronal activation and interaction, in particular. Again, neuronal development is never static but responds dynamically in real time to environmental stimulation and change, or lack thereof.

A provocative argument has been put forth by Allan Hobson who argues that the brain-mind-body checks and elaborates its neuronal networks during sleep, outside conscious direction.[29] Contrary to the Freudian view that dreams presage or mirror intrapsychic conflict, Hobson's thesis, far are more parsimonious than Freud's,[30] is that dreams represent the unconscious checking of routines and circuits needed during the day.[31] An intriguing possibility presents itself that a degree of creative differentiation or articulation in the network might occur as networks are tested, possibly because memories that already share certain elements, facts, or motor systems are close to being connected. Perhaps the bizarre images of dreams as well as the creative insights that seem to occur overnight mean that molecular changes occur within, or between, networks, or perhaps search-and-retrieval mechanisms themselves are being modified, if ever so slightly. That is not to imply that the conscious working of the mind is not the more powerful agent, because it is. But our expanded mental models of the brain-mind-body should allow for unconscious and/or counterintuitive processes.

Research with simple organisms and basic responses suggests *multiple pathways* for information exchange and *multiple biochemical reactions* at the cellular level to process information in neurons.[32] Long-term strengthening of neuronal networks requires genes and proteins not involved in short-term learning. Some effects require "second messengers," even with simple learning in simple animals.

With simple animals at least, the brain-body's response to demands that it do work and learn is represented in physical changes in neuronal connections between sensory and motor neurons. Studies of the *Aplysia* organism and sensitization, a more complex form of learning than habituation, show that a new stimulus activates interneurons to form *new synapses* on sensory neurons. The neuronal network grows and becomes more differentiated as demands are made of it. This idea, that neural memory changes and improves by making the brain-mind-body work, is a powerful concept for educators, one to which we shall return several times.

Selective Perception and the Pattern-Seeking Mind

Both John Dewey and William James, like other philosophers before them, had speculated about the selective filtering of human experience. It fell to Jerome Bruner to create landmark experiments showing that all perception is selective and to argue, more broadly, that human experience is constructed out of many complex sensory interactions.[33] Having a limited attention span, human beings sample lightly from the full range of possible stimuli.

The brain-mind-body copes with a surfeit of information by learning patterns. Selection is aided by "chunking," in which stimuli are perceived in recognized units or patterns, which are learned through experience. While inaccurate patterns may have been learned (and may have to be unlearned), the *selection task* is less imposing. A hypothetical set may develop during attending, involving attention to some stimuli, inhibition of other stimuli, and access to premotor and memory systems that are related to conscious awareness. A continuing set maintains itself, affects behavior and consciousness, and ensures continuity of attention. But if the set is inaccurate, it may lead to misperception and error. Langer's theory of mindful learning points the problems out when patterns or sets are no longer relevant.

I want to change the level of analysis to ask about human attention. The attention system is the primary means by which human beings orient to their environs, and biological limits determine how much information the system can process. Mihaly Csikszentmihalyi provides one estimate saying the central nervous system can process up to seven bits of information at any point, and the shortest discrimination time between one set of bits and another is about one-eighth of a second. It is possible, he estimates, to process 126 bits per second, or 7,560 per minute.[34]

To follow what one person is saying requires about 40 bits of information per second, which is difficult enough. But if the upper limit is 120 per second, only 80 bits are left to attend to postural signals, or, for example, a growling stomach, and to compare the present moment to the memory of an earlier conversation. If, in the next few seconds, the full range of stimuli includes the sound of a bird outside the window, the snatch of a conversation in the next room, and a fleeting sexual fantasy, we understand the importance of the *selection problem*—namely, to attend to the right stimuli from among many competing signals coming from many, many different channels.

The human brain-mind-body has evolved to carefully monitor diverse flows of information, mostly not in human awareness. The nervous system, in particular, has evolved in remarkable ways, and most features are shared among species. For humans, certain signals—a pointed gun, a knife, and a sudden brake light ahead in traffic—seem to cut through normal awareness. That this happens so rapidly, Peter Milner argues, suggests that perceptual channels to and from human senses are monitored constantly but not in conscious awareness.[35] Signals are perceived but not labeled "threat" until a physiological trigger of some sort is pulled. Quick responses are probably instinctual, the result of millions of years of evolution, whereas other reactions are learned from an aversive experience with shock or intense pain.[36]

Humans seek order and direction in life, which is an ongoing struggle because of rapid changes in attention throughout the day as thousands of objects present themselves to the mind. (Estimates are that between eight and ten objects are attended to each second when someone is alert.) The selection task is formidable considering that the stimuli channels according to Hobson include five senses (vision, hearing, touch, taste, and smell), and three data channels within the body (posture, movement, and pain).[37] In addition, the encoded memory of the senses is important (that is, "Is this touch too hot?") as well as of the channels. At any one moment when the organism is conscious, many hundreds of sensory stimuli can be selected, but this does not normally happen, except in the case of organic mental illness or in reaction to psychoactive substances. Thus, extreme deviations in attention, Hobson asserts, are important correlates of, and perhaps causes of, mental instability and psychiatric illness.

The organism samples frequently but lightly from its environs, taking the risk that important stimuli, like a handgun in a dimly lit street, will be missed. Selective perception is a form of unconscious hypothesis testing in which the organism seems especially alert to anomalous sensory information. Bruner notes that we are *hypothesis-generating learners* from just after birth. He calls attention to the actions of the mind as it selectively perceives the world and, together with pre-existing memory, constructs ordered impressions of reality that otherwise could never have been fully or accurately perceived. It is one thing, he notes, to affirm this general principle and quite another to know the rules: "How, for example, do our hypotheses stay so well tuned *both* to the structure of events in the real work and to our biases?"[38]

Human attention functions, to Hobson, as a moving, dynamic tension between *distraction* from hundreds of stimuli and *obsession* with only a few, at the risk of not attending to the real threat of that moose crossing the highway late at night. Based on animal studies of attention and perception, norepinephrine is thought to increase the signal-to-noise ratio, helping the organism focus attention on selected stimuli. If the signals come too quickly, or in ways that cannot be easily perceived by the brain-mind, consciousness will be overwhelmed, as appears to be the case with attention deficit disorder. If, on the other hand, the rate is too little, the organism may be seen as apathetic or depressed.

Specific amines like norepinephrine and serotonin serve as neurotransmitters that facilitate concentration and play a critical role in what Hobson calls the "tuning of attention."[39] These substances help us become alert and precisely oriented to danger. In situations perceived to be threatening, the adrenal gland releases adrenaline, a hormone that raises blood sugar and stimulates the heart. Aminergic molecules are also released throughout the brain and the neural networks that control attention. Unconscious problem-solving mechanisms within the body are thus finely tuned to cope with the threat with hardly any conscious intervention. Finally, the mind-brain senses danger when it reads somatic channels becoming active.

Adaptive Learning

Now I want to think about learning in broad terms, because learning is an organism's most important survival mechanism, and patterns are the means by which we learn and navigate the life-world.[40] Whether lizard or primate, animals need to recognize food and to avoid being eaten themselves. Allies have to be cultivated, shelter secured, the young protected. To survive, all animals must learn from iterative transactions with their environs, and the human capacity for abstract language, shared by some primates, increases that potential. So learning and memory are highly adaptive capacities for animals that must avoid predators and compete for scarce resources. Neurobiological mechanisms underlie mood and attention and are at work processing information for short- and long-term memory. That is, neurobiological events of which I am not aware and do not understand are occurring inside, paralleling a state of motivated learning and the patterns that are being tested and modified.

Moreover, most species share *common learning systems*. Much of the power of that learning capacity, for humans, is not so much that it *can* be in awareness, some of the time at least, but that it resides in properties of unconscious physiological systems that regulate behavior, in general, and attention and mood, in particular. To some degree, mind aside, the brain-body is *always* learning and adapting even as the owners of the organism, so to speak, are oblivious to what is happening.

Interactions with the environment directly influence human capacities. How we construct and read the proximal environment has immediate consequences for muscular and neurological development, even for changes in brain structure and function. Because environments vary for each individual growing up, each person's brain-body neurological structure will, of necessity, be *individualized*. (Keep this notion in mind when in Part III we think about pedagogy.) Gross features and functions are shared. But considerable variation exists with regard, for example, to how brain areas are organized and where memory is stored.

A subtle relationship exists among nervous system function, the near environment, and genes. Adaptive learning is a species' most important mechanism for survival and evolution, and genes carry the most important information. Altered properties of transmitter receptors, as with desensitization, create long-lasting effects that affect gene expression. (That is, the latent effects of a certain gene, which may not have been active previously, are "expressed" because of changes in environmental conditions.) If certain genes are expressed, which implies dynamic interaction with the near environment, we see marked deficits. But new learning can interact with previously latent genes, helping them to come forward and cause new changes. So, in response to environmental conditions, different genes are expressed and the effects can be carried forward in the germline.[41] In yet another way, support is found for the intimate, dynamic relationship between person and environment with respect to how humans learn from, and adapt to, their environs.

Philosopher Daniel Dennett offers an intriguing view of the human mind, in general, and how intentionality in human actions, in particular, has evolved. Concerned with the evolution of consciousness from planaria to primates to humans, Dennett asks about the "birth of agency," a distinctive human attribute. (Later, we call this attribute "self-focusing.") Dennett wants to understand "the intentionality that allows us to speak and write and wonder all manner of wonders," arguing that such a capacity is a late development for the species, a product of many "billions of crude intentional systems" of the brain-mind-body.[42]

Dennett's elegant description of the transducing nervous system in response to environmental stimulation reminds me of Dewey's social psychology, which locates the person in the environment in nonphysiological terms. In Dennett's perspective, which Dewey might have shared, mind is distributed or spread throughout the brain-body into the proximal environment. Emotions, intelligence, and capacity for learning—all are distributed throughout the body, embedded in unseen connections with the proximal environment to an extent that makes no intuitive sense. When thinking of human experience, we do not, therefore, want to draw a boundary at the skin any more than to employ the simplifying, false assumption of anatomical place.

Consciousness and self-identity have evolved as the human capacity for abstract reasoning advanced to labeling objects in the environment, later imagining those objects while problem solving and imagining other worlds, perhaps better worlds. In time, Dennett argues, the labels improve as people use them. Mere contemplation is sufficient to remind us of the appropriate lesson. We learn, indeed, to attach these object-concepts to personal identity as self-descriptions evolve. As we mature, we work internally with invisible, abstract concepts of self and mental models about the world—we create and play with "elaborate exercises of imagination" that use these concept-images of self.[43]

No plausible theory exists about where consciousness exists (in the sense of a discrete, physical brain location). Perhaps what people experience as consciousness, Pert suggests, is a byproduct of a system of systems in the neural network, a control program of some sort that comes to awareness when anomalies are detected by the pattern-seeking mind during routine problem solving. Kandel and his colleagues cite more recent theories, but the exact physical mechanisms of consciousness remain illusive.[44] To ask "where" may be the wrong question, because consciousness may be so spread out in electrical-chemical changes of short duration occurring in neuronal networks that anatomical place is irrelevant.

Researchers have more confidence, limited as it is, in theories about consciousness and the functions that consciousness supports. Self-awareness is an advanced form of cognitive development reflecting humans' evolution as problem-solving animals. While other species show intention, feelings, and perhaps degrees of consciousness, Dennett points to the human capacity for reasoning and abstract language that lets us imagine in "as if" fashion.[45] In this way, humans plan abstractly and weigh consequences without risking all.

Millions of years ago, human beings gradually learned to speak, to declaim and mark things; only lately have we learned to write. Humans arrange the physical space around them, Dennett continues, to contain information that makes advanced behavioral routines possible without having to constantly think. Bruner makes a similar point by referring to the cultural tools that permit the mind to go beyond its limits.[46] The capacity for abstract and symbolic reasoning lets us offload information and tools into the environment where, to protect us from the limitations of the animal brain, we have created storage devices as diverse as books, movies, libraries, archives, maps, and computers to distribute problem solving.[47] Dennett says, "We learn, thanks to this cultural heritage, how to spread our minds out in the world, where we can put our beautifully designed innate tracking and pattern-recognizing talents to optimal use."[48]

Intriguing ideas follow from Dennett's theory. The idea of distributed problem solving in the dynamic culture human beings create to support themselves suggests, in part, why people become so attached to the features of work and living space. That is, the organism comes to depend upon perceptual cues in that environment (the color of a rug, the location of a door), which become an intrinsic part of how we learn and how the memory is constructed. Because the psychological experience is perceived as "internal" to the mind-body, a fallacious impression results—that the human organism is separate from its world, and the information and learning spread in that world. On the contrary and in ways educators only dimly perceive, people live in and through the near environment.

So, behavior depends upon ecological cues, most of which are not in human awareness unless certain thresholds are exceeded. Those unconscious cues, like the color of a rug or location of a door handle, make behavior efficient. A behavioral sequence like walking is embedded, in part, in a specific living room and the location of a rug and door, thus reducing a need to pay attention. The notion of distributed problem solving suggests why it can be enervating and fun to redecorate if we have new furniture, or why foreign travel is so exciting (that is, adaptive learning is constant in new environments). Finally, we have one explanation for why it is disruptive to move the elderly, who may suffer short-term memory deficits, to new environments. Without the capacity to process and store new information, changed environments can be frightening, not exciting.

Motivation, Drive States, and Emotions

Before we think about advanced motivational states, the limits of available theory are worth noting again. Motivation is an inferred state, a hypothetical construct, based on observations that the organism is moving *toward* some goal to satisfy an assumed need, or *away* from a perceived threat. Motivation is inferred when movement, or lack of, is noticed. Internal mechanisms remain obscure, although more is being learned with brain imaging methods.

From a strict biological perspective, motivation is discussed as change in a homeostatic parameter—regulating basic drives like hunger, thirst, and sex—that presumably causes a drive state. An animal seeks water and drinks because, we infer, it is thirsty. Motivational states, at least the simple type, have three components: 1.) a directing function; 2.) an activating function to increase general alertness and energy; 3.) an organizing function to create a coherent sequence.[49] When motivated, general effects are found: increased level of autonomic arousal, decreased behavioral threshold to act, and increased capacity to act. Individual components of a motivated act like eating require a *well-organized, goal-oriented sequence*. Attainment of the goal decreases arousal and/or increases behavioral threshold, and one or more parts of the motivation sequence fall away.

Motivational states are partially determined by homeostatic mechanisms, first studied by Walter Cannon in 1929, that regulate balances in the body of essential needs like water and food.[50] Homeostatic balances are regulated by the midbrain's hypothalamus and its two effector systems: the autonomic nervous system and the endocrine system. The autonomic nervous system, not under conscious control, controls arousal (sweating, mouth dryness, rapid respiration, muscle tension) and controls smooth muscles, heart, and exocrine glands that release hormones. Responding to neuronal and blood-borne messengers, the autonomic nervous system has three subsystems: the *sympathetic* system, which prepares the body for fight-or-flight responses by increasing cardiac response and altering body temperature and glucose level; the *parasympathetic* system, which regulates rest and digestion under normal conditions; and the *enteric* system (not discussed here).[51]

Most empirical research has focused on simple organisms and simple drive states like thirst and tissue deficits. But human beings are not simple organisms and their motivated acts, the important ones at least, are multidetermined. How do we think about complex motivational states in humans, not lab animals? Cognitive purposes may be the shining lights toward which human beings move, but emotions provide the fuel. The emotions are important for learning, aside from being sources of motivation. According to Renate and Geoffrey Caine, learning is helped by active meaning making where patterning is the goal.[52]

Emotions help with the search for pattern while also strengthening connections for the learner to other parts of memory and experience. Educators and counselors help learners refine and test purposes, to be sure. But they also work with emotional states and changes, their own and those of learners. As I have done with neurology and motivation, consideration of emotions and learning has to be limited to a general overview followed by coverage of the most important functional relationships. Emotional states like happiness, depression, anger, and fear—each so variable in intensity—add considerably to the variability and quality of life. They are the most powerful agents in human learning and adaptation. Through experiencing emotions, positive and negative, people evaluate their behavior and the results of choices made. Under most conditions, people want to repeat positive experiences and avoid experiences that frighten or make them feel incompetent.

Neuronal circuits and hormonal pathways control emotions. The pathways have cognitive components, which are viewed as labels for organic changes in autonomic, endocrine, and motor systems. Consistent with a constructivist view of human beings as meaning makers during and after acts (rather than before), contemporary theory views emotions as cognitive labels given to ambiguous and diverse physiological signals.[53] Following James-Lang-Schachter theory, emotion occurs *after* the cortex receives signals about physiological changes. Another counterintuitive notion is that similar autonomic responses, like sweating or breathing hard, can be the result of quite different emotions, such as fear and passion.

Motivational states like curiosity and pleasure are not well understood, especially the way termination of such drives occurs. That is, researchers have an idea of what initiates a motivated activity like eating. But less is understood about why behavior ceases, because complex routines like eating are determined and sustained by more than simple tissue deficits (think about compulsive eating). For one thing, circadian rhythms are biological clocks that *anticipate* deficits, and these rhythms exist for most homeostatic body functions. For another, cognitive purposes like wanting to win an eating contest push behavior beyond biological limits.

Drive states like curiosity or sexual arousal do not have well-defined physiological states of deprivation, but still can be thought of as having both arousal and satiation stages. In particular, pleasure is a poorly understood factor in motivation—after all, it is not hard to think of circumstances in which people deprive themselves, or suspend gratification, to *intensify* drive states and their emotional correlates.[54] Thrill seeking in amusement rides, like a roller coaster, and risk situations, like motorcycle racing, discussed later, may be pleasurable because of the powerful effects of autonomic arousal, particularly if the activity stimulates the release of the potent hormone adrenaline to prepare the body for danger, a response sometimes termed "fight or flight." Similarly, combat veterans sometimes talk about the exhilaration of battle, which may seem odd given the risk of dying that should make them scared. Presumably, this reaction is because of hormonal responses connected with autonomic arousal in life-threatening circumstances or post-trauma cognitive rationalization.

Two lines of research speak to the *pleasure problem,* the truth that researchers do not understand how pleasure functions. Research with lab rats has demonstrated that direct electrical stimulation of the hypothalamus has intracranial reinforcing properties. The poor animals will, in fact, starve themselves to death while activating a bar press wired to the hypothalamus, sometimes called the pleasure center. So, intracranial brain stimulation can work as a potent reinforcer of behavior and, in fact, create its own drive state, which takes us, briefly, to substance abuse. Drugs affect reinforcing centers of the brain, such as mesolimbic dopamine pathways. Humans are motivated by psychoactive substances like nicotine or marijuana, opiates like heroin, stimulants like cocaine, and by alcohol, all of which cause changes in the brain-body to which people can become addicted. Nicotine, for example, increases dopamine levels, an organic opiate, at synapses in the mesocorticolimbic pathway.[55] Finally, it may be that remembering a reward or painful experience activates visceral systems, so-called "gut feelings," in use during the initial events.[56]

Another line of research—studies of the hormone testosterone by James and Mary Dabbs—underscores the intimate relationship between human behavior and emotions, and the near environment.[57] In both men and women testosterone is responsible for secondary sex characteristics. Less well known is testosterone's potent contribution to the level of activity that supports *all* behavior. Individuals with high levels of the hormone are active, if not aggressive, in their environments, which increases performance, other things being equal. With regard to evolution, testosterone is the fuel of aggression and the drive for dominance. Middle school educators witness the dramatic effects in their classrooms when pubescent boys experience a seven-fold increase in testosterone, much greater than the increase for young women.[58] Forget about organized learning—just controlling a class of eighth graders becomes the daily challenge, and large classes add to the problem.

The Dabbs introduce a new method for measuring testosterone in saliva, and this method has let researchers explore the periodicity of testosterone and its changes due to environmental demand. Levels do not remain constant: They decline by 50 percent over the life span, are higher in the morning, and are affected by the seasons. More interesting for my purposes, testosterone level can change in response to environmental demand. High-demand environments like a training camp for bike racing seem to increase testosterone in both men and women, leading to increased performance and higher levels of competence. Testosterone is also influenced by mood, because positive feelings are correlated with an increased level of the hormone. This is not to overstate the complex interaction among testosterone level, mood, and environmental demand. On the other hand, a potent mix of high activation and self-confidence provides the foundation for charismatic leadership in both men and women.

Finally, this important line of research has implications for curriculum design, particularly how environmental demand is structured. For instance, men and women with high levels of testosterone may find it hard to sit still in class, a fact to which high school teachers can attest. But rambunctious, younger students may perform better in less-structured environments that let them move about, at least part of the time, which is acceptable in certain European school systems. Research also points to the value of rigorous physical activity for both men and women to force the brain-mind-body to adapt and learn.

Chapter 5

Psychology of Involvement

Time flies when you're having fun.

—Popular saying

The high points in life come from those few moments when we are psychologically fully involved in an activity. A profound lecture, a great concert, a thrilling soccer game, or a new lover might stimulate involvement. What are those moments like and how do we study them?

Neurobiological mechanisms and dynamics that support motivation and learning are important for educators to understand, at least in the broad outline we have used. How human beings process information exchanges—both internally and with the near environment—has implications for professional practice and for curriculum design, which increasingly will be our concern as we turn to practical applications of all this theory. Now we need understand the psychology of involvement. What is the experience like? How can we think about the experience, especially *changes* in subjective experience? To capture its major characteristics will not be simple because psychological experience is subjective, highly variable, and so much is not in awareness. Diverse examples will let us map an unexplored terrain of great importance to educators.

Three broad topics are ahead: first, characteristics of the psychological experience of involvement; second, the nature of the experience in a wide range of human activities; third, an excursion into theory, mercifully brief, to speculate about the most important dimensions of involvement, defined as a temporary psychological state.

Psychological Experience of Involvement

Involvement is a definable psychological state of being, one involving subtle but significant changes in attention, perception, cognition, and mood. I start with the most intense experiences, although such moments are infrequent. The discussion will concentrate, initially, on attention and mood, because these two dimensions seem most important. Special cases of changed attention are not considered, such as reduced consciousness due to fever and disease or perceived threat.

Why should we care about the phenomenology of psychological involvement? For most of the last century American behavioral psychologists were steadfast in challenging such data, preferring to focus more on measurable behavior than on subjective self-report. Using a wide range of examples, my purpose is to sensitize readers to subtle changes in mood and attention, changes so subtle they pass us by unnoticed. Certainly I did not think of these changes in my own life for more than fifty years. Even today, after years of reading about motivation, attention, and such, I have to concentrate to reign in a restless mind. When I talk about these moments in class, I ask students about their interior phenomenological experience, especially those rapid swings in attention span and degrees of awareness. When asked about such experiences, my students agree on two things: The topic is fascinating, and, most of the time, they are usually not conscious of the states or changes, even dramatic shifts.

The lack of understanding about how the mind and consciousness function is remarkable, especially for educators and counselors who need that understanding to be effective. Teachers do not need to be yogis with exquisite, finely tuned awareness and perfect poses. Rather, small changes in practice are enough to get started. Improved awareness of psychological states in oneself and in others can, for one thing, make one a better listener. One of the subtle tensions in teaching and learning is finding the right balance of talking to the class and listening, really listening, to understand what a learner is struggling to say.

I start with Abraham Maslow's list of the subjective qualities of peak experience reported by people when asked about peak experiences they have had. A long list of attributes of peak experiences were reported by his respondents: wholeness; an integrating experience; suspension of critical judgment; clear perception; loss of ego-centeredness; perception of beauty and goodness; sense of awe; a self that feels active and responsible; a feeling that the person is physically bigger, taller, and stronger; feeling of gratitude; and disorientation in time and space after the peak experience. Often the person feels intelligent, perceptive, witty, strong, graceful, effortless, self-confident, expressive, creative, and similarly positive attributes.[1] Although stated in different terms, Mihaly Csikszentmihalyi's flow experience and Ellen Langer's mindfulness share core attributes reported by Maslow: intense concentration, loss of self-consciousness, loss of time consciousness, pleasantness, and a certain effortless flow to the entire experience.

Whether the activity is climbing or racing, playing music or teaching, psychological involvement evokes positive psychological feelings and cognitive attributions. Consider this example: It is not fun to play the piano when tired; it feels forced, more work than fun. At rare moments like late morning, when perception for me seems clearest and most vivid, I might find myself suddenly, unexpectedly, caught up in the moment. The feeling cannot be forced—it is not consciously directed. I am surprised by *how fast* and *how completely* the changed consciousness takes over my being—I lose any sense of being separate from the music or the instrument. Unlike playing for a teacher or friend, I do not feel either self-conscious or nervous. Rather, I fuse with the rich, layered harmony of the opening bars of Beethoven's "Moonlight Sonata," although that description, strange as it may sound, still does not convey the entire experience, the depth of the merged subject and object. The experience is pleasant and my mood improves. But when I practice a second piece moments later, it is impossible to reproduce the peak experience.

Playing music is only one arena. Doubtless the reader has had comparable experience with teaching, writing, and any number of hobbies that bring us pleasure and meaning. At such moments, I find myself caught up—psychologically captured—by a television drama, a college hockey game when the score has become close, or a Puccini aria. Finding the right words to express the quality of these captured moments always seems impossible. As rare as it is and as challenging to describe, one thing is certain: The psychological experience is profoundly unlike normal experience, even admitting the considerable variability of ordinary lived experience. The sudden onset and spread to other dimensions of being, noted by Maslow, Csikszentmihalyi, and others, are unique.

When a peak experience is intense or prolonged, people report feelings of transcendence, of being removed from the experience, feeling apart from the normal flow of events and time. If interrupted while in this mood, they report feeling disoriented, as when a jazz musician, having finished a set, needs a few minutes to get reoriented. You can see this on stage. Players speak of being "lost" or "out there." Public speakers or teachers who lecture will recognize the same phenomenological shift, finding it hard for a few minutes to reconnect with an eager questioner.[2]

Sometimes peak psychological experience for both students and teacher happens in class. At such moments in a college class, our worldview may be suddenly—unexpectedly—shaken. Reading in class from Shakespeare or Virginia Woolf evokes a feeling of closeness with another mind, another age and distant culture. Suddenly we feel part of a larger human project of great nobility. It can be an emotional moment—I remember moments in certain classes were sometimes accompanied by a shudder or sudden chill even though the room was warm. Because the brain-mind-body is alert and mood is elevated, students remember these moments fondly and want to have them again.

When it comes to learning, involvement is a pivotal precondition but not a sufficient condition. Powerful as the experience is, psychological involvement is not the conceptual learning for which schools and colleges award academic credit. Surely, the organism is adapting and learning, but involvement, alone, is not enough. Hard work will have *preceded* the moment (to master needed technique like musical scales), and work is required *after* the experience for enduring learning to happen (listening to a teacher's critique and trying the piece again at a slower tempo). That is, college-level learning requires additional and *intentional* steps before and after having had a powerful experience.

Returning to phenomenological experience, Maslow, Csikszentmihalyi, and Langer do not address middle-range experience. Discussion of involved moments appears to be all or nothing, peak or no change. Here, I am less interested in exact definitions of these elusive states than in their transforming dynamics—the dialectics—whereby an ordinary behavior like driving or dish washing can be either boring or intensely involving. Perhaps one reason why middle-range experience is not discussed is that the peaks are easier to characterize than low levels or changes in level. Purposive activity is not likely when one is uninvolved, but that does not mean the organism is asleep. As noted earlier, physiological dynamics are not understood except as observations that attention wanders, seemingly without conscious direction, and the mood people experience is variable, neither intensely positive nor negative. Vague feelings of restlessness may be experienced, as if one has watched television for five hours straight. But people may report moderately pleasant feelings from periods of daydreaming, such as when a person consciously elaborates on a fantasy such as new love or an upcoming vacation.

Even in normal, everyday experience, amazing things occur. In the course of an hour, human attention moves rapidly and without discernible order to focus on hundreds of objects. Imagine this scene. I am drying the dishes, my wife asks me what happened at work, and I say "nothing much" (which is not true) while simultaneously thinking about an argument with her two days ago, another argument I lost twenty years ago with someone else, whether I should tell her about that horrid meeting I had with by boss, how she will react, and what my reticence means about our marriage—all in nanoseconds, it seems, mostly without my conscious direction.

Here is another example of changing human experience from my diary. One morning while hiking, I am distracted by a business problem while I begin to focus on glimpses of fall foliage. I am following a creek bed outside Aspen, Colorado, and as the terrain gets steep, the sound of my breathing intrudes and then dominates awareness. My mind roams and I feel good—I am not concentrating on any one object, feeling, percept, or idea.

Or think about learning to drive. As young adults, we learn this new skill, for which we do not yet have patterns. Learning new skills requires intense concentration. Mental models do not yet let us combine smaller skills and percepts (like turning the wheel, touching the brake, and scanning the intersection) into an integrated, unconscious whole (turning the corner). The learning experience is intrinsically "exciting" and this is as true for the psychological experience as it is for hidden neurological events. For the inexperienced driver, shifting a car with manual transmission requires focused concentration—for experienced drivers, shifting is automatic, requiring little focus.

Learning unconscious patterns for complex behavioral routines is adaptive—in the case of hiking, to have to focus on every detail of walking, one foot after the other, would leave an animal exhausted and vulnerable. Sometimes, the mind is too much on automatic. Think about the perceptual complexity of an ordinary road intersection, which people learn to navigate successfully. Experienced drivers have learned physical skills like steering and braking and developed a general attention set by which to scan the environment, often without focused concentration. That is, we are half-aware of coming to a stop, of traffic approaching, and of some movement on the other road. We have learned how to estimate acceleration and braking velocity for our car and those we encounter. By means that are not in conscious awareness, we react quickly to the sudden peripheral image of a child chasing a ball into the street just ahead. If conditions change rapidly, an accident occurs. Better to say, of course, our driver lacked a mental set to monitor the situation, probably representing a lack of experience and reflecting a less-developed neuronal network. Even for the experienced driver, the same behavior, like driving directed by greater focus, high stakes, and lots of practice on a racetrack, for example, can be transformed into high involvement.

So everyday life requires we learn complicated behavioral routines like walking and driving that, once mastered, do not need conscious attention. Not in awareness, the mind wanders, examining patterns in sensory channels without apparent direction. When a person's behavior appears, in this way, to be automatic and there is no active focusing, surface behavior is controlled by unconscious perceptual sets that come to awareness only if some information is anomalous or outside expected ranges. While washing dishes, for example, most people do not think about what they are doing (unless the water suddenly burns them), and the person is not engaged by the activity. By focusing attention in a conscious way, one can make these activities mindful, at least for a period.

When a person begins to focus attention, consciously or unconsciously, perceptual vigilance is heightened and scanning increases. The organism becomes more alert than before and experiences fresh, vivid images. Mood is enhanced, at least if the stimuli do not produce revulsion or fright, which may have instinctual causes. We call the best of these events "fun."

Paying attention, by itself, is not the same thing as psychological involvement. But it is one way the more complicated state of being can be elicited. Although it usually takes a conscious act to try to become involved, like going to the gym or sitting down to practice, flow experience is more play than work once it is begun.[3] The psychological experience feels natural, not forced or consciously mediated.

Finally, our discussion has been brief but sufficient to illustrate the *plastic quality of lived experience* that needs to be better understood both by researchers as well as by individuals trying to make sense of life. Next we consider the peculiar power of psychological involvement in groups, especially when people identify with religious and political beliefs, some quite dangerous to self and others.

Involvement and Religious Experience

Thus far the discussion has centered on psychological experience, using examples to surface inchoate experience that we may not always recognize.

Some of the most powerful human experiences come from involvement with social groups. In particular, many peak experiences throughout history have been interpreted in spiritual terms as visions or the result of prayer.

Earlier we noted William James's interest in religious experience. He wrote about religious conversion more than a hundred years ago and his language is more religious than psychological in its values and vocabulary. People reported peak experiences that they attributed to "God" or the "Holy Spirit," but inspection of the language used suggests the psychological changes are comparable. That is, we can distinguish between the label attributed to a psychological experience and underlying neurobiological and psychological events. Furthermore, James argued that the critical component in conversion is the personal act of surrender to God, of begging for forgiveness and mercy. In psychological terms, surrender to an external, higher authority like a god is no different than surrender to a charismatic cult leader like Reverend Jim Jones.

While some religious experiences share the attributes we have discussed, additional elements are possible. Maslow described a "plateau experience" in religious settings where the involvement has a quiet, reflective quality. The experience is a "serene and calm, rather than [a] poignantly emotional, climactic, autonomic response to the miraculous, the awesome. . . . "[4] The experience is more voluntary than a peak experience, and Maslow describes an involvement in the moment that is more detached, what he terms "witnessing."

Elsewhere, Maslow distinguishes between "transcenders" and "merely-healthy people" who do not have many transcendental moments, or as intense ones. To describe "transcenders" he termed this "Theory Z" (in contrast to Douglas McGregor's Theory Y, then popular as a humanistic management theory). Transcenders have more peak experiences, and having peak experiences has become a central goal of their lives. They tend to use the spiritual language of poets and mystics and to blend the sacred and the profane.[5]

For another account of the phenomenology of religious experience, we turn to a contemporary commentator on religion, Thomas Moore, who has a written a series of popular books on contemporary religious experience that use terms like "soul" and "re-enchantment." Moore worries about how modernity and its cold principles of science and instrumental rationality have eroded human attributes like the playful, erotic, illogical, childish, and spiritual. People would lead richer lives, Moore says, if we could find a "deep, solid, communal fantasy life."[6]

One religious experience stands out, the experience of the *numinous,* an extraordinary sensation outside everyday experience that combines subtle emotional experience and ethical principles of religion. To define it, Moore relies on Rudolf Otto's classic 1917 study of peak religious moments. Often it is an emotional experience in nature that begins the numinous episode, like being startled by the crack of summer lighting while hiking in the mountains (a classic example). Once I had a similar experience at sunset while watching ocean waves roll in on a beach on Prince Edward's Island; I suddenly felt quite small and alone in the world. Otto uses an odd term, "creatureliness," for being in the momentary presence of the divine.[7]

The numinous is sometimes found in calamity, when everyday experience is shattered by events outside control. The September 11 attacks on the World Trade Center and the Pentagon confront us with mortality and chance, events so much larger than self, and with cracks in the perceptual order of the life-world (planes do not fly into skyscrapers, tall buildings do not fall down in a heap). Not only is it difficult to process the feelings from such events, but Moore might add that modern man is afraid to look at—or, once he recognizes the event, to stay with—transcendent experiences like the numinous. Perhaps such moments are simply overwhelming, but another explanation makes more sense: that we are not tuned into changes in attention and awareness.

More generally, consider the functions of prayer in human experience. Prayer or meditation is one of the most personal of human acts. By different names, prayer has a central role in most world religions. Several Eastern and Western religions emphasize elaborate forms of prayer or meditation for the purpose of reaching enlightenment or achieving a state of grace. ("Grace" is a religious term for a psychological state not unlike the peak experiences under discussion.) Terms used to describe the activity vary, but two elements are essential: first, *personal surrender to creed or authority,* and second, *rituals that focus attention.* These two two variables interact to produce powerful psychological identification. (Keep these two dynamics in mind when we later consider true-belief groups.)

Buddhist meditation can produce quite dramatic mood states leading to total fusion with one's surroundings, the loss of subject-object separation that is normal in everyday perception. Small esoteric religions that feature ritual chanting, like the Japanese Buddhist sect, Soka Gakkai, and psycho-therapeutic practices of dubious value, like primal screaming, as well as certain sensitivity-training exercises derive their power similarly.[8] Jim Castelli interviewed twenty-six members of different religions, asking how people pray.[9] He reported many ways of prayer, formal and informal, connected with different rituals and traditions. Few reported prolonged meditating. In the 1970s, the Catholic Church developed "centering prayer," by design a meditative prayer, partly in response to the growing popularity of Eastern meditative religious. As in Eastern practices, the method requires the supplicant to focus on one word by which to reveal the grace of God.

Whether in Eastern religious traditions like Zen Buddhism, or Western ones such as the evangelical Pentecostals, people report powerful emotional experiences in their religious practice. The Pentecostals are America's fastest-growing religion and their ministers include fallen tele-evangelists Jim Baker and Jimmy Swaggert.[10] Begun in Los Angeles in 1906, today 12 million members worship in services that emphasize direct, personal experi-ence and emotional experiences like glossolalia and speaking in tongues, when participants speak an ecstatic language previously unknown to them.

Contrast such a focus on personal, immediate, and transcendent psychological experience to that of traditional churches, like Protestant Episcopa-
lian denominations where worship, by design, is restrained and psychologically
distant. A classic dispute in the history of organized religion is, of course, the
degree of direct emotional experience permitted. By church doctrine and
custom, Episcopal priests are there to both interpret and communicate *for*
the congregation. The hierarchy of so-called high churches will resist anyone
other than a priest interpreting either the scripture or the group's emotional
and spiritual experience.[11]

So, psychological involvement is stimulated by groups, usually toward
goals that benefit both the individual and the group even as the connection
methods vary. Nothing is inherently harmful in such associations and
membership. But it is not hard to think of counterexamples in which
belonging to a group is blatantly harmful, even dangerous, to self and others.
After considering a variety of types of involvement, I will return to the
subject of psychological experience and group identity.

Involvement and Life Activities

Think about ordinary experiences in daily life. The activities people choose
are important with regard to stimulating psychological involvement. Having
a partial understanding of the emotional experience and its ebb and flow,
now we will extend the discussion to how people invest psychological energy
in all manner of life activities.

When it comes to involvement in life, William James would say: Perception is everything! In his classic example, the same event—a pebble bounced
off a windowpane—is experienced as ordinary and forgettable, but riveting
if one imagines the pebble to have been thrown by a lover.[12] The nature of
what we do is much less important than how we *perceive* the event, how we
invest energy in and attach meaning to it. Even so, certain interactive
activities, like dating, or risk behaviors, like racing, seem to stimulate, but do
not guarantee, psychological involvement. What matters most is the psychic
energy invested in life purposes, regardless of whether or not that investment
is conscious or not.

Human culture offers an enormous array of hobbies and pursuits to
motivate, from gardening to hang gliding. Humans develop hobbies and
recreational pursuits to add texture and meaning to life. Often, the valued
hobbies are those life activities that elicit focused attention. A bird watcher
spends hours watching a salt marsh to glimpse a rare bird, thus to add to her
life count. A bow hunter in Northeastern Vermont crouches fifteen feet up in
a tree stand for three hours, scanning the environment for noise or movement, using one kind of attention to scan the environment before pulling the
trigger, which brings sharply increased attention and involvement. (Not
always appreciated are emotional elements in involvement, as when aroused
hunters talk about hearing their heart beat just before taking a shot.) In less

dramatic fashion, comparable experiences can occur while sewing a blouse or planing a piece of white pine to build a small wood box, a gift for a friend. For people who have competitive, stressful occupations, a pleasant day on the weekend may be one of a gentle, meandering attention as one moves from reading the papers to cooking to reading a novel to gardening.[13]

Think about all the rhetorical devices, like anecdotes and sarcasm, in human culture that have evolved to help a speaker capture listener attention. Public speakers learn to vary the tempo of delivery, to use silence and the voice's range to capture and hold listener attention. A good story focuses the attention of a group, if only for minutes. Society's performance artists—a poet, a stand-up comic, and the experienced teacher—all know to use these rhetorical tricks to capture an audience.

Theater, the oldest forum for human entertainment and group learning, is organized to manipulate audience attention, both by dramatic devices and by the issues being dramatized. Before and after the invention of written language, theatrical stories have carried forward human culture. All forms of entertainment, indeed, seem designed to play with human attention and mood. Comedy manipulates attention and mood to entertain an audience, producing powerful emotional experiences. When the shift occurs in a group setting, it seems to be contagious, lifting the mood of the whole group. If psychological changes in mood and attention did not occur, these cultural institutions like theater, the circus, magic shows, and concerts would not have evolved as they have.[14] We call it a "good play" if it holds audience attention, a "good joke," the attention of a friend. Humor and word play bring color and human interest to otherwise boring moments in daily life.

So far I have not emphasized the interactive nature of involvement by which two people, a small group, or an audience and a performer interact to mutually change psychological experience. In the theater and performing arts, performer and audience play off the attention, mood, and behavior of the other. An unresponsive audience contributes to an uninspired performance—and no one has a good time. Take the same play and another evening—now, the evening comes alive for both audience and performer. If prompted, we think we understand group contagion even if we don't know the important variables underneath the phenomenon or are not usually conscious of the mood and attention shifts, up or down. For example, a slang term is "buzz kill," by which something happens to rupture the group "high."

We have all had this experience in social settings, but the reasons are not easy to isolate—perhaps it was something that happened in the city that day, or a more inspired performance that sparks involvement. But now the psychological experience of all participants is elevated because of certain elements in the social interaction. In that spirit, frenetic comedian Robin Williams was interviewed as part of the television series *Inside the Actors Studio*. Williams spoke repeatedly to a theme that experienced teachers understand, the energy he needs from the audience to lift his performance, especially to create comedy, which demands audience involvement.

Solitary activities like reading and playing music can stimulate the imagination in marvelous ways, if one concentrates. Think about reading, which is so important for learning and for quality of life. That experience can be riveting, or boring. If the reader is rested, a well-written story or clever argument fills the mind and time passes quickly. At such moments, a reader savors the moment, not wanting the book "to end." We choose the right time to finish the book, as if we have become emotionally involved with this odd, rectangular object. At other moments, indeed most of the time, people read effortlessly and mindlessly—we are hit with a cascade of street signs, newspapers, and office memos whose patterns we have learned and now anticipate.

A special problem for students, teachers, and counselors is faux reading. Only after several minutes of turning pages does one notice the mind is elsewhere, either daydreaming or going through the exercise. Pages turn themselves. Mind elsewhere, the reader is not conscious that he is not paying attention to the activity, much less learning new concepts for class. To recognize faux concentration in one's own behavior is not simple. Just as it is also easy to misread the surface behavior of students who appear to be paying attention when, in fact, dutiful-appearing students are not listening and not reading. If one could measure the amount of mindless, keeping-busy activity in the school day for both teachers and students, it would be sobering. What is the purpose of education if what results is the *appearance* of learning, not its substance?

The ebb and flow of awareness and attention are hard to follow, especially during the activity. Even changes in emotional mood, which seem less plastic than awareness or attention, go unrecognized. Something seems not right, perhaps, but we cannot spot the cause or interrupt the feeling. Reasons cited are wrong. A teacher hears: "I don't like the book," or "I hate homework." In truth, the student is struggling with an inattentive mind. What learners need at such moments are markers to tell them that they have lost focus (which is partly what teachers and counselors provide). Then students need flexible reading skills with which to self-manage the learning activity.

Whatever the activity and given adequate rest, the conscious act to focus attention can make the mundane magnificent. Situations that require learners to be active—to make *conscious* choices—like gardening, sewing, and painting, elicit psychological involvement. Thich Nhat Hanh, a Vietnamese monk whose life integrates Zen Buddhist philosophy and social responsibility, asserts that washing the dishes, drudgery to most people, can be made a calming, meditative activity if one is mindful.[15] Similarly, interactive, smart machines, like personal computers as well as the web, that make demands of their users offer new forms of human-machine interactivity, which many people find involving because novel stimuli and endless new puzzles are put before the senses.

Interactive situations, which involve other people and the unpredictable stimulation they introduce to the life-world, tend to elicit higher involvement. That is why, in part, people value such activities. While any activity can be boring and invite psychological and physical risk, interactive situations are among the most involving and pleasurable of daily life. Think about the function of games, specifically card games, and how people use them to manipulate psychological experience. Two friends were playing hearts the other night. For two hours, both players were immersed in the game, its mechanical routines like cutting and dealing cards, arranging a hand, thinking about strategy, and playing a particular move. Light banter accompanied the play. Both were fully involved in a cooperative activity that provided an intense, private psychological experience for each. If asked, our card players would say they were "having fun." That fun comes from the interaction of attention, awareness, and mood—a focused flow activity counters the entropy in human experience, which is an uncomfortable state when protracted.[16]

Perhaps the most poignant moments of all in life come from intimate interactions with other human beings. Sexual intimacy or a good conversation with a new friend can be a deeply moving psychological experience for both partners, causing profound changes in mood that last for hours. Perhaps human beings come to value such moments and learn to fully exploit them because of *changes* in attention, awareness, and mood that result. If positive emotional experiences do not result from these investments, we humans look elsewhere. Abundant evidence supports the notion that cooperative interaction helps us solve immediate problems and, over time, helps the species adapt. Perhaps the pleasure we get from such moments in social interaction is, itself, an adaptive mechanism that is not acknowledged.

On the other hand, every day people have phone conversations that do not require concentration, so social interaction hardly guarantees involvement. At such moments, people feign interest and involvement to protect the relationship. The same deception occurs serially at a loud cocktail party where no one can hear any one. That is, we fake it so as to not call attention to ourselves, a fascinating topic later considered in the epilogue.

So, certain life activities stimulate psychological involvement, at least most of the time, and that is why people choose them. Sexual intimacy, gambling, sports, and child's play—all introduce *novel* stimuli that attract attention, especially when people are rested. Animal studies show that normal animals are curious and will explore novel stimuli if the sensations are not too intense. Although the reasons why are debated, primates, at least, seek certain experiences to produce varied, novel, and complex sensations, not just to address tissue deficits in the case of thirst or hunger. While choice of activity is no guarantor of full involvement and attendant benefits of elevated mood, risk behaviors, discussed next, seem to occasion more involvement than solitary pursuits.

Risk situations elicit high levels of involvement because physical danger implicates additional brain-mind-body mechanisms. Emotional reactions are stimulated by danger, real or contrived, and the experience may be even more involving, if not outright pleasurable, than that of quiet concentration, for example, playing a Chopin prelude. Here is an extended example by a motorcyclist finding himself in danger on Imogene Pass in Colorado:

> As we moved up the mountain, the road became more treacherous. Sharp rocks filled the ruts as did water from melting snow. Driving on the crown meant loose sharp rocks. At higher altitudes *down* meant straight down. However, my confidence was growing and at times I ventured close to the edge.
>
> This had become the most exhilarating experience of my life. For more than three hours my senses were at their peak. Every change in the trail meant that there were decisions to be made in a split-second, and then while the body executed those decisions, another decision was being made. And so it was for hours: decide then do; decide then do—always with greater urgency. While this might have been old hat for many mountain riders, it was an unforgettable experience that continues to call to me now.[17]

If we believe the consistent language of such accounts, the act of focusing attention, itself, is pleasurable. A positive experience is made still more intense if serious physical risk is involved because additional biochemical mechanisms are involved, like the release of neurotransmitters like dopamine to alert the body and hormones like adrenaline to prepare it for danger. Before discussing the psychological dynamics of risk, consider another curious example.

Risk and its potent emotional experience motivate people in odd ways. Michael Apter studies the pursuit of excitement and calls this "the danger-ous edge" that people pursue for arousal.[18] Consider this example. Two hundred undercover transit police in New York City's subways have the job of catching pickpockets and muggers.[19] Sometimes, police serve as decoys. When asked why they volunteer for dangerous work, officers talk about idealistic purposes of helping others and how a dangerous assignment can advance a career. They talk, also, about "adrenaline rushes" that accom-pany catching a criminal in the act. So, physiological arousal becomes a powerful reinforcer of the behavior, especially if it is dangerous or novel. But consider this: Burglars have *the same psychological experience* when they can get in and out of an apartment without being detected, especially if the apartment is occupied. This example suggests why we shall want to distin-guish between the psychological experience of involvement in motivated acts and the ethical purposes of that behavior.

Which is more potent: the need for money, for status, or the arousing psychological experience? Human acts usually express multiple motives, to be sure. But psychological process is underestimated as a reinforcer. Both "cop" and "perp" are attracted to risk and the potent emotional experience it stimulates.[20] Perhaps the experiential reinforcers involved in criminal behavior contribute to high recidivism—after all, not many activities in normal life offer moments of such focused attention and excitement. (For a time, the indoor fantasy game, Murder, played in a dark house, was popular because of the potent mix of fear and focused attention. Today, it is paint ball—a form of play war that uses paint guns.) The argument, of course, can be extended to other risk behaviors like white-collar crime, speeding, and violations of social norms like cheating on an exam or a marriage. Apter cites the excitement-seeking motive in rape and murder, observing that excitement occurs in all stages, from stalking to the act to trying to outwit an arresting officer.[21] Then there are amusements parks and roller coasters, where people go to trick the nervous system and mind into responding to fear even though the rides are usually safe.[22]

Dangerous acts demand people pay attention, or else. Why do some people take to hobbies like sky diving, hang gliding, and mountain climbing, and become so passionate in their defense? Marvin Zuckerman argues for a sensation-seeking motive wherein people seek varied, novel, and complex sensations.[23] People take physical risks and social risks to avoid boredom, and the pursuit is active, not passive. Sensation seekers are likely to participate in unusual experiments and experiences ranging from encounter groups to parachuting. People take risks, Zuckerman asserts, because of reinforcing changes in internal physiological states, like the level of endogenous opioid peptides like dopamine. Finally, high-risk behavior may be attractive to persons with attention deficit disorder because of the external pressure to focus.[24]

So, it is the specific nature of the psychological experience that matters most, much more than the activity chosen. Type of activity makes a contribution to motivation, especially interactive or risk situations. But James was right, as in so many things: What matters is the investment of psychological energy.

Human culture has evolved to offer an enormous range of activities that people can invest in and, thus, enjoy a wide range of psychological experiences, some quite powerful because of underlying neurobiological mechanisms. Experience in the life-world is endlessly variable, subtle, and occasionally transforming, affording people wonderful moments that sustain them and let them bear up under difficult challenges at work. Next, we explore how individual psychological experience is shaped by the groups to which we belong.

Involvement and Group Belonging

Now our focus turns to the effects of groups on individual attitudes and behavior. Three questions will guide the inquiry: First, what is the nature of the connections between individuals and groups? Second, what do we learn about those connections from studying cults or true-belief groups?[25] Third and most important, how does psychological experience function to attract people to groups, to hold them inside despite doubts and deprivation, to lead them to self-sacrifice, and, finally, to make it hard for members to leave the group. As we move through these topics, it will be useful to think about the experiential marketplace where groups that manipulate psychological experience compete for member interest and loyalty. It is provocative to look at all groups, mainstream and otherwise, as competitors for participant attention and allegiance.

Social groups bring the best and the worst out of the species, or so it seems. Groups prompt individuals to noble actions that show the best of the species—at other times, groups lead individuals to barbarism. Earlier we considered neurobiological perspectives so important to understanding the process of psychological involvement. Now we ask about the mental models people use to understand their existence in groups. If that experience goes unexamined, individuals do not know how to use groups wisely for their learning. Worse, some people will be vulnerable to the excesses that sometimes arise in social groups like cults and social movements like totalitarianism, whether from the political left or right.

For seventy years or more, if we are fortunate, we move through the life-world embedded in social relationships and groups that provide hidden challenges and support for our behavior. While we experience this passage as an individual consciousness and presume personal control, the unseen forces shaping our attitudes and behavior are social factors, the effects of enduring relationships and groups. In fact, survival as a species depended on our ancestors learning to live together in groups, and so a quick review of a social psychological perspective may be useful. Such a framework, Elliot Aronson reminds us, is well established in social sciences like anthropology or sociology, which have studied the effects of society and small groups on individuals. Individuals are motivated to act and to learn in social groups, carrying forward the values and norms of the group. To understand motivation and learning leads us to the basic elements of group socialization and identification with the group, not the least because the most fascinating facets of psychological involvement are directly tied to social psychological dynamics within the group.

Groups support the most important functions in human development: in every possible setting groups nurture and punish, socialize and educate. Groups come in many different types, of course, and vary with regard to the degree of psychological identification with the group. All our lives, we play, work, and learn in groups. People join social movements like the Freedom Riders of the 1960s, and political parties like the Republicans or Democrats. Raised in families, most people grow up to make families of their own.

Groups bring subtle, powerful forms of influence to regulate individual behavior. Members are not usually conscious of what is happening to them or why. This framework for understanding groups is, of course, well established even as certain implications for our study of motivation and learning are not. Social norms, like proper dress for dinner, send messages, overt and quite subtle, to members about correct manners. When individuals break those norms, positive and negative sanctions are applied quickly, often silently via a disapproving glance or by withdrawing attention. Group norms shape the smallest of human actions like how to laugh at a joke and what to wear to a party. One's peer group, especially, is a potent source of influence and socialization into group norms, and this is true for teenagers and middle-aged adults. Well-established groups like a church or club are organized around a set of values, perhaps codified in a mission statement. Carefully orchestrated rituals transmit and thus reinforce group values and norms.

None of this is controversial even if we underestimate just how subtle and pervasive social forces can be. After considering a few examples, I want to return to this flawed conception and the nontrivial consequences that flow from it. The examples ahead may be unusual, but they serve the purpose of introducing important concepts. Later in Part III we apply these ideas to education.

The fundamental interests of individuals and groups are not identical. Groups shape human motives and actions, and they both advance *and* retard the learning and character development of individual members. Not all members of a group benefit equally—groups operating under competitive norms may harm those members not smart or strong enough to compete. Elementary schools and sports teams stimulate development. The same groups *inhibit* individual development and more.

I wonder if we educators understand this tension, or another, the dark side of group belonging. Families, clubs, schools, and teams—all can restrict the development of individuals because belonging to a group is not without cost. Group norms serve as boundaries to protect the identity of the community. But those boundaries exclude others and hold back develop-ment of the individual unless, as with schools, explicit norms exist to support personal change. A young woman leaves a small community like Grand Junction in western Colorado and its insular norms because she seeks new experience and new learning. She leaves a closed community because she wants to be treated as a whole person rather than as "a Catholic," or "a girl."

The invisible pull of group dynamics can harm as well as help, whether the risk is not developing fully as a human being or losing individuality. Identification with the wrong group—a cult like Jonestown and its totalistic norms—can motivate a person to kill oneself or one's children, thus violating two of society's most powerful taboos. Such is the dark power that groups hold over individuals, or, perhaps one should say, the power we cede to groups.

Alternative Religions, True Belief, and Mass Movements

Groups that are organized around atypical values and norms fascinate a social psychologist. Their very extremes make it easier to see internal group dynamics found in all human associations. For instance, individual liberties, attitude change, and authority relations—all these forces are more visible in a religious cult than a supper club. I have chosen dramatic examples to underscore the curious power that the group holds over individuals where individuals appear, superficially, to give over that power willingly.

Margaret Singer and her colleagues have categorized social groups that employ deceptive and indirect techniques of persuasion and control.[26] While few true-belief groups survive longer than thirty years, their variety is enormous. We need to expand Singer's list and suggest examples: Alternative religions organized around a charismatic figure (Jim Jones and Jonestown, Shoko Asahara and Aum Supreme Truth, Luc Jouret and the Solar Temple, and David Koresh and the Branch Davidians), new religious groups (Bhagwan Shree Rajneesh in Oregon), countercultural groups (the Manson Family), revolutionary groups (Symbionese Liberation Army and Al Qaeda), psychotherapy cults like the Center for Feeling Therapy in Hollywood, and large-group awareness training (est, Lifespring). Mass political movements also manipulate psychological experience, and recruiting depends upon deception and indirect techniques of persuasion and control (Hitler's National Socialism, Mao's Red Guard, and Pol Pot's Khmer Rouge).[27] Not included in Singer's comprehensive survey are single-episode situations that use deceptive methods, like confidence scams, or situations where attention is manipulated (for example, three-card monte).

True-belief groups, to use Eric Hoffer's idea, are not uncommon in modern society, even though the proportion of people who fully commit is tiny. While most of us could not imagine joining a true-belief group, who has not felt the allure of belonging at some point in life, whether contemplating a sorority rush or trying out for a sports team? A special type, the messianic cult, may compel members to the most extreme acts. The dark possibility arises that isolated seekers find their life-project in a true-belief group like Jonestown, eventually harming others and themselves. Jonestown has been well studied, and my characterization below borrows the account by social psychologists Eugene Galanter, Philip Zimbardo and Michael Leippe, and Neil Osherow.[28]

In 1978, Reverend Jim Jones, a community activist from Indiana and, later, San Francisco, led an idealistic community to Jonestown, Guyana. Known for its interracial culture and a peculiar mix of biblical and socialist ideals, the religious community had attracted many hundreds of people in the Bay Area. By time they moved to a South American jungle, however, sinister dynamics had begun. (A deadly drift from the idealism of founding members to paranoid self-destruction is not uncommon. Group culture is seldom static.) Paranoid projections began to consume Jones, called "Father" or "Dad" in the special vocabulary that develops in such groups. Responding to charges that people were being held against their will, U.S. Congressman Leo Ryan and staff flew in to check.

Two families slipped messages to the Ryan party, saying they wanted to leave. As the group boarded departing planes, it was ambushed. Five people, including Ryan, were killed. (Threat from external authorities, another ingredient of in-group formation, was one of Jones's obsessions. After the murders, of course, this threat would become real.) Citing fear and asking his community to make a spiritual statement to the outside world, Jones led 914 members, including 200 children, to take a lethal combination of cyanide and Kool-Aid. In fact, earlier the group had rehearsed community suicide, termed "revolutionary suicide," as a test of commitment to its utopian vision and charismatic leader. Listen to the language: While some members were "assisted" via lethal injections to "cross over," most took the poison voluntarily. Before the group suicide began, the community debated the action. Doubts were expressed, but Jones led the group to his goal. A compassionate "Father" Jones can be heard saying, "Be kind to children, be kind to seniors. . . . " Standing in line, members could see others before them dying in pain and hear children screaming.[29]

What do we think about such a bizarre phenomenon? Why did individuals give themselves over so totally? How do we explain the power of true belief to motivate members to violate society's most powerful taboos: to give over family inheritances and sell their homes and, indeed, to kill their children and themselves in elaborate rituals? More generally, how does the mind work under such conditions?

To start, I believe the mental models people have about their experience in groups, even the pedestrian groups of everyday life, are flawed. The special psychological experience one has inside a true-belief group, in particular, is intense and psychologically encapsulating. To outsiders, details about group life inside, like strange language or customs of dress, seem odd—one just cannot imagine oneself doing such bizarre things (under the presumption that we are independent agents). But outsiders do not see the slow, deepening process of induction, or feel the fear and anxiety that members report when thinking of living on their own again. And I know from personal experience while a graduate student at Columbia that leaving a true-belief group, an anarchist commune, is far more difficult emotionally for individuals than it seems to outsiders. Sometimes the fear is not just psychological. Defectors from Jonestown were threatened with punishment, and armed guards patrolled the camp's jungle perimeter.

Theory exists at several levels to explain these phenomena: *leader goals and character, vulnerability of individuals,* and *influence methods and group dynamics.* Popular accounts focus on a cult leader like Shoko Asahara or bizarre features of the group but minimize the effects of group culture and powerful influence techniques that are difficult to resist once a person is inside the group. With respect to the bad leader theory, certain kinds of controlling personalities do seem drawn to messianic roles by which to meet their own needs, and the group becomes an instrument to personal ends. These leaders are able to build and maintain a complex organization, at least for a time. Such persons are often energetic, intelligent, articulate, and charismatic—useful attributes for recruiting new members and building an organization. That they can build an organization suggests that madness is not a viable explanation—rather, the likely pathology is a personality disorder, malignant narcissism. A cluster of attributes defines this syndrome: self-centeredness to the point of grandiosity, deep insecurity, lack of ethical judgment, lack of empathy for others, and paranoia and aggression, especially under stress. After the tragedy, it seems easy to see signs of serious mental illness, but we should be cautious when distinguishing between leadership of deviant groups versus mainstream groups. In mainstream groups, leader behavior is checked by social norms.[30]

Equally, the attributes of people drawn to total groups and radical movements could be stereotyped. Perhaps risk takers are attracted to such groups. The evidence for a special vulnerability is mixed. Group dynamics wedded to true belief *are* used by leaders in support of extreme ends. Avishai Margalit reminds us that suicide for a religious or political end has been evident throughout human history.[31] In a poignant, contemporary example, Nasra Hassan interviewed some 250 Palestinians from the most militant camps, debunking notions that the motives of suicide bombers are irrational or suicidal in the psychiatric sense.[32]

While the motives behind self-sacrifice for a cause are varied, psychological experience is a potent element in human actions. To stay with the Middle East, Westerners do not understand the word *jihad* for its spiritual and motivational capacity. The popular press focuses on the idea of religious war, not that part of *jihad* that means personal struggle against lack of discipline. Perhaps modern intellectuals and secular humanists just do not resonate to motivating experiences like Christian "grace" and Islamic "*jihad*"—we underestimate the allure of the spiritual in motivating human actions. In the same way, we may not appreciate the appeal of true belief for those who feel alienated by modernity's pace and anonymity. While believers may not be mentally ill, in a strict sense, the alienation they experience in daily life leaves them vulnerable to true belief and the sense of well-being that results. We-feelingness, which is adaptive because it brings isolated individuals at risk into a group, is a potent experience for all who feel the deep human need to belong.

Now we consider the most important social psychological processes involved in total groups. People belong to groups all their lives; few are motivated to violate taboos against killing one's own children. Intentional communities, like monastic orders that are many hundreds of years old, do not go to such ends (even though group dynamics are comparable and individuals inside may be similarly effected, emotionally and financially). One paradox is that people seek an identity by joining a group or social movement that costs them their individuality. Zimbardo and Leippe point to religious cultists like the Moonies, who go to extreme lengths to remove the normal privacy enjoyed by individuals. When individual psychological experience within the group is interpreted by the double authority of sacred text as understood by a charismatic leader, a potent recipe for tragedy emerges, as seen at Waco, Texas, and Jonestown, and, on a large scale, the ethnic cleansing seen in the Balkans and Africa. The psychological experience of belonging is a potent motivator, one easily exploited.

The interlocking influence mechanisms used to attract and bind members have been studied. The Singer report posited a *continuum of influence* to illustrate how indirect and deceptive techniques differ from legitimate means. At one end, imagine nondirective and educative methods that respect the right and ability of a person to make their own choices. Techniques like discussion, information giving, and reflection as used in education and psychotherapy are appropriate. Intermediate zones are advisory/therapeutic; influence is more directive and ideas are recommended. Next comes persuasive/manipulative influence, including rational argument and emotional appeals, even deceptions. At the other extreme, the controlling/destructive type found at Jonestown, indirect and deceptive means may be joined to isolation from social supports, physical restraint, guilt induction, and actual punishment.

Much of the power to change behavior in the true-belief group comes from manipulating member thinking. Writing in the 1970s, Irving Janis defined groupthink as "the deterioration of group efficiency, reality testing, and moral judgment that results from in-group pressures."[33] Eight characteristics are defining: 1.) illusion of group invulnerability; 2.) collective efforts to dismiss negative information; 3.) tendency to ignore ethical consequences of group decisions; 4.) stereotyping of motives and values of other groups; 5.) pressure on individuals to align their views with those of the group; 6.) self-censorship by individuals of deviations from the group consensus; 7.) shared illusion of unanimity; and finally, 8.) emergence of "mindguards" who take it upon themselves to guard the group from deviants. One could take this list and apply it to intentional groups like a sorority or a commune. In combination, this is a potent mix, and it is no wonder individuals find it hard to resist.[34]

Less appreciated are subtle, *unconscious* cognitive adjustments by people under conditions of deprivation, called *self-justification* by Zimbardo and Leippe. A common feature of intense socialization procedures like fraternity initiations and officer candidate training, the individual is first exhausted while group supports are simultaneously reduced by bizarre demands or isolation of the subject who has, by this process, been depersonalized. As people make sacrifices while experiencing themselves being drawn ever deeper into the group, but not without conscious doubts, social psychologists point to the tendency to justify those sacrifices by *increasing* perceived attraction to the group.[35]

To pursue such cognitive adjustments, which respond to experience, would take us far a field. But one self-justification dynamic is fascinating: the way in which proselytizing for a cause or creed reinforces true belief. Leon Festinger, social psychologist and author of the influential theory of cognitive dissonance, and his colleagues found that proselytizing *increased* when a prophecy binding a cult proved wrong.[36] A rationalist theory of human action would predict disaffection and leaving the group when a prophecy fails. By requiring members to proselytize, two essential group functions are covered simultaneously: New members and their resources are recruited *and* convictions of those recruiting are shored up.[37] So it is no accident that proselytizing is a staple of religious and political groups.

And think about the dynamic process by which an individual joins and leaves a true-belief group. Recruiting methods are systematic. People are drawn into the group by a potent three-part mix of physical exhaustion, psychological destabilization, and deindividuation (the loss of individual identity within the group). In an organized cult, individuals are led, step by step, to immense sacrifices—by stages, members are led to question basic values and change behavior to join the group, motivated unconsciously by a desire to belong and to experience the serenity that converts typically report, at least initially. Jones manipulated individuals at all stages as they became integrated into the group. Over several years, he and his lieutenants built a totalitarian organizational culture in all particulars. In small, scripted steps, more and more was asked of members in what was, in fact, a gradual stripping away of personal autonomy.

Deindividuation, the erosion of individual identity, ranges from gradual, as a group develops from its idealistic early stage in a student commune, for example, to forms that are totalitarian and expect increasingly serious commitment. While most people could never submerge their identity inside a cult, we should imagine a long continuum of vulnerability to group forces. Each new demand on a group member has two effects, according to Osherow: the loss of personal assets makes it difficult for a person with doubts to leave the group and the sacrifices increase self-justification. Astonished by the tragic result of an apocalyptic cult, we overlook the systematic process by which a small cognitive-emotional commitment, innocent in itself, is progressively enlarged via influence techniques described by Zimbardo and Leippe.

As psychological identification with the group increases, individual self-consciousness, experienced as uncomfortable, lessens. People feel the pull of groups as they participate in sports, clubs, and religious groups, even if most will never let themselves totally surrender. People who feel the allure of true-belief groups and social movements report feeling part of a project "larger than self," enjoying that sense of belonging. Potent feelings arise, and believers report diminished self-consciousness together with increased psychological attachment to the group and positive well-being. Perhaps such shifts contribute to creativity resulting from reduced self-consciousness and self-censorship. On the other hand, intense identification with a group or social movement can reduce individual creativity because group norms grow restrictive, as Janis suggests.

So, group values and internal pressures themselves evolve *and* intensify. Groups organized around novel and idealistic goals that demand total commitment by adherents create a microculture that becomes encapsulating to both leaders and followers, especially if a paranoid or apocalyptic element enters the belief system. Neither theories of the aberrant leader nor the special vulnerability of believers are adequate to completely explain extreme groups and similar phenomenon.

So, mental models fail in other ways—the emotional power of we-feelingness in a group is *underestimated* just as independence of character is *overestimated*. Fewer people resist group pressure—called brainwashing when first studied during the Korean War—than one imagines because, in part, individuals exaggerate their own strength of character to stand apart from group values and norms.[38] Change groups ties and individual behavior is more plastic than group members suspect, which Philip Zimbardo and his colleagues have documented in innovative experiments.[39] Another source for this phenomenon may be how we perceive the world. Listening to our isolated minds as we construct experience and try to make sense of the world, perhaps we imagine ourselves to be more like separate islands than we are. Lee Ross calls this the fundamental attribution error—observing behavior, we overestimate individual disposition factors while underestimating situational factors.[40]

A few pages ago, I asserted that we educators do not think well about the groups in which we live and learn. Complex motives get expressed in joining and leaving groups, like the need to belong set against the reality that most people function as individuals after leaving the family of origin. Recall William Kahn's observation, drawn from psychoanalytic theory, that people have an unconscious, deep *ambivalence* to belonging to a group. They both want *and* fear group attachment. Perhaps belonging to a group reminds one of the elemental safety of being in a family just as the same experience may be an anxious one because of the demands, in turn, made by the group.

So, how people handle the ebb and flow of existential loneliness is important because group identification may be a seductive solution. When the group adopts familial language and norms, as Jones did as "Father," powerful unconscious appeals are made to family dynamics that go unexamined as we mature. Osherow reported that the Jonestown community's constructed culture imbued "Father" with extraordinary authority. In the case of minor transgressions, for example, Jonestown members were called out in front of the community to confess and to participate in choosing the punishment, as if children. Letting oneself be treated as a child, individual behavior regresses to early stages of development and the freedom to make choices on one's own is lost.

Individuals underestimate the unconscious allure of belonging, which may have roots in the loss of one's own family of origin. One does not have to be a brooding neo-existentialist to recognize that individuals face a very personal existence largely on one's own and are made uncomfortable by this fact. Being embraced by a new community and having instant companions, or so it seems at first, are hard to resist emotionally, at least initially, when the charismatic leader and the group lavish attention on prospects. Though differing in degree, to be sure, the process is not dissimilar to the excitement of taking a new job and the attention one gets.

Human beings are vulnerable to intense group experiences, and I have argued that we underestimate the power of such moments to shape attitudes and life choices. Primate survival depended on working in groups, and that was as true when homo sapiens emerged from the African savannah 100,000 years ago as it is in the urban jungle today. David Gutmann would remind us that the allure of the power-bringing moment is emotionally seductive.[41] Gutmann says people are "magpies for power"—the emotional power of belonging to a group or cause may lead them, ineluctably, to betray values dear to them. The power of the involved moment comes from its sharp contrast with personal depression, or a boring period of one's life. Part of the power comes from the manipulation of peak experiences by a leader like Jim Jones or Luc Jouret, who suddenly treats you like a long-lost friend. Innocent people, perhaps those overwhelmed in life, are drawn to the experiences, false or dangerous as later they may prove to be. Psychological involvement in the moment and the deep process of identification with the group are stimulated by peak experiences in-group rituals, whether the formal events of a high church or the unrecognized communion of a rock concert.[42]

At Jonestown, many forms of social influence were exerted in interaction, and partialist explanations will not suffice. Such was Jones's actual power and personal charisma that even well-educated members who doubted his motives felt drawn to commit, leaving their own children vulnerable to corporal punishment by "Dad." Survivors report that some people had doubts that persisted even as they took the poison. Some were prevented from leaving by being in Guyana, by the jungle and the guards, and because they had no money of their own.

But for most members, the power came from self-justification dynamics, connected to cognitive and emotional events, which provide unconscious rationales for personal sacrifice. The demanding environment of Guyana and the hard work expected of members fed self-justification, which increased attraction of the group even though living conditions were atrocious. Although we might argue over the relative contribution of mechanisms of self-justification and other influence dynamics, social psychological forces in groups are intense, powerful, and underestimated.

We are not quite finished with theory. Group identification is associated with psychological involvement, and authority figures use group dynamics, ritual, and creed to control the psychological experience of members. Groups and movements that help people manipulate and interpret experience compete with one another for the attention and emotional experience of potential converts. Modern society features quite different social institutions to stimulate transcendent experience and to help people make sense of human existence: organized religion, education, psychotherapy, political movements, the theater. Gutmann might add cultural practices like rock concerts, sports events, political conventions, protest marches, and such.

Groups and organizations in society compete for members by manipulating psychological experience.

Whether one thinks about an evangelical church, higher education, or psychotherapy, where the manifest purposes of these three human institutions are so different, consider the latent functions each serves. Each provides an experience venue and rituals designed to help people have psychological experiences, which are then interpreted in the context of that institution's values and norms. Values, norms, and rituals are codified. A priesthood exists, or emerges, with titles and formal training to lead group rituals and mentor learning (recall Janis's mindguards). Stages of joining the group are, in time, codified as novitiates move into the group, and separation from the group, especially intense groups like cults or monastic orders, can be emotionally wrenching.

In fact, social institutions like organized religion, psychotherapy, and the theater have internal debates of long-standing about how, exactly, to manipulate participant experience, how to find the right balance of emotional attachment and cognitive involvement, and how to consolidate participant learning. Little is left to chance if the goal is building the organization. Organized groups of these types are most careful about how they perpetuate the group via the recruiting and socialization of members. Whether it is a benign neighborhood church or a demonic cult, psychological experiences, emotional, physical, and mental, are manipulated precisely to attract and hold converts. Through cognitive mechanisms like self-justification, which we have discussed, individuals come to believe in what they are doing, and what is more, take to their hearts a belief and symbol system—arbitrary as it is—that brings a measure of comfort. So the institutional manipulation of human psychological experience is *intentional, systematic, profound,* and *undeclared* as such, even if dressed in positive terms such as those that adorn religion, therapy, and education.

Belonging to a group is neither inherently dangerous nor wrong. On the contrary, belonging to groups is essential for human identity and the building of human culture. Groups provide emotional succor and intellectual challenge for people who might otherwise be alone. Human culture would not exist and could not develop without these imperfect institutions. For most types of groups, individuals find the support and companionship they need. At the same time, group goals and the degree of individuation allowed within are worth noting. That said, educators need to understand how such institutions and group dynamics function. Our purpose is to understand the role of psychological experience in human motivation and learning, and how these social institutions create conditions, first, to *change* psychological experience and, second, to help people *interpret* that experience.

More generally, I have argued that psychological identity is highly dependent on the nature of groups and the personal relationships in which people live and learn—becoming educated requires people to understand this fact. An authentic individuality is created in creative tension with the seductions of group identity.[43] In broad terms, then, each person's life-project must struggle anew with the ancient theme of individual in society. Television ads that define individuality in consumerist terms—that lovely friends and success are yours for the taking if only you buy the right beer—falsify the charged relationship between individual actions and group identity.

If would not be right to close without noting threats to democratic society posed by extreme groups and radical social movements, about which political theorist Benjamin Barber and many others have written. Total groups and totalitarian social movements pose severe challenges to democratic values and social order, whether the values are expressed in small cults at Waco or in large social-political movements like ethnic cleansing in the Balkans. Utopian solutions to modernity's dislocations do not admit, indeed will not tolerate, the inherent messiness and indeterminacy of democratic change. For example, paranoid thinking in the cult Aum Supreme Truth led the group on March 20, 1995, to kill twelve commuters in Japanese subways using Sarin, a lethal nerve gas. True belief certainly figured in the minds of Al Qaeda members who flew passenger planes into the Twin Towers, the center of American capitalism, and the Pentagon, on September 11, 2001, and history will surely record new statements by persons and groups protesting modernity.

Consideration of such groups introduces, once again, the critical distinction between being psychologically involved, which many groups stimulate for their own purposes, and being socially engaged. A moral questions looms: "Engaged toward what ends? *Whose* ends?" The values and purposes of Jonestown, a socially engaged community in some respects, led that community to extinction. On a larger scale, totalitarian political movements with a "moral" agenda of stated values of the last century in Germany, China, the Soviet Union, Cambodia, and the Balkans killed millions. Many millions of German citizens who supported the Third Reich believed they were doing the right thing, fighting the Bolshevik menace from the East. And history will surely witness new barbarisms. Choice of values is paramount for both individuals and the groups and movements they come to join.

Dimensions of Psychological Involvement

We have been considering the special power of groups and social movements and the ways individual psychological experience is affected. Some of my examples may be difficult to set aside abruptly, but one theory topic remains: the dimensions of psychological involvement.

When thinking about so-called higher, or deeper, levels of human potential, as Maslow did, it is tempting to make a romance of the highest levels—that rare peak experience, its psychological characteristics, causes, and consequences.[44] Rather, we want to understand *intermediate* states of motivation and its components, the ebb and flow of psychological involvement that define ordinary human experience and give quality to life.[45]

But unitary constructs like peak experience or flow are misleading. To suggest how complex things can get, imagine four correlated dimensions of psychological involvement: *attention, awareness, mood,* and *self-focusing*.[46] It is not difficult to imagine the utility of other factors in psychological involvement, like feeling self-confident about a purpose or having the raw energy to just get going on a rough morning. My purpose is more heuristic than to build formal theory. We are working with hypothetical dimensions of being and behavior whose existence cannot be observed directly and must be inferred from behavior, and these components are nearly impossible to isolate.

Before defining each of the four dimensions, recall a distinction made earlier between two broad types of personal involvement. *Psychological involvement* is defined as a distinctive, transitory *state* that does not require social purposes of any type.[47] Involvement is stimulated by sustained, purposive attention, and accompanied by elevated mood. The psychological state of involvement is made up of more than transitory changes in attention or mood. *Social engagement* is defined as a learned character *trait* that connects the individual's developing life-project and psychological involvement to the community's welfare. Social engagement is a special case of focused involvement, differing in three ways from involvement: the ethical purposes chosen, like helping others; the spread of involvement to other interests and pursuits; and the cultivation of this character trait over many years.

What is psychological involvement? Imagining one undifferentiated category, motivation or involvement, is too general. Earlier, I used two dimensions to discuss involvement—mood and attention—both attributes varying from person to person. I described how the attention system, which responds to threat, novelty, and complexity, sets the rhythms of daily life and gives quality to lived experience. Because sustained attention is usually accompanied by elevated mood, for reasons only partly understood, people want to repeat these experiences. Other things being equal, purposive attention in the face of obstacles leads to improved task performance and achievement, in general, which bring (we hope) material rewards, social contributions, and increased popularity.

Motivation is complicated and human actions do not require conscious purposes because the organism initiates many, perhaps most, acts without obvious reason. But intentional acts involve *choice*. People make choices about goals and actions needed to reach them even if the acts are as inconsequential as brushing one's hair. In general, we want human behavior to be purposive even if the goal is vague or intangible, like "having fun" or "killing time."

Attention

Second only to self-focusing, the attention system is the most important component of motivation. Paying attention, that mantra we use with students and ourselves, means focusing on a few signals and ignoring others, which humans cannot do for long. By "attention," we refer to the direction and degree of focus on information provided by the senses: sight, taste, touch, posture, and sound. Most of the time we attend to many things at that same time, none with focus unless it is a perceived threat, like an oncoming car. Threat signals, Peter Milner speculates, are not mediated through consciousness until after we have acted to turn the wheel.[48]

Like motivation, attention is inferred from observable behavior. That is, we see others "paying attention" or notice ourselves watching something intently and are perhaps surprised by the concentration. Attention is a hypothetical construct referring to varying degrees of concentration by the organism for a period of time on a relatively isolated set of stimuli. Attention is not necessarily, or even primarily, conscious—and it is ephemeral, a state easily lost by the fickle mind moving on to consider other objects or percepts. We talk about attention span, and that span is seldom long.

The ability of human beings to control attention—its focus, type, and duration—is not well understood. We can follow two conversations, which is valuable in social settings. But to follow three or four is nearly impossible. By acts of will, one can override biological limits in signal processing and force attention upon a tired nervous system, but there are limits. When deprived of sleep, our ability to pay attention degrades quickly. If we lose several days of sleep, perception is radically changed, even to the point of near-psychotic states.

At any point in time, the organism is bombarded by information, both internal and external. Hundreds, perhaps thousands, of signals impinge. Just sitting quietly, David LaBerge argues, the brain-mind-body monitors many scores of signals simultaneously, mostly not in awareness.[49] The attention system wanders from signal to signal, or perhaps samples among groups of signals. Not always with conscious intention, we notice—suddenly, it seems—the sound of the air conditioner, a beautiful passage of music, or a yellow light at an intersection. The percepts just appear to us, as if miraculously, and the mind stays with the image briefly, measured in seconds or less. Ideas may be mulled over for a few minutes before the mind is on to the next percept or thought.

At other times, people consciously direct attention when, for example, we proof the spelling of words in a sentence. Professional writers know that proofreading makes unrealistic demands of the brain-mind-body because it is hard to concentrate for one page, much less proof an entire paper, especially if it is one's own work. As in other parts of life, we humans invent artificial conventions to force concentration such as using a ruler and reading word-by-word backward in order to minimize distractions from the paper's content. Better, we read passages aloud to another person who has the text before them, which seems to focus two wandering minds on the task.

Hobson reminds us that human attention functions as a *moving, dynamic tension* between distraction from all the hundreds of stimuli and obsession with only a few. Proper orienting is important for staying calm and thinking on a moderate course. Humans enjoy the innate trait to project meaning on ambiguous stimuli in the form of sets and expectations. The brain-mind-body has to depend for its orientation on "a construction that we have to fabricate upon awakening every day."[50] Orientation, Allan Hobson says, breaks down rapidly if a major piece in this cascade of sensory images changes.

Attention can be intense and stable for a short period, as when we follow directions to a party. It is easy to get lost. We listened to the directions but did not work through the new information hard enough or long enough to remember it. Human attention span is so mercurial that people seldom pay attention perfectly or completely for more than a short period, and much modern work does not require concentration. For both reasons, it is important to *learn* to manage *intermediate* attention levels and the information they yield.

Finally, can human beings pay attention without being *aware* of paying attention? To an extent and for brief instants only, attention is subject to conscious control, as in the exhortation in tennis, "watch the ball," or when a teacher calls on a student by name in class who then consciously pays attention for a short period. But little is known about how the attention system as a signal recognition and selection mechanism(s) functions. Monitoring and signal selection likely require multiple, redundant mechanisms that have evolved over many tens of millions of years in other species as well as ours. Awareness, discussed next, is still more obscure than attention as an adaptive learning mechanism in human beings.

Awareness

Of all the categories we humans employ to understand existence, awareness or consciousness has the most vexed history. Thinking of types or stages of consciousness, Eastern and Western religious figures have explored the topic with more subtly and elegance than my brief discussion reflects. "Awareness," the term I will use because it has less baggage, is another hypothetical construct referring to a special quality of human experience when we *notice* that we are paying attention or feeling something. That is, at such a moment we are aware that we are thinking, we have a fleeting feeling of being separate from the moment and its information or consequences. That awareness is sometimes experienced as being in the "back of the head," although its physical location is unknown as are the neurological and chemical mechanisms of awareness. When most aware, the organism is alert and aware of *where* it is and *what* it is doing.[51]

Martha Nussbaum argues that awareness may contribute to a subtle sense of personal identity. At such times, we sense that one special person with a particular history is coming into a particular moment doing this one thing, not something else, and we feel connected and present.[52] Daniel Dennett observes that self develops early from "semi-understood self-commentary." He adds that most people have the ability to call images and ideas to mind, saying, "One of the things we know about ourselves—that we all enjoy engaging in elaborate exercises of imagination carefully tailored to meet our interests of the moment."[53]

If moments of peak experience are rare, what is the mind doing the rest of the time? How do people move in and out of different levels of both attention and awareness, sometimes in the course of seconds? Unfortunately, the mechanisms are not known, either philosophically or physiologically. Although its mechanisms are obscure, the subjective experience of mind can be described. Over the course of the day, even when fatigue or hunger set in, the mind moves automatically and continuously, like a sand shark needing to keep water moving through its gills. Only a portion of that time, when an external event or internal command demands we concentrate, is there anything approaching conscious direction.

Somehow, it appears to us, the mind acts as if it has a "mind of its own," seeming to run ahead of awareness, attending to this and that without conscious direction. One can grab the reins with effort and for a time hold on—seconds, perhaps minutes—but both attention and awareness keep rolling as the organism moves through the life-world. So it goes all day long—periods of roaming awareness punctuated by sharp, intense moments of focus, each so quickly lost without apparent cause.

Awkward and incomplete as my subjective terms may be, I want to capture one part of the involved experience, what Ellen Langer and Thich Nhat Hanh mean by "mindfulness" (to be fair, Langer weighs cognitive flexibility more heavily than the holistic, Buddhist concept of which Hanh writes). Subject and object are not fused as they might be in a peak experience as described by Maslow or Csikszentmihalyi's flow.

Awareness varies at least as frequently and subtly as does attention, both facets of psychological involvement only occasionally under personal control. As I write this paragraph, for example, awareness shifts as I think about what I want to say.[54] But my mental state gives way quickly to doing the writing without distance on the activity. As I yank my mind back, as I must, to think about my experience, awareness seems to require *active* choice to be conscious in the moment. If not directed, awareness comes involuntarily and episodically, always briefly, during the day as I move through my environs.

Mood

Attention and awareness, along with self-focusing, refer to mental and cognitive facets of psychological involvement. Emotional states affect motivation and learning. First, even the word "emotion" by itself is cluttered with meaning. Intense emotions like fear, anger, and joy are not uncommon in human experience; they accompany, and perhaps cause, motivated acts like aggression. From dark depression through a moderate sense of well being to feeling elation and joy, the range of human emotional experience is vast. (Some scholars believe that mammalian species like dogs and primates, with which we share so much neurobiology, experience a range of emotions, although perhaps not the self-awareness of homo sapiens.) Positive moods, broadly speaking, are easy to recognize: happiness, certain forms of arousal experienced as excitement, calmness. Acts that stimulate such feelings are valued because we enjoy these emotions and seek them out.

Negative moods like anxiety, depression, feeling blue or "not right" may operate in different ways. We may not identify these moods readily or understand the connection to our actions. Examples can be found of people tolerating, perhaps seeking out, such moods, even though that seems counterintuitive. Then, too, anxiety and depression are much different experiences. A degree of anxiety may be experienced as slightly positive, as when one is about to go on stage.

But again, I want to focus less on peaks and valleys and instead think about intermediate-level emotions, particularly subtle *changes* in mood. In one respect, mood seems easier to understand as a component of involvement because it is closer to daily experience: People talk about being in a good or bad mood. Mood, a temporary psychological state, is the subjective label attached to the dimly felt, emotional experience of the moment, reflecting underlying mechanisms like the degree of arousal or the effects of hormones on the body. As we have seen with attention and awareness, intermediate values are the most important in understanding the vagaries of human existence. But mood is a powerful factor, if sometimes unrecognized at the time, because humans interpret and evaluate whether they like what they are doing. For example, even though I may not, unless asked, know how I am feeling while working today on this chapter, my motivation to write is increased if that mood is positive.

Mood is not subject to conscious control, certainly not to the extent we tell ourselves. Nussbaum says we may learn to understand our feelings and the behavioral conditions surrounding them, which means we can change our feelings, or at least some of the conditions. Perhaps we cannot change the angry feelings had in a fight with one's partner, but we do not have to act on them. One may, however, be able to change the stimulus conditions that accompany or affect a mood state. Passionate injunctions like "Feel better!" are much less effective than suggestions that follow from understanding how the brain-mind-body and its adaptive learning systems work. That is, if I want to change my mood, it is better to go for a run to trick the brain-mind-body into neurobiological changes that elevate mood.

Finally, compared to the subtle, rapid changes in either human attention or awareness, mood is not plastic. While anger can start suddenly, sometimes surprising us by its onset and intensity, mood does not change quickly or often. Unlike rapid shifts in attention or awareness, a bad mood can linger for hours, even days. The physiological mechanisms underlying mood do not change quickly, except for instinctual fight-or-flight responses powered by hormones like adrenaline.

Self-focusing

Before discussing the fourth component, consider this: Neither attention nor awareness by itself brings purposeful direction to human existence. Mood does not either, though we may unconsciously avoid activities that leave us depressed. To explore direction in human affairs—why one course of action is chosen over another—we study human agency, and it should not surprise that this executive dimension must, sooner or later, find itself at the center of most theories of human behavior.[55] Maslow posited a self-actualizing personality and Csikszentmihalyi advanced the idea of the autotelic personality. Both theorists were looking beyond momentary psychological states— peak experience and flow, respectively—for enduring personality traits. The definitions used vary, and most such personality constructs have at least one type of measurement, usually a paper-and-pencil attitude scale, and claim empirical support (usually correlations). Few constructs acknowledge their competitors or can show empirical evidence of independence. The point is not to intercede in this contest to name human agency. Any psychologist or educator, sooner or later, must confront one problem in living, *the steering problem*. How do we describe that part of human beings that sets goals for the organism and helps it stay on course? Let's introduce and build upon a construct, self-focusing, by two philosophers, Charles Guignon and Dirk Pereboom, who are interested in existentialist philosophy.

Guignon and Pereboom want people to be self-focusing, to follow a "coherent set of commitments that shape the past, present and future into a unified flow."[56] In the best case, self-focusing helps us to imagine ourselves as "works of art" that are being created.[57] Self-focusing is a *learned* attribute, certainly more so than awareness or attention, and cultivation of this attribute is the principal aim of an education.

Self-focusing requires explicit purposes *and* the psychological and physical energy to pursue them. Without purposes, self-focusing has no signposts. Self-focusing seems to require articulate purposes. (If I have learned to value certain purposes, I can work to make them come true. No purposes, no focusing. No focusing, no involvement.) Self-focusing may require, or stimulate, self-confidence, an idea we cannot explore here. (If I have a purpose *and* feel confident I can perform, commitment comes easier.) Finally, self-focusing plays the major role in social engagement because the life-project must be sustained over time, cope with failure, and show a degree of coherence. Self-focusing gives direction and integration to life activities while sustaining effort in the face of fatigue and distraction. Another role is to cope with the variability of attention and awareness (as well as mood). Perseverance is paramount in the life-project.

Whether we select the construct of self-focusing or Julian Rotter's internal locus of control (and there are many others), the problem in living is the same. Educators want to help learners to become self-aware, to learn about capacities and limits, to ask better questions, to make better choices in the life-project. Moreover, the goal is not just to get learners involved in some activity, although that is a reasonable intermediate goal. Rather, educators want an engaged learner whose life-project integrates service to others and personal development. To be engaged also goes well beyond the narrow involvement in family and career that Jurgen Habermas dismissed as civic privatism.[58] This ideal learner-citizen is involved with building the human community, not just psychologically involved for the moment in risk behavior. So, social engagement is not the transitory involvement of shopping or mountain biking, even though people use these pursuits and hobbies to focus attention and improve mood.

So much for theory. We have reviewed different psychological experiences and states of involvement ranging from utter boredom to peak experiences in creative work, sports, and risk activities like rock climbing. Even if certain dimensions of the interior psychological experience I have described are tentative and better terms come to mind, the quality of this "theory" is less the point than the general value of playing with our mental models. Every educator should play with the pieces of the puzzle to reach their own understanding of the *steering problem*, a central topic in human affairs. If we educators have one job in society it is to help students become self-focusing. The purpose of this brief exercise in theory building has been to explore different facets of a core problem in human existence. It is not controversial to say that human beings have wide-ranging perceptions, thoughts, and emotions as they move through the life space (although to mark them with reductionist terms like "perception" or "emotion" does not reflect the *holistic* nature of human experience).

I have made the point repeatedly that positive mood changes from activities that ask us to concentrate seem to reinforce those behaviors, thus motivating us to develop a sport like tennis or hobby like sewing. Educators may not always appreciate the power of unseen reinforcers as they shape student behavior and learning (and their own behavior and learning). But in the best case, direction in life—not just the aimless wandering of our sand shark minds—comes more from choice of daily and life purpose than the incidental reinforcement of a given activity, purposeful or not. But how are alternative purposes formed, grouped, and evaluated?

Social engagement is not psychological involvement, and for that matter, paying attention for a brief moment during an activity is not involvement. Consider an additional example, this time a sport like tennis, where many skills are needed for effective play, especially the ability to concentrate on the point as it develops over two minutes and twenty or so shots. This small example should also make us cautious with regard to the complexity of phenomenological experience and the challenge of building adequate theory. Attention roams among a number of channels, including posture; the pace, spin, and location of the ball; the blurry movement of an opponent; cognitive images of possible shots; and self-exhortations to "stay positive." The brain-mind-body perceives sounds from other courts and may be distracted by watching the play nearby. In this example, involvement is more purposive than chained-together moments of focused attention. Only when many such moments of psychological involvement, pleasant as they can be, are put together with other purposes and activities to help others and benefit society could we think of social engagement.

Part III

Motivation, Learning, and School Culture

In the varied topography of professional practice, there is a high, hard ground overlooking a swamp. On the high ground, manageable problems lend themselves to solution through the application of research-based theory and technique. In the swampy lowland, messy, confusing problems defy technical solution. The irony of this situation is that the problems of the high ground tend to be relatively unimportant to individuals or society at large, however great their technical interest may be, while in the swamp lie the problems of greatest human concern. The practitioner must choose.

—Donald Schön[1]

High-minded ideals about learning and making an engaged life are well and good. But teachers and counselors live and work in Schön's swamp, that messy world of imposed deadlines, boring meetings, and always-hurried encounters with learners. What we have read so far has emphasized theory in the form of incomplete, sometimes complementary, perspectives about motivation and learning. The best ideas are interesting, a few useful. But practical consequences of theory have been neglected.

The characteristics of peak experiences have been discussed and consideration given as well to a far more important topic, *intermediate and dynamic changes* in involvement and awareness in the ebb and flow of daily life. We explored philosophic topics like the limits of language and method, which are necessary asides for such studies, and a special topic so important to motivation theory, namely, the values reflected in human choice. The full study of motivation, I argued, requires us to understand psychological process *and* to evaluate moral purposes. Both *techné*, the techniques by which something is done, and *telos*, the choice of goals, call out for study.[2] To think about motivation in ethical terms, some purposes being better than others, inevitably took us to criticism of modernity, particularly the organization of schools, colleges, and modern organizations as they prepare citizens for fast-paced, consumer society.

Now two broad topics lie ahead. Drawing upon insights covered earlier, our discussion turns to ten considerations for creating lasting learning. Following this discussion, a small companion chapter approaches the topic differently, and here we focus on the culture of a school or college and implications for designing optimal learning settings. The examples ahead come from where I have worked—higher education, in general, and progressive colleges, in particular—but most of our considerations for better learning have applications for elementary, secondary, and corporate settings.

Here is *the* question every educator must face: *Which educational ideas create the most powerful learning environments?* Each of our ten considerations contains within it creative tensions that are more important to explore than any one idea. When it comes to educating human beings of any age, the search for hard-and-fast principles will frustrate; besides, I doubt if any theory is precise enough to let us derive precise principles. The nature of human beings and the culture we create inside any institution forces us to think of models that allow for intricacy and some subtlety. Experienced educators know that the art in curriculum design comes from finding just the right mix of elements. If we are smart, we assemble that mix while expecting interpreting human beings to challenge all prescriptions for learning, especially so if students become the active learners we want them to be. That last sentence is not hard to write, but finding that artful mix of elements for learning while negotiating the movement of agency from teacher to learner are human challenges of immense difficulty.

Chapter 6

Ten Considerations for Better Learning

Tell me, and I will forget. Show me, and I will remember. Involve me, and I will understand.

—*Saying attributed to the Lakota Sioux.*

We turn to practical ideas to increase the probability of learner and mentor motivation, organizing them as ten considerations for better learning, summarized in the following list:

TEN CONSIDERATIONS FOR BETTER LEARNING

1. Learning needs purposes
2. Learning needs individualization
3. Learning needs predicaments
4. Learning needs mentors
5. Learning needs small spaces, human places
6. Learning needs process before academic content
7. Learning needs reflective experience outside class
8. Learning needs reflective experience in class
9. Learning needs feedback
10. Learning needs theory

Our goal is to improve the mental models with which to design learning environments that motivate learners. Each topic is framed as a consideration because the ideas in play are objects to be manipulated, not fixed certitudes. Simple-appearing ideas, like the importance of purposes in learning, as well as subtle topics, like the creative tension between the authority of the learner and the teacher, are considerations, weighed this way and that, when designing learning situations. So, our purpose is heuristic more than prescriptive: We ask teachers and counselors to play with the pieces of the puzzles we have opened, looking for fresh combinations.

Mine is hardly the first such list.[1] Readers should add and subtract as they go, substituting ideas that make sense from personal experience. Unless one has become discouraged, we educators worry about how to be effective even if the daily choices about theory and method are made more from unconscious habit than conscious choice. Ethical dilemmas arise every day and good educators I know agonize about the quality of their work. Whether on the backs of envelopes, or in proposals to a distant committee, educators try to think through the dilemmas that block the way to better practice in order to design high motivation settings.

To that end, we consider shortly a handful of curricular ideas rooted in progressive education, its high ideals, and substantial contradictions. How we *think* about motivation and learning is more important than individual ideas or methods, which always change. For instance, we will draw upon ideas and practices in progressive education founded by John Dewey in the 1930s. While coming from an important current in American education, progressive schools are difficult institutions to sustain.[2] I am more interested in Dewian ideas for increasing motivation than in how the concepts have been used, or abused.[3] Each idea is examined in terms of its potential for increasing motivation and learning, noting inherent problems attached to the best idea. That is, any reform brings unintended, perhaps iatrogenic, consequences that it would be best to anticipate.[4] No perfect curriculum exists—all models have strengths and weaknesses, as do individual ideas within.

Perhaps negative criticism of educational practice comes easier to mind than positive theory for educational change. It is easy to hide behind a self-righteous critique of conventional education, which only makes colleagues defensive, rather than live in the open, looking for better practices while accepting the limits of human invention. Parker Palmer makes the point when he describes two powerful learning experiences of his own, one close to the progressive model, the other a conventional lecture done well. Although quite different learning situations, each had the capacity to motivate, connecting him to noble purposes and the human community.[5]

Curriculum design is an educator's first responsibility, and Seymour Sarason sets forth two challenges: "What is the overarching purpose of school, a purpose which if not realized makes the attainment of other purposes unlikely, if not impossible? What are the characteristics of contexts of productive learning?"[6] Many answers are possible to the first, but the most powerful is to say, "Make better learners!" Details aside, a school should cultivate, test, and refine the enormous capacity human beings have to learn. To reach this goal leads us to design learning communities that inspire hope, self-confidence, and hard work. The rest of this chapter is given to answering Sarason's second question, how to create "contexts of productive learning."

As we proceed down the list for better learning, please think about learning as making connections. Learning that lasts *is* connected learning.[7] Recall our discussion in Part II of the multiple connections by which the brain-mind-body creates and reworks memories in neuronal networks. Rather than short-term, surface learning, which is found in many schools and colleges, learning that lasts is what Theodore Marchese calls deep learning, where connections are made to as many facets of being as possible.[8]

Consideration 1: Learning Needs Purposes

Optimal learning communities are suffused with a defined set of purposes, values, and norms. The values a community stands for are apparent not just in class and lab, but in every facet of campus life. A rich, thick learning environment results, Art Chickering contends, when the institution's mission sets clear and high purposes that attract and socialize teachers and staff, whose shared values and aspirations attract and socialize students.[9]

The mission must be alive in the entire institution. Roles are defined and a rich ethos for learning has evolved. If the community can reach a consensus about direction and values, a college's mission statement will be more powerful than the parsed statements for which planning committees are justly known. Perhaps the most important function of a school's mission is that its values stimulate self-selection by students and teachers of a particular type who want to learn in this particular community. When these two cohorts arrive, peer pressure works on members of both groups to extend the connections.

How we think about a school or college focuses excessively on students, neglecting the other groups that pass through the culture. A college's nested learning communities serve more than just students. A school's curriculum is not merely an obstacle course designed to educate or socialize just students. In the best case, a school offers cogent values and a certain regimen to everyone: teachers, staff, administrators, and students, alike.

More often than is recognized in conventional thinking, a college's impact extends beyond the school to family, friends, local businesses, and human service agencies. In full definition, the school or college is a *community* institution situated in history, a living human culture that shapes values and skills in ripples extending well beyond the school.[10] The learning culture reflects a set of conscious, agreed-upon choices about what is important to learn and how best to proceed. In the best case, a college's values live beyond a given cohort of faculty and students. We see this in a college town like Yellow Springs, Ohio, the home of Antioch College, where the bohemian culture of the village has been shaped over many years by the college's values and aspirations and the artists, intellectuals, and activists attracted to the vision and its community.[11] The New School, located in Greenwich Village, shares the same intimate connection with its urban community.

An education needs more than clear purposes. When a college's mission and academic culture encourage pedagogical ferment, expressing a certain restlessness about educational means and ends, teaching and learning are kept alive. Because one's own teaching or counseling is seldom consistent or ideal, it is valuable to compare personal values and teaching practice to the pedagogy and values of the school. To cite one example from my own university, debate is passionate about the extent to which the university administration supports the academic values of the Graduate Faculty, the successor school to the storied "University in Exile" of the 1930s, when The New School admitted 180 intellectual refugees from Europe.[12] Socialization into the academic values of a school might come from seminars for new instructors or just be "in the air" because community members talk so much about history and traditions.

Good teachers worry about pedagogy. Faculty practice is improved if nagging questions bother us about how to define learning, or what is the best way to integrate experiential methods in a certain content area like chemistry. At Goddard College, faculty members argue over what John Dewey meant by "progressive," and whether or not he would be comfortable with modern-day progressive politics (probably not). Arthur Morgan's ideas about co-op education and community development, which transformed Antioch in the 1920s, are still debated on that campus. Professors at Evergreen State College and Stony Brook University think about learning communities and the best way to design interdisciplinary studies. Sterling College teachers and farm supervisors worry about designing experiential learning exercises and sustainable agriculture. And so on.

Finally, a learning community is strengthened by having had to argue to the point of agreement on curricular purposes. The same principle applies to individual learners for whom the curriculum should structure that kind of reflection. And I do not mean the superficial reflection on learning purposes that is the case in routine college advising. By now, the reader will anticipate a call to ontological questions, that *all* community members are asked to think deeply about *who* they are, *where* they are going, and *what* they need to learn (not when to take chemistry, in the case of students, or what major to pursue, by far the smaller questions).

Consideration 2: Learning Needs Individualization

The mission and purposes of a great institution should be alive in a school's particulars. The good regimen-curriculum reflects a consensus of values, goals, and means that shape the behavior of teachers and students, staff and administrators. Put in other terms, it is a mistake to envision a curriculum, much less a reform, as something done to the students, or to oneself, as if human beings were objects, not individual beings. On the contrary, we teachers work with pattern-seeking, whole, individual human beings, not static vessels to be filled or water spigots to be turned on and off.[13]

Learning is ubiquitous in the way humans constantly adapt to changing circumstances, internally and externally. One type of learning, abstract or conceptual learning, that is valued in college requires additional and focused work by the brain-mind-body. But whether learning is incidental or directed, our earlier review of neurobiology underscores two powerful ideas: that human learning is holistic, not exclusively cognitive, and that learning is uniquely organized when it is first acquired as well as reworked in memory. So, *all human learning is individualized*. That idea is hardly radical until we think about the ways schools and colleges are organized so as to violate that order. Other than lip service, very little about contemporary education would seem to say that as educators we value individual experience in learning.

I want to return to certain ideas from existentialism, particularly Sartre's notion of an authentic existence. How does one begin a conversation with a learner about the life-project, its means and ends? What are the needs and purposes of the individual learner? Getting students to state their interests is only the start of a longer, more demanding dialogue. Emeritus Goddard professor Wilfred Hamlin would tell us that student *needs* are not the same as student *interests,* which can be transitory, impulsive, half-considered. In practice, the progressive mentor begins with the first interests or passions of students, which are not easy for most to articulate. These needs should be defined anew for each student, neither presumed nor taken for granted. That is, educators learn to ask questions—and to listen and *wait* for an answer—before prescribing a course of study. No distribution grids here! If the listening is active and sincere—if the mentor's mind is open—it is an elemental act of recognition of the other, a sign of respect that is motivating, as William Kahn observes.[14]

But are respect and authenticity possible, given the way schools and colleges are organized today? Whether in school or the modern corporation, the relentless momentum of production slowly saps the will, wearing us down, depressing our hopes for ourselves and for what we might give back to others. Racing from class to class, paper to paper, where is the time and space to ask questions like: "Who am I?" "Where am I going?" "Why?" Fundamental questions about being and human existence *demand a structure for authentic contemplation of the life-project.* If that place and time are not obvious and protected, those first questions about direction and meaning in life we spoke about earlier hang about, unanswered, as daily refrains. The worrying that results is hardly the quality of reflection needed to change behavior.

Even experienced teachers might forget just how naked a learner feels in front of authority and his or her peers. Becoming a "good" student may mean learning to hide the self, not disclosing personal details. (A faculty member told me she was astonished to hear students ask permission to use the first person pronoun, "I," in a paper.) For this and other reasons, the implicit message of schooling is this: "Conform to the drill. Don't stand out." Students may master the essay or literature review, but having learned these academic forms, voice is submerged. Too often, teachers then receive an inauthentic collection of half-digested ideas, a mechanical recitation proffered to meet a requirement with which the student does not identify.

From using retreats to encouraging learners to use personal experience in class, the progressive learning community I imagine offers diverse tools for reflection. To stimulate and structure reflection and inquiry, the mentor can ask students to keep a diary for personal reflection, or write integrative papers that draw from both personal experience and academic content. Two types of papers can be used: one that integrates theory and practice in a subject matter, and one that applies a body of thought to personal experience.

Drawing on personal experience in academic studies, however, is more difficult than it sounds. The best work is lively and stimulating because the application of theory is grounded in real, as opposed to scholastic, problems. Average work meanders, to be sure, and here, neither the personal nor the academic voices are developed. Unacceptable products do not move beyond passionate opinion and undigested experience, which are worth about as much as a mechanical literature review. Many students find it difficult to write papers that integrate academic and personal knowledge in a balanced way, acknowledging that both voices are emerging, provisional domains.

Surely, teachers want students to be able to think and write with care. We want them to know what they think about a matter, and why. We seek *active* thinkers. The goal, then, is to ask students to master technical forms like the essay or research paper while simultaneously cultivating a mature, personal voice for the appropriate time and place as an argument unfolds. The earliest writing voice is undifferentiated and undisciplined—teachers work hard to get learners to develop just enough distance with an analytic approach. In this way, we hope to combine the motives of romance and precision in student scholarship, as Alfred North Whitehead terms it.[15]

If we educators want to develop an individuated, mature voice, repressed subjectivity must be confronted, as suggested earlier in my opening example of teaching at Harvard and Antioch. Students who survive a conventional curriculum, especially in the best schools, have learned to a fault what authorities want. They struggle to learn the arguments of a discipline, to write an essay or literature review. To learn a discipline and its forms is important. But do we help students integrate personal values and feelings? What results, one fears, is a thin, inauthentic narrative because learners are not involved in the connected scholarship. The very best students rise above mere conformity. But many more learn to hide beliefs and feelings behind academic conventions, even though no one intends that sad outcome.

Finally, an authentic existence requires more than honest, searching conversations, or a probing relationship with a mentor. Social context is needed: Learners need to work as effective team members in groups and to give back to society. A theory of human nature must, we have argued, reconcile individual needs with those of society. Although a central tenant of progressive philosophy, the cultivation of individuality is also its most vulnerable feature when, for example, a school is riven by student passions, becoming impossible to govern because of idiosyncratic demands by staff, faculty, and students for special treatment without end.[16] An authentic existence connects the learner to the community in the spirit of "giving back," not "taking from."

Consideration 3: Learning Needs Predicaments

Let us stay within the existentialist spirit and ethic. How should a good curriculum relate to our lives as developing human beings? How does it support, or better said, test, the human spirit? The word "regimen" is not a modern word, but I use it to underscore the value of setting clear, high standards with which to test the character, motivation, and skills of students and teachers. The conventional term "curriculum" feels insubstantial for what is really needed, existential predicaments that test students and teachers.

Consider the next example, a most demanding curriculum that, superficially at least, is not like most college experiences, not to mention progressive education. (Ideal cases, even extreme examples, let us surface hidden assumptions and help us explore curricular principles.) The Marine Corps has a grueling training exercise called the Crucible, which caps sixteen weeks of basic training. Designed to simulate combat conditions, running more than fifty hours, the Crucible features sleep deprivation, long marches, and built obstacles to be overcome by individuals working in small teams. Exhausted, bedraggled recruits endure a seven-mile, forced march with pack and weapon back to the base, after which each recruit is awarded his or her first insignia by the drill instructor. The physical stress is extraordinary. Men and women are trained separately—all show tears when honored in front of new comrades.

Why is this example so interesting? One could argue that military training is hardly the same thing as higher education, but for this comparison, I am more interested in similarities than differences. For me, the example expands mental models about learning in line with concepts discussed in Parts I and II. First, high expectations are held for all. One can survive a crucible, literally, that tests human character. But no one can master each phase. Second, individual recruits learn to work in teams, both to solve obstacles and to support each other when tired or ready to quit. The curriculum demands group experience and learning. Sleep deprivation limits cognitive mastery of topics like map reading, or even the theory of group dynamics that recruits studied earlier in the training.

A holistic experience on this order tests physical and mental limits. Having been passed, the curriculum increases self-confidence and in-group solidarity because of the silent effects of dissonance reduction. That is, Marine recruits have suffered mightily and now justify that investment by increasing the perceived value of the Corps, its traditions and values.

As we do in civilian education, military educators use group dynamics to build and sustain motivation. We understand, now, why recruit morale is high and why Corps members—those that survive such rigorous training, anyway—forever feel they belong to a special institution, one which sets an implicit standard for challenges later in life. Marine Corps military training is a uniquely demanding setting. But its dynamics are comparable to those found in all intensive, holistic learning cultures: college team sports, outward bound experiences, mountain climbing expeditions, medical residencies, and intensive residencies for adults in distance education programs.[17]

So, a good curriculum, first and foremost, probes and challenges the human spirit—it is not a set of courses, a collection of professors, or a degree earned, all of which are reified conceptions of the modern school. Content to be covered, like Victorian literature or college algebra (or military tactics), is secondary. Good learning settings test character traits, perseverance, and organizational skills—the important learning, far more so than the content of a major. Similar to Dewey, Roger Schank and Chip Cleary argue that we learn by doing and, indeed, we learn best from failure, when our mental models are insufficient for the task.[18] The ideal curriculum does not feature talking heads but involves the learner in role-playing simulations that occasion failure. Chickering, among others, asks us to concentrate on generic learning skills because of the short, half-life of modern knowledge, which is soon out of date.[19]

No effective reform can proceed from a cynical, behaviorist understanding of human nature. Feeling stuck inside an uncaring institution, learners with potential learn to "beat the system," focusing their learning on psychic escape and evasion, itself a type of learning. As curriculum designers, why do we assume the worst in human nature? Why do we design curricula that presume students cannot be trusted?[20] Better to reach for the highest standard—and expect disappointment—than assume the worst in human nature, and then have to settle for the mediocre work learners produce.

We want learners to struggle to make better questions, not to find right answers for the standardized exams that are so convenient when batch processing large numbers of students. Such exams should, in fact, be understood as control systems of the factory school more than essential elements for academic quality. In this regard, the American obsession with testing in elementary and secondary education is short sighted, yet another technical solution to much deeper problems of diffuse goals and lack of funding. If anything, writing should be the national obsession. Writing stimulates critical thinking and learner involvement far better than most forms of testing.

An education helps students choose how and why they exist, nothing less. It reaches for the future, for the person we want to become, what Maxine Greene calls the person she is "not yet."[21] Learners are held accountable for their choices, gently supervised while they make educative mistakes, in the sense that we often learn the most from mistakes. We seek better "choosers" who understand how they learn.

Existentialism as a body of values and ideas points us toward a wide-awake life-project, hand built of well-considered choices. Greene says we want engaged citizens, not passive consumers of ideology. The good curriculum is made of ever-better questions put to learners, and iterations of choices and mistakes, better choices and more mistakes, and so on. If the menu of existential choices is too structured, if the choices are safe and convenient, most students will not be motivated—and most will not, in turn, challenge the preset curriculum, or their teachers, which is the dark compromise of which Theodore Sizer has spoken.[22]

People sense when they are taken seriously as full beings rather than as half-people, half-objects to be processed, given a small window to make an impression. If the curriculum treats human beings as objects, they adapt to expectations and perform as objects. Eyes lose their light and a motivational stand off results.

The hidden curriculum, what John Dewey called collateral learning, produces passive citizens. The particular cultures of schools and colleges are instruments for political socialization.[23] Rather than confront, students retreat in the face of authority and institutional convention, becoming passive with regard to their own responsibility for their choices.[24] That many graduate to become active consumers, but passive citizens, should not surprise.

Progressive colleges err in the opposite direction. A process-based curriculum is vulnerable because it may not provide enough structure for learning. To admit students as legitimate partners, if not co-architects, in learning makes the process dicey. A long, patient dialogue is needed to help a naive student explore the realism behind a newly excited enthusiasm. Costly mistakes are made, especially early on. Compared to a conventional college, a progressive curriculum does not protect students (and parents and society) from poor decisions. Safety nets are not provided, unlike the Marine Corps curriculum, which is an artful mix of high demand and support for learners.

A second problem follows from the humanistic values of progressive education. Student *intentions* as a whole person are valued more highly than *performance* on a difficult assignment. Indeed, the progressive institution, be it school or Sengian learning organization, lives on enthusiasm and learner passions, which provide ready motivation for learning.[25] But because the curriculum is radically student-centered and driven, hither and yon, by student passions, the teacher may withdraw, not set limits, or withhold credit for a failed study.[26] In the progressive school, teachers risk being disempowered because the role of mentor is so much more demanding than that of conventional teacher.

Consideration 4: Learning Needs Mentors

What do we want from an educator? The conventional idea of teacher is defined by the courses one teaches, or an academic specialization like social psychology. Few of us go beyond that circumscribed, narrow role as we prepare for teaching, if indeed we get any real training in pedagogy or human development. A tiny conception of this powerful role in human affairs leaves hidden the attributes of master learner and existential counselor. The conventional role definition of teacher is one who transmits facts and culture, Hirsch-like, to the next generation. But imagine the role of mentor as defined by Laurent Daloz or of coach as defined by Donald Schön.[27] A higher standard is needed than culture bearer—faculty members and staff alike should be exemplars of engaged living, mentoring students as they make their own life choices.

Consider this: Teachers have had, in their own time, to confront the self-same existential dilemmas as their students. They share with students a common humanity and comparable problems in living, but with the advantage of greater distance and experience. From the assumption of common human experience, advising should be less about setting degree requirements than a master learner helping a less experienced learner. Using Goddard terms, the focus should be *quality of being,* broadly defined, and the quality of person the learner wants to *become.*

Advising in most schools and colleges is a last-minute clerical exercise. To be critical of my own institution, New School has eight academic schools and colleges. Advising for undergraduates is done rather differently in each, and rather poorly in all, at least by an ideal standard. In one of the professional schools, academic advising, defined mostly as course selection, is done by part-time staff at a ratio of about 1 to 200. Questions about career and life are handled by classroom teachers, or not. One of our liberal arts colleges does it better: Here each full-time faculty member advises sixty students for a half-hour each and conversations can be wide ranging.

Across the board American teachers are given little or no special training on advising or human development. Individual teachers may make extra effort to advise and individual students may be unusually assertive, but advising is not a featured part of the curriculum. Losing the opportunity to connect with a mentor means that students lose valuable learning outside the classroom. When advising is mechanistic or haphazard, students lose *the* critical element of a life-changing education.

Beyond superficial matters, what separates teacher and student is generation or age, not the nature of life problems. Students, staff, and teachers—all human beings inside a school—have more in common than is acknowledged, notwithstanding differences in age, gender, or race. Consider this implication: Students and teachers alike feel powerless inside the modern school, trapped by bureaucratic forces that compel allegiance and proper behavior. The pell-mell pace of the school day pulls everyone along. All members of the college community also share a responsibility, in some degree, for the learning process, as Carl Rogers suggested to generations of teachers and therapists, citing his model of person-oriented learning.[28]

Students and teachers are human beings, "all too human" as Nietzsche puts it.[29] All lives are marked by mood swings and fantasies, by failures that haunt us endlessly, punctuated by sudden bursts of creativity. While each person has a role to enact, teachers, students and staff all face similar life problems: not having enough money, dealing with illness, competing with peers, being alone in modern times. Rather than reify formal roles that separate people, such as student versus teacher, or teacher versus administration, the better assumption is to understand all persons as imperfect beings who face common life predicaments. Learners need exemplars of engaged living—exciting, real-life models upon whom students can model themselves, both consciously and unconsciously. We want teachers who are endlessly curious, compassionate to a fault, vital human beings who serve the college and the community with commitment and great personal discipline. As teachers and counselors we want "better persons" rather than "better specialists."[30]

Perhaps a certain naiveté is understandable, and preferable to the cynic's frown. One might just stumble upon fresh questions about education and society on the way to becoming a better person. Learners come to school to encounter teachers as whole persons. Teachers as mentors bring subtle, underestimated learning about life to students. First-generation college students, in particular, benefit from modeling themselves after a certain manner, curiosity, way of dressing. The role model should be able to advise the student directly about how to manage the transitions being faced: how to handle the stress, or to reach for a new level of being. In this work, having a role model is an important, but passive, function, whereas being a mentor or coach requires active counseling, as Schön and Daloz argue. What teachers have to teach, ultimately, are who they are and how they cope with life's endless challenges.

Unfortunately, the idea of advisor as life counselor has been eroded by production imperatives to mean "curriculum technician." Sometimes, full-time teachers no longer do the advising because they do it poorly and a dean hires "advisors." Neither is the spirit of the ideal met by occasional advice on getting into the next school or finding a great job (more likely, a student is referred to a guidance counselor).

For their part, college teachers are hard-pressed by pressures to publish as well as by the scale and momentum of production teaching. They grow impatient with inarticulate questions brought by students, especially those not tied to class content. Students, too, learn the rules of engagement and do not learn how to frame good personal questions. Not seeing the importance of getting students to ask *more* questions about life, those deep and messy questions, and not rewarded for doing so, counselors withdraw (like the ways learners withdraw to a reified conception of student). Individual student requests for help may, in fact, be labeled "needs therapy." Referral is made to another specialist.

The progressive mentor wants to begin where the learner *is*, not where he or she *should* be. The mentor, first and foremost, helps the learner work through misconceptions and reduced self-confidence resulting from earlier experience. Teachers find this challenging, if not scary, because it turns the conversation toward murky psychological topics. "Edutherapy" is an ugly word, but it suggests just what is needed because schools often damage student self-conceptions.

Think about the memories we have of school and college. The damage shows in many ways: Adults returning to education bring painful memories of formal learning, inaccurate estimates of their skills and abilities, and repressed dreams of the kind of person they want to become. Adults recall thirty years later being called out by a tactless teacher in biology lab, or by an aggressive coach at soccer practice. Psychological damage is suggested when learners say "I'm not good at . . . " and fill in the blank with "math," "science," "foreign language," "sports," or "school." While such self-assessments are deeply held and reflect poor skills or motivation at the time, what an educator hears is more about poor self-confidence than native talent. So, teachers have to work directly with poor motivation and crippling anxiety before students step up to challenging content. That is the damage done by Fordist, assembly-line education.

Given a grim portrait of an education that does not inspire, an educator's first assignment is to spark involvement, to do what is necessary to break through negative self-concepts and repressed dreams. Progressive reformer Sizer says, "How to stimulate engagement is the first question every good teacher asks."[31] Students adapt to school and college by being passive—most have learned to not confront an advisor, usually someone older from another generation, who is presumed to know so much more, a false generalization from the teacher's academic discipline and technical expertise to all areas of human experience. After all, that intimidating statistics teacher may, in fact, be immature, lacking any useful life experience to pass on.

To be educated requires active self-reflection. By what means, however, should educators encourage authentic self-reflection? How can we create the right distance, that creative mix of subjectivity and objectivity? How do we cultivate Schön's reflective practitioner? The best way to work through the damage of schooling, seen as a set of psychological barriers to learning and human development, is to build many overlapping ways for learner reflection.

My fear is easily stated: The pace of production education leaves students and teachers mindless, going quickly from class to class, assignment to assignment. Any sense of a living philosophy of education being put into practice and extended is lost—educational practice is not made vital by pedagogical and epistemological concerns. Who has time for ontological reflection about the quality of existence, even to look up the words—"ontology" and "existence"—and to think about what they mean? Sizer, Stanley Aronowitz, Meier, and other critics of production schooling point to adaptive learning by teachers *against* quality. Sizer calls it Horace's compromise, the sacrifices a well-intentioned mentor makes, like not assigning long papers to cope with the pace of the line.[32] Students, too, make their compromises with a production culture. A cynical manufacturing process unfolds that traps both students and teachers in reified roles they unconsciously learn, enact, and pass on to the next generation. The noble idea of school as a good and just place for human development is abandoned.

The most powerful teaching relationship, Robert Kegan says, is a mix of support, reflection, and confrontation, where the timing of each piece is an art form that takes so long to learn.[33] A student may develop an intense, emotional relationship with his professor, which is best understood from the perspective of transference relations in psychotherapy.[34] The clever dualism, "sage on the stage" versus "guide on the side," provokes us to think about the nature of the role set and its reciprocal responsibilities.[35] Like all dichotomies, clever phrases call attention to the relationship, its parts and dynamics, but falsify it. The teacher-student role set is an archetypal human relationship, only partly resembling other educating relationships like that of parent and child or supervisor and worker. The easy dualism does not, for example, help us understand the *evolving* emotional attachment, positive and negative, between student and teacher that, with strict boundaries regarding intimacy and sex, is so important for transformational learning.

First attachments outside the family by learners to a teacher or authority like a coach are important, first, to motivate action and development, and second, to help the learner evaluate competing life purposes from which the learner will have to choose, consciously or unconsciously modeling the respected teacher's behavior. A colleague tells about how, as an undergraduate at Columbia College, he became enamored of the work of Mark Van Doren, then in his last semester of teaching. My friend read everything Van Doren wrote, took notes (and later elaborated those notes), and attended every one of his professional and social occasions to which he could gain access. The enchantment led him to a life calling of teaching.

Not all teacher-student relationships are straightforward. Everyone has had a demanding teacher who motivates us to work hard but who seems distant, capricious, even cruel. Consider this example: The professor was a charismatic man who set impossible standards for the quality of student work and confronted students in class. Lowly graduate "ants," as we were called, wrote detailed predictions for experimental variations based on social psychology experiments covered that week, many first published by, yes, that professor.

The course of study was meticulously organized. As guides for each class, four pages of questions, single-spaced, requiring twenty anxious hours a week to answer, were given to students. Because questions always went in order, clockwise, students argued before class over which seats around the table to take in order to avoid being called on for a question they could not answer. As anxious as the classroom experience was, my friend learned theory construction in that demanding crucible led by an autocratic character.

Mutable and not-simple relationships evolve between student and teacher, usually a mix of positive and negative experiences, resulting in increased motivation and performance. Some teachers and coaches take drastic steps to reach the learner, to the point of what some observers consider abuse. In-your-face confrontation is sometimes necessary but easily abused. Consider the intense, personal way basketball coach Bobby Knight engages and motivates his players compared to the carefully exerted authority used by the legendary John Wooden. Think about *the space between* the conventional definition of student and teacher. The effective teacher will be a student of this most ancient human role set, one that has the unique capacity to motivate and enrich both actors. Power evolves and changes hands, for example, as the learning relationship matures, but one seldom thinks about the transfer of power and its subtle dynamics.[36]

Each of the roles inside a school, however, has certain responsibilities, and it is also a mistake to force egalitarianism as a politically (or philosophically) correct solution. Teachers *do* bring special expertise and life experience. We *are* gatekeepers for the award of credit; administrators are supposed to be leaders; the staff has special skills and assignments; and students come to school in a short, compressed time to learn, and they pay us for this opportunity. What must not be missed is that role-based differences should not be allowed to define the humanity in practice of a school.[37]

As pivotal as the mentor's role can be, the influence of peers for good and ill should not be underestimated. Students new to a school are quick to orient to students their own age and one grade ahead. If the experience of parents I know is valid, students choose colleges because they want to be like the students they see on campus during the visit. Peers embody the organizational culture of the school—if they are seen as working hard and careful about alcohol, new students do not have to be told what the school stands for, its norms and values. As active learners, students will model their behavior on their peers and the age cohort just ahead.

What can be done to explode the technicized role of teacher? Robert Tremmel advises teachers and counselors "to let go of the security of technical rationality and make the leap of faith *backward* to reflective practice."[38] Putting it so, Tremmel asks educators to slow down, to execute "a backward step into the self" rather than look for magical, "high tech, high dollar" solutions from somewhere "out there."[39] In pointing teachers toward self-knowing, toward understanding how our developing minds work as we teach and advise real students, Tremmel like Jacques Ellul, warns against the seductive lure of technical solutions to human affairs, like new computers, the Internet, or even group dynamics exercises that descend upon the stage, *deus ex machina,* to resolve a play poorly written to vague purposes. But *techné* should not be valued over *telos,* explicit purposes to drive learning, certainly not at the expense of human experience with ever-new technology.[40]

Consideration 5: Learning Needs Small Spaces, Human Places

Learning is most likely in manageable settings of human scale, described by George Kuh and his colleagues as "small spaces, human places."[41] So many pedagogical and logistical problems follow from having schools and colleges organized toward mass production that this one notion is worth any five of the rest for its contribution to quality learning.

"Small is good!" is a worthy principle for human learning. Deborah Meier's innovative work with a small, elementary school in Harlem can be extended to secondary and higher education, even though higher education folk are skeptical of ideas not from their sector. Small schools encourage teachers to be thoughtful and responsible about their practice rather than resist change mandated from above. Public school teachers are buffeted by mandates for curricular change from on high. Classrooms are packed with imposed initiatives. Meier wants teachers to work collaboratively and cooperatively, not have to hide from a remote administration. Having thoughtful, empowered teachers is needed to change school culture. Meier continues, "Large schools neither nourish the spirit nor educate the mind; except for a small elite who run the place and claim (falsely) to know everyone, what big schools do is remind most of us that we don't count for a lot."[42]

Learning communities of human scale do not require elaborate governance structures and numerous committees. Small schools encourage mutual accountability because teachers have access to each other's work. Faculty work is more visible to the community than in a large school, and thus, community accountability is increased.

Small schools let teachers know a student by name, letting them recognize subtle changes in mood, or a different learning style. Listen to Meier speaking of her students: "we know their moods and styles—whom to touch in a comforting way and whom to offer distance and space in times of stress." Later, "small schools offer safety—plain, ordinary physical safety" and "there is less theft, vandalism, and graffiti in settings where people know us by name."[43] Finally, the small school that offers an organized academic culture based on the school's mission has a better chance of competing against the peer culture, which is as true for higher education as for elementary education. About the large school, Meier adds:

> Adult and student cultures rarely interconnect, much less overlap. There is *no thick, complex and powerful counterculture* to balance the one that has been developed for adolescents only, no counterforce representing serious adult ideas and concerns to which these novices might now and then apprentice themselves.[44]

To attract students to faculty "love affairs" with literature and history and math, the life of the mind, Meier seeks "joint membership in an attractive community representing such values as well as a myriad of interactions across generations."[45]

Thinking about American high schools, Sizer makes the same point, asking that secondary teaching loads be reduced from 100–180 students per teacher to 80 so that students can be known as real persons. His fictional teacher, Horace Smith, sees five groups of twenty-four students each for less than an hour. (In poor urban schools these are small classes.) The relentless pace of dealing with students-as-objects forces Horace to compromise quality. Sizer asks: "How can teachers know the students, know them well enough to understand *how their minds work,* what they are and are not disposed to do?"[46]

Finally, size and scale are problems for university education. College chemistry lectures of 800 students, like high school civics classes of 35, are difficult environments for students whose skills are uneven or whose motivation is not robust. In one department at the University of California at

Berkeley, teaching assistants have a form for undergraduate students to fill out if they want to see the professor for the purpose of getting a recommendation. Individual differences in intelligence, motivation, and learning style cannot be recognized. Subtle changes in a student's mood or behavior—possibilities for transformation—pass by unseen.

While small classes, alone, do not assure personal attention, much less academic quality, what purpose is served by treating human beings as objects? I believe an insidious social message is being sent. Although not intended as such by any person or social institution, the result is the same: Students must learn to cope with modernity's impersonal, mass institutions. Having to learn to maneuver inside the bureaucracy, another latent social function can be seen. As students survive mass institutions they learn, anarchist critic Guy Debord asserts, to be compliant consumers, well-adjusted types better prepared to be consumer-spectators than engaged citizens of the republic.[47] A Fordist curriculum does not encourage question posers and social critics.

Empirical studies of higher education by Kuh and his colleagues and Ernest Pascarella and Patrick Terenzini support small learning communities.[48] Even inside a state university or large corporation, small communities with which participants can identify can be built. A mass institution can overwhelm, but Pascarella and Terenzini argue that *psychological size as perceived by learners* is most important. So, the involving college will create interlocking networks of academic and social communities for students and teachers, whether in academic departments, labs, or residential houses.[49] To create Meier's "thick, complex and powerful counterculture" the school within a school has to have power over decisions.

Another large-scale, empirical study of school size in 2000 finds that smaller schools reduce the negative effect of poverty on achievement.[50] Using the school as the unit of analysis, the study looked at 13,600 K-12 schools in 2,290 districts in 4 states: Georgia, Montana, Ohio, and Texas. Small schools, 700 students or lower, reduce the negative effect of poverty on achievement by 30–50 percent even when controlled for race and class size. Some evidence was found to suggest that small classes increase the benefit. Moreover, the benefits are notable in middle school when performance problems mount, leading to school dropout.[51]

Finally, size of learning community has implications for the quality of human interactions inside. The progressive community seeks to reduce the distance between people in order to encourage full, authentic communication among developing, whole persons who know each other as real people. Does this sound utopian? Perhaps, but the patterned expectations of social roles like teacher or student, their seductive facticity, make it difficult to see the whole person, especially as that person is responding to life pressures. To the progressive educator, hierarchic, status distance between student and teacher diminishes the possibility of authentic communication, never easy or assured, between teacher and administrator, staff and student, client and therapist.[52]

Consideration 6: Learning Needs Process Before Academic Content

Here is another essential idea to progressive educators: The process of human learning is more important than the content of what is learned. This one principle, by itself, leads to a host of curricular ideas that may not be immediately obvious. To be an effective mentor, we need a sophisticated understanding of the dialectic between the two learning elements of learning process and learning content. Progressive educational philosophy gives primacy to personal experience in learning and thus, it follows, to the needs of individual learners. A learning experience that encourages the learner to learn more about a subject, or to invest in new domains of understanding that arise during a study, is educative—to Dewey, it is *progressive* because personal experience is progressively incorporated in human development.

Motivation for new experience is the important element, the driver. Without new experience, no possibility of integration exists. Quality of learning process as it motivates the learner is given primacy over learning content, that is, the skills and concepts to be acquired in a certain domain of knowledge. About the dialectic, Martin Heidegger said, "Teaching is more difficult than learning because what teaching calls for is this: *to let learn*. The real teacher lets nothing else be learned than learning."[53] Dewey makes the same point, saying the most important educational outcome is "the desire to go on learning."[54]

If we think in terms of process versus content motives, we introduce another pesky dichotomy that works only so far. For the moment, I want pull the terms apart. Imagine *learning process* as a hypothetical continuum of learning outcomes from low to high where the highest level is a learning setting that encourages a learner to become self-focusing, self-confident, and intrinsically motivated to continue learning. At the lowest level, the learner drifts, lacks self-confidence, and is only motivated by grades or other extrinsic rewards.

Learning content refers to a second continuum where the highest level is a learning setting that encourages mastery of advanced theory, concepts, and methods appropriate to a knowledge domain. At the lowest level, few concepts are learned and difficult topics are avoided. The terms are posed as a dichotomy, making my argument easier; but as we will shortly see, the two dimensions are not entirely independent.

To be an effective mentor requires a teacher to understand and probe the relationship between process and content, the primacy given to the former, and the consequences we want for optimal learning and human development, depending on how one mixes the two design principles. First, aroused motivation should precede task performance or academic content, although motivation and task performance often develop and expand interactively. Second, learning that is not self-motivated may not persist because it was learned for extrinsic purposes, such as to earn a grade or a promotion. Third and most important, attending to learning process focuses both student and mentor on learning-to-learn skills, which are far more important in life than most academic subjects. Content areas like English literature, biology, and social psychology are of greater value, in this regard, for their potential to stimulate and refine general thinking and organizing skills than for their pure content, which is so quickly out of date.

That is not to deny the importance of knowing a body of material, or the deep satisfaction we get from conceptual mastery of a topic. Maxine Greene believes that we may be provoked as learners, unexpectedly, to challenge the taken-for-granted world by imaginative literature, soulful music or great art, almost always without intending this or expecting it.[55] A poem by Rainer Maria Rilke touches us, suddenly and unexpectedly, because of a hidden psychological conflict it surfaces, or a half-forgotten romance comes to mind as we listen to Mitsuko Uchida playing a Schubert sonata. If only for a moment, our expectations for quality in lived experience are heightened—we look with fresh eyes for beauty or intensity at other moments, which seems to me to be the greatest promise of a liberal education. Finally, studying a discipline like music or literature—any discipline, in fact—helps develop character, the most important part of an education.

I want to return briefly to our two dimensions in the learning dialectic, process and content. Imagine two barometers, one measuring learning process and the other, learning content. Each imaginary instrument is arranged vertically, measuring one of two dimensions, from low to high. In the best case, both our meters should be as high as possible, beginning with learning process. The ideal learner is self-motivated and focused and is learning the most advanced material. But tradeoffs quickly appear in real-world education—after all, it is challenging, if not impossible, to have the best content joined to the best process for any one student, much less for a captive class of thirty-five. As Donald Schön said in the quote that opened this chapter, teachers have to choose. They choose what to emphasize, and in my teaching, coverage of content suffers somewhat because I design to stimulate intrinsic motivation and elicit individual student needs (as opposed to designing learning settings that require demonstrated *performance* on a *teacher's* tasks). Because of this emphasis, I cannot cover the same range or depth of material without alienating all but the most involved or prepared students.

Hoping that motivated students will get advanced content on their own, I make a choice as to what is most important. For this educator, process comes first. I am satisfied, most of the time, if students are motivated to pursue "their" studies, meaning they identify with the work psychologically. At the same time, I worry that enthusiastic students caught up with the romance of their studies may not choose the best focus. Purposes may be vague or grandiose. They may not consult diverse sources, especially classical ones that may not be easy to read or digest. Finally, the class cannot cover the range of content if I do not lecture, or we spend time on learning process. But I take the risk, telling myself that a passionate, life-long learner can find the full measure of content later on their own, hoping that Alfred North Whitehead's precision motive, if nurtured and balanced against romance in small studies, can be applied later to complex projects.

The relationship between process and content to create learning that lasts is not straightforward in another way.[56] If, for example, I lay out a detailed course of study, one that makes sense when we have a body of technical or abstract content like inferential statistics, not much room is left for the individual learner to choose content to meet his or her needs. As a teacher, I have to work that much harder in a structured course to motivate a learner whose stance is, in response, passive, tending to lay back and watch me work for both of us. If I slow the course pace to involve more students, coverage of content suffers. If mastery of advanced texts and methods such as multiple regression is required, which are conceptually challenging for student and teacher, students may do the work required of them but not engage the material. They comply to "pass the course" but invest little more.

If the learner is not involved in choosing the content to be studied, mastery is technical, at best, and not connected in the mind—not burned in emotionally, neurologically—with other domains of memory. Perhaps that is why course-knowledge decays rapidly when class is over. Still, to build a course from student needs is slow going, involving negotiation among student interests, which can be inarticulate. The process may not serve better students well. (Better-prepared and motivated students may not like my attempts to involve the group. Impatient and focused on their needs, they say, "Move on.") Every teacher has, of course, to find through trial and error the best way to balance process and content, individual and group needs, whether in counseling, teaching, or advising. To teach topics like statistics that frighten students, for example, I like to involve them in an applied project of their design, such as a survey of attitudes toward student services.[57]

Educators face another dilemma and it will serve to highlight the problematic relationship in the role set of student and teacher. In conventional colleges, the risk of insubstantial (or dangerous) studies is less. Teachers are in control and their psychological involvement is greater, even if, at the same time, student motivation is thereby weakened. Like the artful balancing of process and content, an unrecognized dialectic in education is the complex relationship between student and teacher motivation and development.

Finally, we want to think about how and when to offer appropriate self-directed study inside conventional curricula. In conventional curricula, electives are too few, too small, and come too late. They hang like ornaments on a Christmas tree rather than follow from a searching commitment to developing autonomous learners, with all the inefficiency and frustration that this path brings. Independent study for lifelong learning is essential work best begun early.

Free time is hard to find in a residential college. Most colleges plan a tightly structured curriculum for students. For motivated students with good skills, every semester features a set of intense competitions that carry the student along, breathlessly. While such a drill will test motivation and discipline, it has an unrecognized problem—even the best students will not have had to wrestle with structuring their own time and interests, except in choosing weekend recreation. Preoccupied with running the steeplechase, learners will not have had to struggle, deeply and personally, with their life-project, which exists, if at all, as a job label ("be a lawyer"). To survive a race built by others, students focus on the lesser challenges of knowing and doing—ontological challenges of *being* and *becoming* are set aside.

Progressive and student-centered study assumes—indeed, requires—uncommon maturity because students are asked to design their own learning plan, a task for which they are not prepared, however. Intrinsic motivation and personal discipline are necessary, which learners do not bring with them in full measure. When not caught up with a college's rock-and-roll intensity, many students are passive when it comes to studies they might design on their own. First efforts are less substantial than they imagine and credit is withheld.

But that does not mean, at the same time, that nothing has happened. First and most important, students are learning to develop learning plans. Second, not having the structure of a class to carry the work, they must learn how to motivate themselves daily and weekly, which is a major life skill. Third, they learn project production skills, to be used in writing a play, producing a lab project, or producing a video. Finally, they have to find resources on their own, whether in the library or on the web. Independent study stimulates process skills that will be more valuable than the content of even the most well-crafted course designed by someone else. More generally, the good curriculum will integrate faculty-organized learning, expressed in courses and labs, and student-organized learning either within prepared courses or preferably in independent research projects on problems that students select.

For all these reasons, added value comes from requiring senior papers, theses, and culminating studies. Whether in high school, college, or early graduate work, schools should ask advanced students to produce a semester-long, complex project. Such a project adds cost because faculty supervision will be needed, but it is a worthy investment. We want graduates at all levels, after all, to have skills planning and executing projects because, in part, that is what the workplace will expect of them. Surviving lecture classes and rounds of tests are not skills that have much validity for the real life tasks just ahead. It is easier, finally, to organize and manage independent projects by students and to provide close supervision, if the college is organized in small, human-scale academic units.

Consideration 7: Learning Needs Reflective Experience Outside Class

Learning that lasts connects the full use of human experience with critical reflection. Most educators would support this proposition, but we want to look more closely at the internal tensions or dialectics when we admit personal experience into learning. Dewey's philosophy gives concrete, lived experience the central role in learning. Rather than focus on the teacher's good intentions and the academic content to be taught, progressive education begins with students and their needs. To put this value into practice is most challenging.

That facile phrase, learning from experience, contains troublesome topics such as the nature of the relationship between experience or practice and theory. Although learning to some degree is ubiquitous as the brain-mind-body continuously adapts to its environs, conceptual learning requires conscious effort of two broad types: *inductive logic,* to examine and distill lived experience to find higher-order concepts; and *deductive logic,* to apply concepts and theory to lived experience. We want to ask: Which logic is better under what circumstances? How do the two elements, theory and experience, interact? At what level of analysis? Maxine Greene discusses the nature of *dialectical logic,* a powerful tool for teachers and counselors but an illusive concept to master:

> A dialectical relation marks every human situation: it may be the relation between individual and the environment, self and society, or living consciousness and object-world. Each such relation presupposes a mediation and tension between the reflective and material dimensions of lived situations.[58]

Greene adds that both elements, theory and experience, are important: The "tension cannot be overcome by a triumph of subjectivity or objectivity; the dialectic cannot be finally resolved." The dialectical tension between theory and practice forces us to think hard about dynamic events and processes rather than static things. That is, dialectical logic is better than formal logic because the former focuses on process in learning and the nature of change. Dialectical logic drives creative thinking and ever deeper understanding of difficult relationships between self and the object world around. Greene concludes, "If we teachers are to develop a humane and liberating pedagogy, we must feel ourselves to be engaged in a dialectical relation."[59]

Consider how we might improve the use of experience in learning. Most experiential learning settings use a soft inductive logic by which learner experience—for example, a winter outdoor expedition at Sterling College in northern Vermont—is the subject for group discussion and general reflection. But the process is soft because students are not expected either to examine their experience closely to derive new concepts or to apply formal theory to their experience, what we might call a hard dialectic. Antioch College, famous for its use of co-op education in liberal education, uses soft deduction by which students are asked to make plans and set goals for an internship, and then write a modest paper upon returning. A co-op faculty member once told me that a "loose dialectic" is better—it does not force a restrictive praxis in co-op jobs. But I would argue that work-study programs only achieve full potential when the learner's experience, powerful or mundane, is embedded in a curriculum with clear learning purposes, one that supports reflective learning and the development of theory from the experience (or application of formal theory to experience).

Educators need better theory about how to fully use student experience, and much better supervision and mentoring models. As it turns out, learning is more *retroductive logic* than either purely inductive or deductive.[60] That is, learners have tentative purposes in mind when they go to an internship, which are then refined by the field experience, the reflection and theory-building occurring in successive iterations, not unlike the way social research unfolds (as opposed to the falsified, hypothesis-first concept of how research is conducted). One place to look for best practices in supervision are graduate social work schools, which have refined methods of case supervision for students working in field placements. As we search for better mental models of experiential learning, and the changes needed to develop Schön's reflective practitioner, we think about coaching more than teaching.

Our conceptual difficulties are not over. Subtle problems appear about the nature of experience, past or present. Powerful emotional experiences, past or present, are not to be confused with learning because learning, especially in school or college, requires intentional reflection and some effort. The brain-mind-body must do work to learn. Students struggle with this stricture because emotional content seems so real, so overpowering, to them that it must be learning, somehow. The fallacy of the emotional moment—that something surely has been learned from this much pain or joy—is common in young adults, perhaps because emotional experience is so vivid at this age. Learning, physiological at a minimum, has occurred at many levels. But *conceptual* learning, the focus of most college learning, is missing or half-done. At the same time, emotional experience provides the motivational energy to do the hard work of thinking about experience. Raw pain or pure delight do not merit academic credit. On the contrary, college learning requires systematic reconceptualization of lived experience of all types.

What can we do to help students integrate personal experience in their learning? We look to the fertile intersections where work and study mix, using campus work programs, co-op programs, and internships.[61] This motive is more important than the teacher's experience or the experience of the ages, important as it is, recorded in books. So, we are asking for a curriculum to be learning-centered more than being either faculty-centered or student-centered because both terms falsify the dynamic, interactive nature of the human learning community.

Public service and good citizenship as core tenets of the curriculum are being reemphasized in hundreds of American universities. In 2000, more than 900 institutions were connected to the Campus Compact, a national group devoted to community service founded in 1985.[62] Some 374,000 students worked up to 32 million volunteer hours last year. Course catalogues listed 11,876 "service learning" opportunities. Tufts University has created a new University College for Citizenship and Public Service, funded by a recent alumnus who made his fortune by having created eBay.

So, the challenge is to integrate a student's lived experience, cultural history, and the wisdom of peers and other generations. We should not make a shrine of naive student experience; rather, we begin with the learner and reach for an active interplay among competing realms of learning: self, others, history, and the immediate environment. While personal experience is integral to all learning to some degree, even in a lecture class, the progressive school has explicit and interlocking mechanisms for reflection on experience, ranging from student diaries and concept logs to formal supervision in a campus work program at Berea or Blackburn College. To ask students to be self-reflecting cannot be incidental or accidental, as it will mostly be in conventional education. Rather, the progressive educator looks for openings, Greene might say, to stimulate self-reflection.

Work of all kinds—farm, office, and lab—provides learning settings of unrecognized potential, not just with regard to narrow vocational skills. If supervision is provided and self-reflection built in, learners can explore and understand motivation, group dynamics, and leadership and "followership." After all, work roles perpetuate silent stereotypes about gender and social class. Ask a young man to sew curtains, a woman to tune an engine, a middle-class student to clean toilets, or a teacher to lead a painting crew—all the sorting mechanisms of modernity's job system come alive for both students and teachers. Such moments make for potent learning predicaments. ("Why do *I* have to do this work?" This question implies its powerful companion: "Who does it for me at home?") Using learner experience does not, of course, assure that learning will occur—rather, work settings open a grounded context of learning that can be more powerful than that found in conventional classrooms. What will be challenged are the implicit, unexamined gender and class-based skills that students have learned.

Less than ten American colleges require on-campus work by students: Alice Lloyd, Berea, Blackburn, College of the Ozarks, Goddard, Sterling, and Warren Wilson.[63] College work programs reduce the cost of education and build a stronger sense of community than if hired staff do the work alone. Several buildings at Goddard were built by students and faculty, and alumni/ae reunions feature a work day where volunteer crews work on repair projects around the campus. At College of the Ozarks, students are required to work fifteen hours a week. They run the college's fire department, airport, and restaurant, and raise cattle and pigs, some for the college's food service. Curiously, most preschool days end with "clean-up-time," when children learn to put things back where they belong, wipe worktables, and so on. Such learning and responsibility taking, however, is rarely continued beyond kindergarten, to the loss of both learner and institution.

Students are much less likely to vandalize a facility they have built or have to clean tomorrow. Before choosing to create a campus-based work program, however, a codified curriculum about work, supervision, and the campus job system is needed. While faculty-specialists in work supervision are needed, the academic faculty, in particular, must be visible—the program will atrophy if students, alone, do the work, or certain kinds of work.[64]

Work programs also involve all community members in shared work, thus increasing the possibility of a synergic spiral of engagement.

Cooperative work projects increase long-term identification with the college and its mission. Even the most mundane job, such as working on a wood lot crew, has potential: College-level learning requires a structure for reflection by which a conceptual understanding is constructed by the learner (goals for the event, additional reading about forestry, supervision around the work and dynamics of the team, and self-evaluation of the work).

Cooperative or co-op education, another type of work-study program, is used in professional and engineering schools. Antioch College, a liberal arts college, requires students to work off-campus six terms in order to test new skills and motivation. Since the 1920s, "co-op" education has been the defining characteristic of Antioch's curriculum since it was brought to the college by reformer Arthur Morgan.[65] On a large scale, Northeastern University considers itself the largest cooperative program in the world, enrolling 50,000 students in a wide array of degrees and majors, with alternating periods on campus and off in a work setting.

Work programs change a college in enduring ways. According to Morris Keeton, Antioch's co-op program derived its power, unintentionally, from reducing faculty control of the curriculum, countering the tendency of some teachers to focus too narrowly on the content of academic disciplines. The student role changed because they came and went to different job settings so often. As a result, Keeton says, student interests became legitimate topics inside the learning community, and student authority in the community increased. The co-op requirement forced students to be active learners, creating their education and laying the foundation for the life-project. A good deal of the learning was no longer under direct faculty supervision (for good and ill). If you speak with Antioch alumni/ae of any generation, they remember most fondly their co-op assignments, much more than the major or their professor at the time.

Consideration 8: Learning Needs Reflective Experience in Class

How should class experience be constructed to motivate students and improve learning? Dewey believed that all learning begins with the learner's experience in the learning setting, broadly defined, not what educators *want* that experience to be. Conventional colleges provide structured learning settings in labs, lectures, and discussion groups but pay less attention to the lived experience of students (as if to say, they either learn from what is proffered, or not). If the group is large, experienced teachers know it is difficult to know what students are thinking or feeling. If class size is between fifteen and twenty-five, we can work with students to create a flexible array of learning settings, in and out of class, that balance process and content. That is, the learning experience integrates didactic experiences, such as lectures, with in-class experiential exercises, such as reflective exercises, or small group assignments that have the promise of increasing personal involvement, albeit at the risk of less time to cover content. Experienced teachers learn to read class mood carefully. In planning a class, we anticipate the needs of the group with respect to attention span and group morale. Many of the tricks we learn from experience have the purpose of getting or holding class attention.[66]

College teachers in education and the social sciences have full command of experiential methods. Role playing, guided imagery, and working with small and plenary groups are valuable pedagogical tools. While experiential methods can be used to increase psychological involvement, they should be used with care. For one thing, participants need to know that they do not have to participate. They have a right, in the first place, to say "no" if asked to participate. Today's college students, some reports suggest, are not comfortable with experiential or collaborative learning methods, which my generation learned in the communal Zeitgeist of the late 1960s.

Group exercises can increase learner motivation. Small group exercises stimulate broader participation than even a class discussion. Learners have more chances to use concepts they are learning and to serve as mentors for each, also learning as they do. But when it comes to academic or conceptual content, a group consensus of casual opinion can be substituted for the hard, lonely work of scholarship. Consider this example: A group of graduate management students meets off campus to discuss the problems of modern bureaucracy. In subgroups, participants list problems on worksheets put up around the room. The learning process has been fun, motivating active discussion. Few members hold back. But there is no close reading of Max Weber or Peter Blau, difficult texts by scholars of organizations. Moreover, students had not heard what the professor learned from his research about bureaucracy (he saw his role as group facilitator, not scholar). In short, the workshop design focused too much on process, too little on content.

Finally, all teaching innovations, if we view them as Jacques Ellul might, as technical interventions in human affairs, have unintended consequences and the possibility, as well, that students adapt to them, making the innovation less effective over time. I find I have to search for new ways to get and to hold the attention of restless students who adapt quickly to any method favored by a teacher. Every class is different and has the possibility of drifting toward stale process precisely because teachers and students are continuously interpreting their environment.

Consideration 9: Learning Needs Feedback

Having clear, high expectations for performance followed by timely feedback enhances learning.[67] On this, educators would agree, if about little else. But how that feedback is given to students varies, and progressive educators reject evaluation methods like grades and grade point scores. Conventional grading focuses student and teacher attention on one summary score (the "grade"). The focus is formal, summative evaluation rather than informal, formative evaluation during the term, which is far more important for motivation and learning.

Perhaps teachers who were excellent students in their day are less sensitive to the impact of grades on marginal students. When a nervous student challenges a teacher about a plus or minus on a grade, a demeaning experience results for both parties. The possibility of a rich conversation about ideas and values, theory and method, is corrupted by bartering and haggling over power and rewards. At such moments, authority issues surface quickly. Worse, conventional evaluation compares students against one another, even if a grading curve is not used. What should be given more weight than comparison to an external standard, usually quite arbitrary, is improvement measured against the learner's starting point, and his or her purposes.[68]

Educators of the second wave of progressive education in the 1970s experimented with narrative evaluation to replace grading. Grades were eliminated in favor of written paragraphs about student performance, and many students (and teachers) welcomed the change. Grades were rejected, in particular, by students who had dropped out of conventional schools and colleges and by adults returning to education.

Rejection of traditional methods of objective test and grade follows from a radical assumption, namely, that students are, or can be, intrinsically motivated. Under this assumption, progressive educators do not need to employ extrinsic motivators like working for a "good grade." Faculty members in unselective, conventional schools complain endlessly about unmotivated students. Students are "lazy" and "don't care." But our good colleagues do not question the problem's source, the production school's necessary reliance upon extrinsic motivators like grades and objective testing.

After a rocky start, perhaps, students in progressive schools, or adults returning to college, will be better motivated than traditional age undergraduates. Why would we want to use grades or objective testing? A more relevant tool would be the narrative. Done well, the narrative will be a small essay crafted almost as a personal letter to the student that discusses development holistically and in detail. The best narratives offer differentiated feedback on many aspects of the student's performance, including choice of goals and motivation. Students read the narratives many times and usually write their own, which the faculty member asks to see (and also evaluates). Daloz might say that a narrative evaluation helps move a student spiritually in her personal odyssey.[69]

Students are asked to write narrative evaluations of their own, which will contain valuable information to be shared with the instructor. If an honest self-evaluation is written, and compared to what the mentor has written, a dialogue opens between student and teacher. The views of performance might be quite different. To be sure, students new to narrative evaluation will be uncomfortable evaluating their own performance. A few may be too harsh, others, too casual. But learner self-assessment is, in itself, an educative experience.[70] Whether no internal standards can be articulated, or those that do exist are too harsh or too low, is less important than the conversation with the mentor about the student's emerging theory of learning. Evaluation and feedback systems must, we have to believe, return people to human encounters about important matters, to existential predicaments, even as such moments are unpredictable.

The principles for effective feedback are not complex. Feedback should be:

Timely, because feedback should occur as closely as possible to the behavior in question;

Balanced by offering a mix of support and criticism that students understand and accept;

Directional, to suggest what needs improving;

Holistic in considering all forms of development; and

Detailed with respect to specific aspects of the experience or learning.

Learning improves through frequent, differentiated, balanced feedback. Against this standard, formulaic or sugary narratives convey as little useful information about learning as one summary score or grade for the work on an entire class or project. While many students welcome personal feedback and evaluation, we have enough experience with narrative evaluation to know its limits as a feedback system. Narratives, done poorly, violate our evaluation principles. The result may be worse than grading: because narratives take time to write, teachers may be late submitting them; if faculty loads are high, the narratives may be formulaic when teachers use computer macro commands to insert favored paragraphs; problems arise when inappropriate or personal language is used in a permanent institutional record; a humanistic teacher may be leery of being critical in an institutional record and so the narrative is packed with euphemisms; and the narrative may be long on laudatory phrases but short on specifics of what was studied and to what extent the student applied herself or not.

We have other problems. It takes institutional resources to train, and retrain, the faculty to learn the method, especially new or part-time faculty, and time and cost to produce, store, and transmit narrative evaluations, which can be several pages. To get consistently high quality narratives also requires faculty time and frequent training and monitoring, which leads budget-conscious administrators to question narrative evaluation and then suggest grades as a labor-saving change. Narratives also require innovation.[71]

As students learn narrative evaluation, they will not be satisfied with empathic, humanistic phrases. The opening tone in most cases should be positive. This may be important for students newly returned to learning, and anecdotal evidence suggests that women may be more likely than men to react poorly to personal feedback. Most students, especially experienced ones, will spot the faculty member who is not being candid, however.

Grades are crude, blunt things, but narrative evaluation can be equally miseducative. Like all pedagogic choices, narrative evaluation has intrinsic limits and unintended consequences. Perhaps the most difficult balancing act of all is to provide Kegan's "ingenious blend of support and challenge."[72] Most students are eager, albeit apprehensive, to learn about the smallest matters regarding their performance. Just look at a student who skims through a paper just returned, looking for the smallest comment. An offhand phrase on a paper or in class by a teacher can produce hours of personal doubt (not always a bad thing). When one is using summary quantitative measures, the numbers are remote, if not cold. One grade stands for a total behavioral performance, which is, in fact, a mix of many strengths and weaknesses. If the advisor has the in-depth and personal knowledge of the learner, even the best performance will necessarily be a mix of progress and regress that a grade cannot capture.[73]

When designing feedback and evaluation systems, more weight should be given to *formative* feedback than to *summative* evaluation. Formative evaluation asks the faculty to create ways to give feedback early and often in the semester. Giving formative feedback takes time to do well, and thus, we have another justification for working with human scale learning communities.

A third way of assessment and feedback is needed, one that goes beyond the limits of traditional grades, on the one hand, and the individualized, but labor-intensive, practice of narrative evaluation, on the other. Another progressive idea is to not interpose a paper-and-pencil evaluation system between human beings—where possible, one wants to encourage face-to-face, reciprocal, real time, candid discussion about goals and performance. Similarly, the existentialist spirit leads us to seek authentic discourse between real people about shared human problems.

So, why do we educators seem to back away from authentic connection with students? Perhaps it is easier to let technical matters separate face-to-face dialogue in human relations, thus to pull us from authentic moments that are, however, unpredictable, though worth the risk. Perhaps we find it easier to measure and move on. We let *techné* and the seductive promise of efficiency enter all aspects of our lives, not seeing the invisible connection to our own loss of relationships and community.

Before closing our discussion about evaluation and feedback, I want to make the strongest possible case for making writing the curriculum's absolute center.[74] Writing, more than any type of testing, leads to active engagement with concepts and critical thinking. In fact, it is the best form of testing, inefficient as it seems to be in the short run. To do this right is expensive because writing is more craft than mass production. Helping students become effective writers takes time and makes more demands of an educator's skill and energy than lectures and tests, the instruments of mass education. (Lectures can be entertaining and inspiring, but they do not stimulate active learning.)

To learn to be a better writer means to be a better thinker and active learner. Becoming an active and self-confident learner can lead to becoming involved in the community. If we are serious about improving the quality of education, which sometimes seems more rhetoric than substance, we start by improving writing-thinking, which usually involves the integration of all realms of human experience. Size of learning group, quality of writing, and quality of thinking—all go together if we make the investment. Good writing is like making one's own clothes or buying bespoke garments rather than buying off the rack; handmade clothes cost more but fit better and last longer. We value what we make all the more.[75]

Consideration 10: Learning Needs Theory

So much of what students gain from school and college depends upon how they *think* about the experience, especially the extent to which emerging mental models help them navigate the passage. Mental models are the major building blocks of the life-project because they carry purposes and justifications needed to motivate new investments of scarce time and energy.

At all levels of education the first responsibility of a teacher is to stimulate, manage, and evaluate the learning process. We want to understand the many rhythms and flows that shape the possibility of learning in ever-changing, temporary human groups. That means, in turn, that we teachers should know ourselves as learners, having had to struggle with the ebb and flow of our own motivation at different stages of life. And most important, using their mental models about motivation and learning, we should know how to stimulate and sustain motivation in students, too many of whom come to school damaged as learners. Being a *master learner* also means that we understand how to work with the ebb and flow of mood and attention in a group or class. The considerable variability of attention and mood in both individual learners and in the group as a whole cannot be ignored. Rather, the effective teacher manages those flows.

Students, like their teachers, should be expected to learn about themselves as learners. One of the unrecognized advantages of student-centered programs is the emphasis upon learning-how-to-learn, if this technical knowledge about learning is joined to a moral and social vision. Though rarely as formal or articulated as it might be, students learn about their strengths and limits as learners, developing and refining their own mental models about motivation and learning. Advances in our understanding of individual differences in learning styles, intelligence, and other capacities underscores the need, first, to see each student as an individual and, second, to ask each learner to explore and refine their mental models about motivation and learning.

Learning how to learn is the only graduation requirement of lifelong consequence. Students and teachers need to learn about learning, building this competence into the curriculum from start to finish. After all, which outcome is more important: to know the essential dates and themes in American history, or to have an informed understanding of oneself as a learner and human being in a modern society? Because good process in learning is so important to educators, we want to help students and teachers enjoy surfacing, testing, and making explicit their personal theories of learning. At the very least, society expects this of an educated man or woman who will need these skills—and is able to teach these skills—in fast-moving, modern society.

Learning to learn is important for another reason. It connects to the surprising holes that exist in our understanding of ourselves, ranging from the simplest biology to advanced topics like the nature of consciousness. For educators, especially, better mental models are needed with regard to human motivation and learning. Many different ideas for motivated learning have been advanced in the foregoing, and the reader has added his or her own formulation. The purpose of the discussion is not to prescribe one or another solution—rather, educators are asked to create their own list, to play with the most powerful variables, and to keep a curious, open mind about learning.

Finally, how we think about learning *while we are learning* points to a different type of degree planning and advising process. Learners need more than a degree plan limited to a given semester or even four years. The progressive curriculum should begin with, and consistently return to, *life planning* with which to advance the *life-project*. Before students attend their first class, indeed, before they develop a degree plan, they might just write a life plan. Perhaps it will sound innocent or intrusive, but students should be asked to set forth their dreams, deepest values, and life purposes. The dialogue that ensues between learner and mentor should return to the student's whole life at the beginning and end of each semester. If approached this way, life planning becomes a conscious, natural part of life, standing in adamantine opposition to the pull of the given world, its many seductions and noise, the "terror of daily life" that so worried Glenn Gould.

Chapter 7

Institutional Culture, Motivation, and Learning

Educators are in reality competing with other forces in the student's life for a share of that finite time and energy.

—Alexander Astin[1]

It is the *culture of the whole institution*—its values, norms, roles, and ethos—that educates. That intentional culture must compete effectively with the dominant culture and the values and norms that surround a school. We began Part III with ten considerations, and the reader has no doubt crossed out several, substituting better formulations. Now I want to think about how to create Deborah Meier's thick learning culture as the whole learner experiences it. We have a substantial task, how to coordinate emerging student character traits with important transactions with the environment such as friends, academic studies, and on- and off-campus work. For this discussion, we will use George Kuh and Elizabeth Whitt's definition of culture: "the collective, mutually shaping patterns of norms, values, practices, beliefs and assumptions that guide the behavior of individuals and groups in an institute of higher education and provide a frame of reference within which to interpret the meaning of events and actions on and off campus."[2]

Evidence is growing for the concept of the involving college.[3] Ernest Pascarella and Patrick Terenzini used multivariate methods to study the net effects of a wide array of student outcomes in 2,600 studies over a span of twenty years. The transformative power of the school experience, they find, lies with *the total level of campus involvement more than any one type or vehicle*. First, college is far more than just the academic curriculum. Second, psychological involvement can begin in one area, such as sports or clubs, and spread to other areas, such as academic study.

A school curriculum is a nested set of opportunities to elicit involvement in learning, broadly defined. We need better ways to assess human development, not just cognitive development, as it may be advanced in college and other learning settings, especially given all the attention that accreditation associations are giving to outcome measures rather than input measures. Indeed, more colleges, like the work colleges previously discussed, could stipulate and evaluate holistic learning outcomes that occur outside class.

For example, Goddard College faculty and staff meet weekly to discuss students, using the language of knowing, doing, and being, thus referring to content areas, skills, and qualities of a whole life.

Measures of emotional and spiritual development to assess the deep purposes of college are needed. Certainly colleges recognize the value of multiple activities, but most hang back from holistic purposes as well as from assessing varied types of learning. If educators took whole-person, ubiquitous learning seriously, a rich menu of cocurricular activities and assessment strategies could be set forth, awarding credit for what is learned. Academic credit is important—in schools and colleges, the award of credit says what we think is most important.

Criticizing the status hierarchy of higher education, Alexander Astin argues for a talent development model of education, which he contrasts to the industrial production model adopted by conventional colleges. His thesis is simple: "Students learn by becoming involved." Many forms of involvement are possible, and, within limits, good: academics, campus activities, governance, sports, and part-time work. Drawing upon his longitudinal studies of higher education for empirical evidence, Astin argues that involvement serves to increase persistence and to produce better-than-average achievement.[4]

Involvement comes in many forms, such as studying hard, working on campus, being active in student organizations, and frequently interacting with other students and faculty. In Kuh et al.'s study of fourteen four-year colleges and universities, two-thirds of traditional student time is spent *outside* the classroom. The authors do not argue for one best model but rather recommend that involvement to a *moderate* degree both enhances academic learning and improves retention. Involving colleges share five characteristics:

1. Student learning in and out of class is seamless.
2. Students know how to work the institution.
3. Students take seriously the expectation that they are responsible for their lives and learning.
4. Students learn as much from peers and others outside as in class.
5. Student subcultures are complementary to the college's mission.[5]

Astin's theory of involvement, supported by Kuh's research, points us toward reforms. Astin argues that the most important source of influence on student development is the college peer group, more so than the faculty. Involvement measures are positively associated with retention, involvement both in entry activities and during the middle years. In contrast, outside employment and television watching are negatively correlated. Astin speculated that involvement in cocurricular activities contributes to developing a philosophy of life, comparable to what we have called the life-project, that arises out of existential dilemmas encountered in studies, reading, and dorm conversations.

Astin's theory is not stated in formal terms, but its ideas are useful in thinking about a progressive curriculum. First, he asks educators to focus more on behavior than on interior states of motivation, which are not easily observed. Second, he calls attention to the importance of formative feedback on different forms of student involvement, which is more important in shaping behavior than end-of-term evaluation. Third, involvement theory applies *equally* to the psychological investments made by students, staff, and teachers. Astin suggests the use of time diaries to help students assess their use of time. Experienced teachers know they compete for student energy and attention with outside interests like sports and parties. Looking at the whole culture, the involving school will create ways to involve *all* community members, to offer assessment about degrees and quality of involvement, and to reward those members who are involved, especially students and teachers.

Astin writes about the civilizing potency of a college culture where individual pieces of the culture interact to form a more powerful whole.[6] Haverford College is noted for the potency of its Quaker-inspired culture. Quaker values like simplicity and loving acceptance are pervasive in the campus's understated architecture and muted palette, an honor code that respects students, reduced campus hierarchy, respect for political engagement, and in liberal academic values and high standards.[7] So, to understand the potential of the college experience as a holistic, life-changing experience, we want to understand a powerful interaction among four variables:

1. The extent to which a college's mission, purposes, and culture self-selects students with certain abilities, dispositions, and emerging life purposes.
2. The effects of potent peer group interaction among admitted students with similar characteristics who socialize with one another, compete endlessly, and refine latent abilities and emerging purposes.
3. The effects of a curriculum for social engagement, one designed to involve students in varied pursuits, both academic and cocurricular, on and off campus, where timely feedback is provided on both the choice of purposes and results.
4. The tonic effects on individuals within this group who work especially hard at being involved (that is, students who are active and work hard inside a well-organized curriculum will get the most out of the first three conditions).

In the best case, interactions among these four factors are not simply additive but multiplicative. That is, in the case of involvement, "the rich get much, much richer" when learners become active agents in a curriculum of diverse, lifelong experiences organized around integrated values. Such a curriculum encourages involvement at every turn where involvement *qua* involvement is the college's meta purpose, which is what Ernest Boyer, Arthur Chickering, and Seymour Sarason ask. The involving curriculum is not, in this way, the usual hodgepodge of bits and pieces tacked together, reflecting years of competition among academic departments with some time allocated, grudgingly, to sports and student life activities. (Chickering calls this a "junkyard curriculum.")[8] To be sure, an eclectic curriculum organized toward diffuse purposes will be better than an unstructured setting to promote learning and character development. It is not, however, the focused learning community of principled ideals, high demands, and defined purposes that most students, teachers, and advisors need.

Now we have plausible ideas for creating an involving school or college. But the discussion has sidestepped certain theory problems. How should we think about the transactions between the institution and its involvement platforms, so to speak, and psychological consequences for learners? Several dimensions of self are involved. Self-confidence, self-understanding, the quality of one's imagination and goals, and skills like critical thinking—all are intrinsic causes and consequences of involved learning as a dynamic interaction between learner and his or her immediate environment. Under the best circumstances, students gradually acquire concrete skills, thus increasing self-confidence. If they are asked to understand themselves as learners, as we have suggested, and also are asked to explore their dreams and passions, the possibility of increased performance is improved, which in turn increases self-confidence.

We cannot consider classic theories of human development from Freud to Kegan, which try to capture the important transactions between the emerging self and involvement with an academic culture. But less agreement is found about the essential pieces, either within the self, or in the environment in which the self invests time and energy in different activities. As yet, no unequivocal specification of dynamics between person and environment is made, much less a calculus that links developing character traits with involvement in the community and the many, many feedback loops that result and that, in turn, shape character, which affects investments.

A personality theorist would argue that the self is formed out of such interactions. But person-environment transactions are so complex that all we have to work with, in the end, are general effects and apologetic speculations about interesting problems found along the way. The two-dimensional, graphic representation in Figure 7.1 underestimates the complexity of what we need to understand. But a few points can be made about the iterative transactions between person and environment within a learning culture.

Imagine five correlated aspects of character development: life purposes, self-focusing, self-confidence, belongingness (to social groups and movements larger than self), and learning skills. These five variables contribute to an emerging sense of self, an idea of oneself as a distinct, authentic human being with needs and talents, limitations, emerging life purposes, and expanding skills. Life purposes, such as wanting to work with the poor, are shaped by interactions with peers and mentors and present new opportunities for learning from experience.

Self-focusing in this model is a conscious construction consisting of both explicit purposes and an understanding of self in the world that is used to interpret past and present experiences while projecting direction into the

Figure 7.1: Hypothetical Feedback Relationship between Emerging Self and Psychological Investments in the Environment.

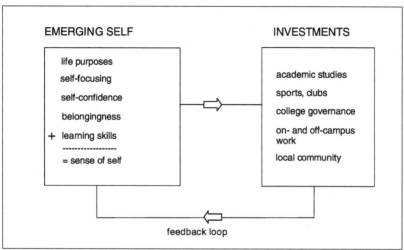

1. Only general direction of effects shown between different facets of the emerging self and investments in different activities in the environment.
2. Not shown are complex feedback loops in which positive or negative experiences with investments lead to changes in self, which lead to enhanced or reduced investments.

future. Self-focusing is, in turn, correlated with emerging self-confidence with which to make investments in the environment, to take risks by engaging in activities that are new or anxiety-arousing such as volunteering for a committee or trying out for a sport. As self-confidence builds, the learner is emboldened to look to additional arenas, thus enlarging the range and scope of learning settings.

Another facet of the developing self is the emerging connection, the belongingness, the learner feels to other people, groups, and social movements. This connectedness is important because students are more likely to invest in activities when they belong to a human group and are lifted up by its purposes. Young people need to affiliate because, having left the family and high school networks, they are lonely. Similarly, adults returning to college are often in major social transitions, such as divorce, and feel a need to connect with new networks and friends. Perhaps educators are tempted to *overestimate* the impact of teaching on learning and transformation, and to *underestimate* the power of friendship networks and peer comparison in learning communities. So, we want learners new to a learning community to get involved quickly in new social networks to spark and sustain motivation and learning. This goal is important for individual learners. For the institution, student involvement increases retention and attainment.[9]

Finally, the learning skills shown in the model form the foundation for self-confidence and self-focusing. Literacy, numeracy, skills with modern technology, organizing skills, and learning-to-learn skills—all are essential. If a learner cannot complete complex projects as they move into new learning settings, their psychological investments, described next, will not be productive or prompt positive feedback loops to strengthen emerging attitudes, values, and traits. Psychological energy to drive person-environment transactions is missing.

One could attach different labels to these facets of human development, and the relationships among them have not been discussed. But for present purposes, let us move on to consider involvement with the surrounding environment. These attributes create the foundation for different psychological investments of time and energy in the near environment: academic studies, cocurricular activities like sports and clubs, college governance, on- or off-campus work, and local community. While each has the potential to stimulate new learning, the learner must choose among interests, given limited personal time and energy, forming them into purposes and connecting purposes to the emerging life-project. Much early college experience focuses on just this ordering of priorities for personal investment.[10] If the learner has, for example, an exhausting, off-campus job, energy left for academic study or campus governance is reduced.

More importantly, the model assumes that involvement can begin in one arena, such as school governance, and generalize to other activities, such as improved learning. Students who belong to teams or who participate in school cocurricular life persist longer and do better academically.[11] The emerging self is thereby stretched, extended in successive iterations, as the learner experiments with investments in new life activities. As Dewey would put it, one learning experience sets the stage for the next in a rich, progressive curriculum for learning.

Intermediate levels of involvement are best. If learners spend too much time in off-campus work, Pascarella and Terenzini report, persistence and achievement are reduced. Too much, or too little, involvement has a deleterious effect. The same could be said for narrow investments in any arena of college life, even academic study, because of the reduced potential for holistic transformation. To the extent that a college only values cognitive development or academic learning, its students may not find the support to expand the boundaries of their interests and personality, thus losing the potential for deep learning when different learning settings interact.

What drives this model of human development? It is the quality of the feedback received by the learner from so many different transactions. What is being learned in each area? How is that knowledge received and integrated with other life experience? Some learners, after all, do not read their experience well. Others are acutely sensitive and quick to withdraw, leading them to not invest as much as they might. A subtle dynamic not depicted in the table follows from the self-observing nature of human beings, one of our leitmotifs. That is, learners watch themselves perform in different areas, and, to an extent, they monitor the feedback from different investments. If that feedback suggests they are not welcome, or are not competent, the deflating psychological experience reduces self-confidence. It may redouble self-focusing, of course, or it could lead to reduced investments and reduced opportunities for educative experience. Our crude model does not account for this possibility.

Perhaps other paths for competence and self-confidence open up—for example, belonging to a fraternity or a gang—and quite different purposes and life prospects result. Perhaps as self-monitoring learners, we carry a rough scorecard through life, one that summarizes return on psychological investment and samples how we feel about ourselves and the quality of the emerging life-project. We have a "good day" or a "bad day," reflecting this most personal accounting. If my assessment is positive, renewed investments are likely, leading to more feedback and more learning, and so on: It is a good day. If, on the other hand, I feel overwhelmed or ineffectual, investments are scaled back, or shifted to other objects, including those that take the learner from prosocial learning. Redirected investments, for example, into criminal behavior lead to learning that is self-destructive.

By way of giving emphasis to the importance of school culture, imagine an ideal academy for whole-person learning, one consistent with John Dewey's philosophy of learning from experience. In this exercise, please suspend judgment as to whether a utopian academy is realistic. Sober realism and practicality are not the point: The goal is to play with ideas about motivation, learning, and curriculum design.

The progressive academy is not the conventional production site with which we have grown up, consider as given, and expect to find. Our imagined school begins with the subjective life-world of each individual student, not a preordained curriculum of another generation. The teacher begins by asking each student who *she* is, where *she* is going, and what *she* wants to learn. The learner is required to be an active agent in charge of her self-development as a whole person, and the curriculum is co-constructed by teachers and learners to encourage active learning and the full, reflective use of human experience. Students are understood to bring rich experiences from their past and to have equally rich experiences in the present—what is missing is critical reflection on prior and present experience, which points to the mentor's role helping students become self-reflective and self-focusing.

Call this a progressive school, not for its political values but because experiences that students and teachers have encourage *new* experience and the possibility of *new* learning in a progressive connecting of experience to ever-expanding mental models. Both teachers and students come to school eager to have the involved psychological experience of learning and teaching that awaits them. Neither students nor teachers are bored in our energized community, and all students do well.

Imagine a spiritual community where students, staff, and teachers are joined by an articulated mission based on clear values and agreed-upon means. (Recall Sarason's first challenge to educators to set clear purposes.) A college at its zenith offers a culture of hope and generosity, inclusion, and social idealism to evoke Maxine Greene's ethic. Teachers, parents, and students who make up these communities of commitment, as Fred Kofman and Peter Senge put it, rely upon hope for a better day.[12] Besieged American schools and colleges, especially poor or isolated institutions on the margins of society, need a renewed spirit.

Schools and colleges *are* spiritual communities. Whether denominational or secular, these are social institutions created to nourish, test, and extend the human spirit. The best schools are, indeed, *spirited* cultures where a number of attributes combine to pull the most from the generations of students and faculty who pass through. Spirited schools share certain features—they are organized around clear and shared values, look at their members holistically, set high expectations for growth, test motivation and skills, and look after members in the community who may be struggling, perhaps silently, at a point in life.

Seen as a spiritual community, a concern for basic welfare extends to all members of the institution even though such policies bring additional cost. Progressive schools want to treat students, faculty, and staff more similarly than not. While there are different roles to be enacted, the school aspires to treat each person holistically and from the perspective of a humane learning organization. Viewed in such terms, the difference between secular colleges and religious schools, or between schools and churches, is not as dramatic as it might first seem.

Such a high and noble academy for learning and the best of human culture does not exist. Utopian institutions do not long survive, given limited resources inside most schools and fallible human beings. Educational experiments are born of romance for a better life, what Gerald Grant and David Riesman called the "perpetual dream." But they do not endure more than a few generations, if that, because pedagogical assumptions prove too idealistic. But those two limits should not constrain our idealism, that restless search for better lives that animate a good school.

Most of all, we hope to improve student quality of being in the world and ask of students that they be awake in the world with regard to how they invest themselves. Being in the world is influenced directly by how we imagine a better life, which introduces the category of becoming, because the direction of the life-project is expressed in emerging purposes as to how to use one's time. In this regard, being and becoming are the most important dimensions of learner development—we should not be content with assessing the lesser categories of what one knows or can do.

Epilogue

My life is one of low peaks, high valleys, and a continual stream of diverse rewards and enthusiasms; this isn't Maslow's ravishing ideal, but it more nearly reflects the life that many of us lead.

—Eric Zencey[1]

Many pages ago we began by asking about problems in living, particularly self-motivation and learning. Large questions were posed in the form of puzzles and dilemmas. Few have convincing answers and if an answer appears, one should be wary. Not lending themselves to pat answers, such perennials help us ponder tangled ethical and social questions. "Are human actions determined by external forces?" Well, yes and no. "Can individual and organizational needs complement one another?" Perhaps, but it is unlikely to happen anytime soon. And so on. We need now to wind the project down. I use my closing chapter to reconsider the problems of self-motivation and social hope and to highlight unresolved issues or emerging questions.

Many folders lie open on the desk. Wanting to understand motivation and learning, I have posed questions not common in educational or counseling texts, where the discussion is dominated by methodological debates. For hard-pressed teachers and counselors, escape into method and technique is understandable. Rambling ontological questions about being in the world and problems in living are too remote from the press of work and the production imperatives that drive modern institutions. Arguments about educational means, the choice of a reading method or curricular innovation, are less threatening, serving as pragmatic responses, if incomplete, for impatient Americans. Perhaps in a multicultural community we doubt our ability to negotiate, fairly and without rancor, the political fights that force their way into the conversation when educational goals must be decided. Maybe we argue about means and methods because setting goals for human institutions will be too contentious.

Problem of Self-Motivation

Self-motivation is rarely as easy or straightforward as it seems. Sometimes one is fortunate to have an inspirational supervisor or staff that makes one want to work harder and longer. More often, organizations follow their own imperatives and just assume worker motivation, and colleagues are often distracted by their own needs. So, most days it is up to the individual to generate direction and movement in the life-world, and if one is a leader, to bring to work the right spirit with which to motivate others. We know this story, but it is worth repeating because when it comes to motivation, educators have several responsibilities: to design motivating curricula, to help students learn about self-motivation in their studies and life, to motivate colleagues, and to motivate ourselves.

Human beings manipulate psychological experience all day long, and modern work and culture are organized in ways that seem to require we do so. Left unconsidered has been the not-small matter of how individuals adapt to the organizations where they work, study, and play. How do human beings—interpreting, pattern-seeking creatures that we are—adapt to organizations and to the demands of the workplace and learning place? What directions emerge by which we educators might construct better mental models, first, to inform professional practice and second, to improve quality of life?

Now I want to think about the organizational climate of the modern school and workplace, and the ways in which people learn to adapt to those conditions.[2] No study of human motivation and learning would be complete if we did not understand how motivation and learning help us manage, for better or worse, the contradictions of modern institutional life. Alienation from meaningful work, in particular, and from society, in general, has been studied extensively by social scientists like Richard Schacht, who emphasizes the ways experience at work affects quality of life and even personality development.[3]

Most jobs do not wear like a handmade suit. Even the best work requires considerable adjustment on the wearer's part. Of course, the interests of impersonal organizations are not the same as those of individuals. Of course, this fact forces us to adapt, if not compromise, private dreams and change personal habits. What is curious to my mind, however, is how we humans struggle so with this reality, finding it difficult to think clearly or deeply about lived experience at work and our problematic lives inside the modern institutions we have created that then come to delimit human existence.

How do the mind's pattern-seeking and signal selection capacities allow people to work on multiple tasks? All forms of work require that one pay attention, at least minimally, to tasks at hand. Examples of jobs that require high and consistent levels of attention, one hopes, are not hard to find—air traffic controllers, pilots, surgeons, machine tool operators, race car drivers, psychotherapists, and teachers. At the other extreme, mundane tasks like mowing the lawn or washing dishes in a restaurant require almost no focused attention (although they require focus when being learned and can be made involving for a time, if one concentrates).

Most institutions require workers to monitor multiple tasks and informa-tion streams simultaneously. The worker must focus quickly, accurately, on a few channels, usually scanning for anomalies. Being a mother or single parent with children in the home is one of these occupations. Women learn to handle multiple tasks like working on a house project and answering the phone while attending to young children constantly in motion.[4] This selective vigilance, so necessary to modern life, is learned. While it can be adaptive, some people do not like the experience of fragmentation, or lack of focus, sometimes calling it alienating.

Modern work is organized in segmented ways that do not expect much from workers, and William Kahn says institutions make much less than full use of human capacities.[5] Personally, I look at people in jobs different from my own, wondering what the work feels like. Where I can, I ask what the work is like. Think about a sales representative in a department store who waits listlessly for customers to approach, or a cop who stands alone at a traffic intersection, just watching hundreds of people pass. (Cops talk about their work as long periods of boredom punctuated by instants of terror.) What do hotel maids think about all day long, moving from room to room, cleaning up after strangers? Most modern work is boring, or perhaps we just do not know how to make it otherwise.

More interesting than a ditch digger bored to tears who daydreams about deer camp are those adaptations that evolve with jobs of moderate complexity or novelty that seem to require a degree of focus less than full. We have learned the repetitive routines such jobs require, like filling out a car rental agreement if one is an Avis agent, but a degree of alertness is necessary. Perhaps a customer wants directions, or we notice a piece of anomalous information that suggests some process has broken down. Other occupations, like running a print machine in a one-hour, photo shop, require specialized concentration as quick judgments are made about images on the monitor, one array of twenty-four images after the other, every fifteen seconds. Leaving the question of mood variability aside, little is known about attention variability in the workplace or school other than the near-universal experience that daydreaming and unfocused attention are commonplace. As one learns a new role, a huge space develops for mindless worrying and daydreaming, and not much is known about this adaptation to modern times.

So, we humans have to learn to motivate ourselves to do boring if not unpleasant things, to endure stress and danger, and to work hard and attend to complex stimuli when the brain-mind-body is tired. Peak experiences at school or work are so rare and unpredictable—the cold demands of the authorities, the "suits," seem relentless. Faced with the demands of the modern organization and its fast pace, it is challenging to build an authentic life.

Alienation from society has many forms and some variants are not obvious, like alienation from meaningful language and the objectification of self. In the former instance, alienated workers do not develop the concepts needed to understand how their labor is used, and the concepts they do have falsify the nature of the power relationship between owners and workers, and the social consequences. In the latter instance, for most forms of modern work, at least those parts with which we do not identify, we learn to treat the brain-mind-body as an object to be hurled this way and that. No one is harmed by changes in psychological experience that help us adapt to stress, or that give pleasure. If, without awareness I throw my brain-mind-body into work, as if a foreign object, and then, to cope with work stress, throw myself into mood-altering experiences, the downward spiral of alienation and bad feeling can only tighten and accelerate.[6] This is why self-focusing or, more generally, mindfulness, are so important to cultivate because only with those learned capacities can life investments and rewards be weighed against costs.

One final form of adaptation is worth noting. In all that has preceded, one theme has been steady—we humans learn to manipulate psychological experience to cope with and to enrich the life-world, the subjective experience of reality.[7] Edward Khantzian advanced the self-medication hypothesis by which people use a variety of legal and illegal substances such as caffeine and cocaine to treat underlying bad feelings traceable to attention deficit disorder.[8] Let us treat his idea somewhat differently because *self-medication* is one variant of a larger propensity to manipulate psychological experience. People self-medicate to cope with work stress and boredom, using caffeine, sugar, nicotine, and alcohol, not to mention prescribed drugs like Prozac and illicit drugs like cocaine. Types of adaptation are wide ranging, from occasional abuse of coffee to heroin addiction.

What mental models could we use to think about the many ways people manipulate the brain-mind-body and its hundreds of information systems? I want to distinguish between mood-altering experiences, which produce *endogenous* substances like the neurotransmitter dopamine to alter attention and mood, and mood-altering substances, which introduce to the body *exogenous* substances like caffeine. Both are psychoactive interventions intended to produce changes in human consciousness, some profound.

Growing up, we *learn* to use exogenous substances like caffeine, alcohol, and nicotine, and *learn* to use physical activities like hard work or sports to manipulate psychological mood and attention via endogenous neurotransmitters and hormones produced by the body. While motives like financial reward, attention from friends, and perceived prestige are potent, our concern has been the psychoactive behaviors we humans pursue, mostly unconsciously. The unconscious manipulation of lived experience for its effects is constant.

All day long, people manipulate mood and awareness: coffee to wake up, the effects of sugar from breakfast cereal, a power walk at lunch, a piece of chocolate mid-afternoon, a cat nap late afternoon, tennis before dinner, a beer or two with friends. Bored at school, young people drink sodas like Mountain Dew that are laced with caffeine—facing the workday, their parents load up on coffee every morning. Many smoke for the psychoactive effects of getting "high," calling it a habit, overriding thoughts about health risk and smoking's unattractiveness. "Sugar highs" come from soda and sweet desserts like ice cream. Children and parents, alike, daydream about a new purchase, using the fantasy to create small pleasant moments in an otherwise boring day. To feel better on the weekend, we go cross-country skiing, or hike a mountain, intense aerobic activities that stimulate the release of neuroactive peptides as well as a cognitive sense of accomplishment, combining to give us a feeling of well being.[9]

Life activities that help us focus attention and improve mood are valued. People are motivated by these psychological experiences—we call them fun—because of mood changes that result. Conversely, the psychological experience of a wandering mind, the vague anxiety we experience, is not "fun." People go to an amusement park for the thrills even if the salutary effects are temporary. Perhaps fingers are pointed at others and we say those poor souls over there are "addicted" to mood changes, as compulsive thrill seekers, or "addicted" to alcohol or sharp, intense rushes caused by illicit drugs like crack cocaine. If I am honest about my own use of psychoactive activities and those of students and colleagues, these are differences of degree, not kind, in the human propensity to manipulate states of mind.

Another insight has emerged. When I look casually at a human foible like shopping at the mall, or think about rare self-destructive behaviors like self-mutilation, one idea now seems so obvious to me—the extent to which human beings try to be attention-managing creatures. We move through the experiential day trying to be intentional but so easily captured by its events. Our mind functions, in one respect, like a camera with automatic focus—moving through the day, the focus changes constantly as different images come into the viewfinder, in and out, back and forth. Most of the time, we do not notice these changes in response to new stimuli. That is to say, human beings are unconsciously motivated by attention mechanisms of two types: first, to find focus in hobbies or reading that calm us, and second, to find both focus and arousal in brain-mind-mood states stimulated by aerobic sports and risk behaviors. When we look at the rhythms of a simple day or one's entire life, these two mechanisms emerge as powerful, if unacknowledged, motivators in learning. Educators who understand how they seem to work can, in turn, create better learning environments for others and for themselves.

While the lineup of daily activities and motives may have endless variants, the learned habit of manipulating psychological experience is consistent. Even if the linkage is neither in awareness nor understood as a mechanism, Mihaly Csikszentmihalyi points to the deep human need to control psychological experience.[10] Now extend this idea to how human beings adapt to alienating work conditions and institutional life. Within limits, self-management of mood, awareness, and attention is important for both the quality of work produced and quality of life. A Puritanical work ethic, for example, does not permit a nap at work even though quality of both work and personal experience would improve. Perhaps it would be utopian to expect that, some day soon, modern organizations will balance corporate efficiency with ideal human development. That failing, at least we can organize the work and school day to recognize how the brain-mind-body functions.

Organizations built to satisfy *collective* needs set expectations for *individuals* hired to pay attention and work hard when people might not choose to do so on their own. That idea will not surprise. But if pushed a bit, the notion leads to one consequence that is not obvious: Growing up means one learns to fake it, to dissemble and lie. One inevitable byproduct of mass education, if not modern organizational life, is that people learn the art of impression management.[11] To fit in, we learn to feign participation and to fake paying attention. Early in life, young people fake involvement in class or a conversation to avoid being conspicuous and to avoid being punished by an authority. Teachers and public speakers had better learn that attentive faces and nodding heads do not mean either agreement with the speaker's points or that the listener is paying attention.

Feigning involvement is not necessarily inauthentic but an example of normal coping by individuals finding their way through the life-space, with all its uncertainty and changes. Individuals need private space, especially given the pressures of group life. We should celebrate the marvelous nature of how the human mind functions and work with it, not against it.

Still another adaptation to alienating institutional life is unseen. Compare the quality of psychological experience outside school in sports and social life with the requirements and monotony of the impersonal Fordist classroom. Now we understand why restless minds are drawn to the self-stimulation of daydreaming and fantasies. Hidden behind social masks not obvious to teachers or supervisors, daydreaming is commonplace and not entirely escapist. Rather, it is part of the mind's essential work because daydreaming can bring creative insight as well as help us understand how we think. Daydreaming about a new car, a baseball game, or that trip to Italy becomes a way of focusing attention, curbing the anxiety of wandering consciousness. Preparing a shopping list for tonight's dinner serves the same purpose.

One's private mental space, so to speak, is not valued in modern society, as if human beings by nature are undisciplined or worse. It is not hard to understand, then, how that mental model becomes a self-fulfilling prophecy. Students will do better if teachers assume a higher standard that to some degree everyone works on self-discipline toward some purposes. Better to risk disappointment when an ideal assumption is frustrated than assume the worst and realize it too readily because of our own expectations. Learners are not "paying attention" to the institution's demands, it is claimed, when they are attending, in fact, to what is more interesting to them than a dumb drill that does not treat then as individuals.

Certain individual adaptations to modernity provoke interesting questions. Is there a difference between involvement in a hobby, sport, or career and those behaviors that are judged addictive, neurotic, or ultimately harmful? Committed athletes work out daily to prepare their bodies and to enjoy the increased levels of neuroactive peptides produced by the exercise and the feeling of well being that results. They can become psychologically dependent upon this enhanced mood and how it functions to bring pleasure during the day, leading them to neglect other supports for quality of life.

What do we say if our earnest athlete works out twice a day? Three times? What about the committed cyclist who avoids going home to a noisy dinner table, or has to work out before he can cope with the stress of a job interview? Suppose our athlete works out alone because he cannot sustain a conversation. The line between healthy self-focusing and neurotic compulsion is not easy to draw. Maxine Greene might remind us that people are not perfect beings, surely, as they adapt to modern times. She merely asks that we become awake in the world, reject the habitual, and make conscious choices of how we work and play.

The distinction between healthy, involving activity that adds human development and those activities that limit development is easier to define, in general terms, than to evaluate in real-life examples. Work that requires us to solve novel puzzles everyday may be more involving than circumscribed, repetitive work. But a certain level of routine helps us feel competent and provides some rest. One criterion is whether or not the pursuit gets out of personal control, limiting other life experiences, which is the conventional standard used by psychologists. But a different rationale exists. If running or skydiving becomes compulsive, or serves as a substitute for other responsibilities, like being a good parent, John Dewey would call it regressive rather than progressive. Such activities are regressive because the narrow limits in one's purposes reduce learning from *new* experience.

Where are these developments in self-medication, or, if you prefer, the control of psychological experience, going? In the last fifty years, the ability to shape psychological experience has grown dramatically, and the reasons are several: growing popular interest in psychology and human behavior; availability and use of psychoactive drugs, legal and illicit; and advances in human neurobiology, especially those of the last twenty years. If anything, brain-mind-body interventions of the new century can only become more deliberate, more sophisticated, and more invasive than those of today.

Problem of Social Hope

Existentialists struggle with a difficult problem in living: the means by which individuals justify personal existence in a world bereft of external moral authority. More than most topics in education, this one is central to helping students find their own way in the life-world. They struggle mightily but unsuccessfully with the dilemma of implicit individualism, a vulnerability for any theory of learning as well as for philosophies and religions. If individuals are ultimately alone in the world, people need only worry about themselves. Existentialist philosophy could justify solipsism ("I alone exist"), or excuse the rapacious consumption in America of the late 1980s. Even admitting the power of external social forces, the existentialist says, "Yes, but you are still alone."

The fundamental responsibility for constructing an engaged life, it could seem, is personal, not social. Whether this life is a worthy one or not—

whether it leads to happiness or success—is an inescapable, individual responsibility. If one's constructed existence is always solitary, does that mean that others and society are not intimately involved in both learning and meaning making? Of course not. The radical social psychologist in John Dewey directly tied individual learning and development to the quality of social life. While the responsibility for choosing worthy purposes is ultimately individual, human beings live and learn in social groups. Both ethically and developmentally, individual well being is inseparable from the groups that surround and support human behavior.

Although imprecisely linked, progressive development of the individual can be tied to progressive development of the group, if not the larger community. It is difficult but not impossible for the isolated individual to advance very far if the welfare of the group is left too far behind. For instance, a student's performance is dependent upon his or her family, the quality of classes and teams, and the quality of the college attended and its networks. If the groups in which we live and learn are at risk, so is the learner. If we humans are alone, we find aloneness tolerable only in the company of others while working, in some measure, to improve the well being of all.

Other arguments support an ethic of reciprocity, sometimes expressed at school graduations as "giving back." Like all young animals, human beings are raised by others in a social group. Except in the most abusive situations, everyone is "given to" for most of the first quarter of life, and this is done without expectation that the social investment will be paid back immediately. In this way, social reciprocity is a general evolutionary adaptation that has benefited the species. People who cooperate in the face of an external threat, like fire or attack by another tribe, are more likely to survive.

We have considered the classic, existentialist notion that the modern self cannot avoid anxiety, the necessary product of a discrepancy between the facts of the world that surround and the human impulse to change existence.[12] Except for brief moments, we confront a discrepancy between the world we find ourselves in, its facticity, and the world we want. And the discrepancy only grows and deepens the more one is educated even though some peace obtains, perhaps, in knowing that this gap will be inevitable, even good. Unless a belief system is embraced that serves to bridge the discrepancy between the given world and the imagined world, existential anxiety is inevitable, and so the definition of an educated person is that mind and conscience are alive!

Critical reading and social action cultivate existential anxiety. Individuals can choose to create an emancipated consciousness, even try to change what they do not like. If these choices challenge the routine, the world as it is, responsibility is assumed for others and the larger community. In this way, transcendence or personal transformation begins, as Maxine Greene and most social critics believe, with criticism of the world. By calling for change, transformation connects the individual to a larger community, but this does lessen the alienation.

Isaiah Berlin calls attention to an "uneasy conscience"—the necessary burden of the intellectual who would cultivate an enlightened mind in a world of suffering and inequality. In pointing out the seductive nature of totalitarian beliefs, a refrain in his work, Berlin returned time and again to the responsibility of making choices whose consequences cannot be known in advance. Human beings are, he said, "doomed to choose." Elsewhere Berlin said, "The hope that perfect knowledge of ourselves and all the options open to us will free us from the anxiety or choice because we shall see exactly what we must do is simply delusive."[13]

About individual happiness, however, existentialists are silent. Happiness is an impossible abstraction, an archaic motive manipulated by consumerist forces to stimulate buying ever-new things to distract. How can an educated person who is aware of self-in-community be happy given the scarcity and inequality in the world revealed to all in the human tragedy of the week? Can one be happy if millions are starving in Central Africa, or when we learn that mass rape is an instrument of war in Croatia? The answer is "no" if we assume a human nature in common. If this argument is reasonable, we seek a self-sacrificing, noble human purpose that stands in opposition to the egoistic pursuit of happiness and personal fulfillment.

But what about hope for the future, for a better life, which human beings need to give lives direction and energy? Surely, to read descriptions from the existentialist perspective will make the most cheery reader uncomfortable. And yet, the sparse, unsettling assumptions are reasonable because the existentialist perspective does not require elaborate metaphysics or articles of faith like an all-knowing deity. Existentialism does not accept religious metaphysics, rejecting patriarchy and the seductive projection of warm, family dynamics onto those of cold, impersonal nature.[14] Thus, the existentialist perspective as theory is more parsimonious in its assumptions than many religious perspectives, which rely on faith statements when the logic in the belief system turns awkward.

Rather than leave us feeling pessimistic, the skeptical existentialist stance in life is oddly reassuring. Like the clean lines of a glass and steel house by Philip Johnson, the modern mind wants to be free of ornamental superstition, especially compared to religious or political explanations offering false comfort, which seem tailor-made to reduce ambiguity and loneliness. Small relief is had just this way: The true accounting for the immense universe, ever beyond human ken, and for one's short life in that cold void, cannot be much worse. A certain nobility obtains from facing down a lonely existence without blinking, as the Japanese filmmaker Akira Kurosawa put it.

There is no one existentialism, no text or creed. In contrast to my severe characterization, Emmy van Deurzen-Smith, an existentialist counselor, underscores the flexible nature of human beings and their capacity for personal change.[15] All people try to create meaning and order in their lives—what varies is the clarity and accuracy of that self-understanding and the meaning and value of the direction chosen. Whether a person lives to attend the weekend dog show in Stowe, Vermont, or works with teenage prostitutes in the slums of Bengal, people construct an order about their day and week.

Though more optimistic than I am about the human capacity to change, van Deurzen-Smith criticizes the arrogance of humanistic psychology, saying this school exaggerates human potential and importance. The humanist posture encourages a false sense of the primacy of the human species on a fragile planet while diminishing real barriers to a full existence, like grinding poverty. So, the Continental existentialist worldview is both more restrained and sober than that of American humanistic psychology.

In this regard, we return to Abraham Maslow and what he wanted to accomplish with his work. Maslow saw humanistic psychology and his attempt to theorize about a positive, ideal existence as leading to a new, balanced existentialism (in contrast to a morbid, fatalistic existentialism). Writing in the 1960s, Maslow had a mission that is apparent in his later work. But the larger movement toward a humanistic psychology, noble enough, veered toward technique, even individual hedonism, when it sidestepped contentious social issues like racism, sexism, homophobia, genocide, not to mention the unpopular war in Vietnam. The focus, instead, became humanistic technique such as role playing in Gestalt therapy.[16] Humanistic psychology lost its critical edge and became marginalized— preoccupied with means more than ends, the theory swung toward personal growth in a vacuum. Left behind are protracted social problems like racism and the moral dilemmas that quickly follow.

Odd thing, such an end was surely unexpected because encapsulation in technique is what humanists criticize in the rationalized, modern world. It is not hard to find academic or popular compendiums of motivational methods.[17] But in the spirit of Jacques Ellul's critique of modern society, we ask, "Self-directed toward *which* goals?"[18] "*Whose* goals?" Distrusting highbrow topics and the intellectual's stance, Americans feel more comfortable with *techné* than with *telos*. In that regard, Jack Mezirow argues curriculum theories should offer a social context and critique, rather than focus on technique *qua* technique.[19]

I want to press the question of hope, so important for teachers. William James, writing in the early 1900s, argued that religion brought hope to people, both in terms of the immediate and tonic experience of faith-states, and in the comforting idea of an afterlife where one will be rewarded. James also wrote about the secular self-help movements of his day (the "Mind-cure" movement, "New Thinking") that focused on the benefits of "positive thinking," and it is not hard to find parallels today in secular motivational retreats, some, like est, that were organized on a massive scale.

Is there room for hope in the existentialist perspective, which treats human beings as just another animal, as Richard Rorty suggests, fragile creatures facing poverty, injustice, and modernity's fast pace?[20] The answer is "yes," or at least "possibly," because the alternatives of blind faith in popular nostrums, or faith in afterlife theology (or political totalitarianism), would seem to deny both reason and individual responsibility, two of the most human of characteristics. After all, what choice is there but to think rationally about a problem-filled existence—and the short path given each person—and place one's bets? Once admitted, no alternative remains. "In the best of all possible worlds," social psychologist Morton Deutsch said, "one has a choice of problems."[21] In that regard, human beings face a dreadful freedom to either minimize personal responsibility and disengage from society or choose a course of understanding and social action that may not bring happiness. But choose, we must, says Berlin.

Come back also to Csikszentmihalyi and his assertion that individual happiness is the central motive in his theory. Surely, all deserve to feel better about their lives and work. Who can argue against such a vision? But to make happiness the central motive in human experience, and put a hedonic ethic, not service to others, at the theory's core, narrows and weakens the framework. Recently, Csikszentmihalyi moderated his position, saying, "One cannot lead a life that is truly excellent without feeling that one belongs to something greater and more permanent than oneself."[22] With the decline of traditional meaning systems, Csikszentmihalyi adopts a familiar theme, that people need to find new values to connect individuals to community. Applying systems theory, Csikszentmihalyi goes on to say that helping improve flow for self and others holds off entropy and the dissolution of focus and energy.

Meanwhile, the question of happiness haunts my imagination. Happiness is an impossible standard for most the world's inhabitants, who find that food, water, and a job are more immediate concerns. Even among the advantaged, the reality is that most days, one is caught up in a routine—hamster on a wheel—trying to be productive, having fleeting moments of pleasure and creativity. What is more, the happy life is a distraction from the small moments that one *can* enjoy. In that regard, Ellen Langer and Thich Nhat Hanh remind us of the quality of life that can be gained from mindfulness in daily living. Listen to Hanh:

> Every time we have 15 minutes or a half an hour we run away from ourselves. We turn on the television, pick up a novel, eat, have a drink because we do not want to go home to ourselves. Going home, simply being with ourselves fully, might be painful, but going home in mindfulness can bring us peace.[23]

If basic needs for food, drink, and shelter are met, a central paradox faced by human beings is this: Everyday we have lots of choices, and none at all. Through acts of will we can choose to remake our lives. We can change a career, take a spontaneous trip to Montreal, or volunteer at a nursing home. One can enroll in college, or find a counselor to help manage conflict at home. Yet, radical choices are not made easily.

If existentialists are correct—if there is no grand design and no paternal figure to guide and pardon—for what is there to hope? If not working for heavenly reward or fearing damnation, what keeps human beings from doing only what they want, when they want? The idea that God and ideology are "dead" (in the sense that neither is enough to justify human action) leaves humans alone with uncertain choices. So, we teachers face an elemental motivational quandary: What is the justification for hope in a world of tired belief systems even as we understand more about human development and the nature of consciousness?

Students need hope to justify the painstaking work of personal transformation and so do their teachers. Lacking hope that life will somehow improve, that perhaps tomorrow will be better than today, students are not motivated to work hard, to search deeply within. They have learned how to look busy, but they are not engaged. In addition to what is on the syllabus, what teachers have to offer students is hope for a better life. Teachers are both coaches and cheerleaders.[24] Instrumental hope, important as it may be, does not, however, carry the weight of the *social* hope that Rorty and Dewey imagine.

Creating and nourishing hope is important for both individuals and the school, which seems straightforward and reasonable. But we ask: "On what values will the community of the school be built and how do those values mesh with those of other social institutions like the family, business, and larger civilization?" The values of different institutions will, in fact, not be compatible. If one cannot assume a common human nature or a common set of moral principles, how is it possible to build that sense of community that isolated individuals, in search of guidance and succor, need so badly? It is at this point, of course, where many explanations signal retreat.

Rorty stands his ground. Consider his philosophical argument for social hope, which takes us to epistemological debates, alluded to earlier, in the natural sciences, social sciences, and humanities in the 1970s and 80s. Rorty argues that the scientific method, which in the nineteenth and twentieth centuries gradually challenged contemporary religious systems of meaning by explaining natural phenomena, has brought manifold benefits, albeit underestimated, even as some, at least, enjoy longer lives and a higher standard of living. Social scientists like Auguste Comte, who also challenged the authority of the Church in state affairs, borrowed positivist assumptions for their work. But the *savants,* as Comte put it, have not been able to demonstrate the predictive validity of the scientific method when applied to human behavior and social problems, leading Foucault and others to suggest that hermeneutic and qualitative methods are preferred.

Rorty argues that neither camp can claim superiority, saying there is no "principled distinction between explanation and understanding, or between two methods, one appropriate for nature and the other for man." Rather, the social sciences and humanities are more continuous than not, simply offering different vocabularies for working on Kuhnian puzzles (rather than hard science versus sloppy subjectivity). Rorty continues, "Vocabularies are useful or useless, good or bad, helpful or misleading, sensitive or coarse, and so on; but they are not 'more objective' or 'less objective' nor more or less 'scientific.'"[25]

To return to social hope, both the social sciences and the humanities serve to enlarge and enrich a sense of human community.[26] Rorty lauds Dewey, in particular, for believing in the moral mission of the social sciences to extend both community and democracy, challenging religious, political, and educational dogma. Rorty praises Dewey, specifically, for having "worked out the vocabulary and rhetoric of American 'pluralism.'" Dewey's ideas made "the first generation of American social scientists think of themselves as apostles of a new form of social life."[27]

Rorty praises Dewey and Foucault for "the attempt to free mankind from [. . . what Nietzsche called mankind's] 'longest lie,' the notion that outside the haphazard and perilous experiments we perform there lies something (God, Science, Knowledge, Rationality, or Truth) which will, if only we perform the correct rituals, step in to save us."[28] In addition to valuing political liberalism, Rorty argues that a tenuous social hope comes not from faith and true belief but, paradoxically, from questioning.

Lab and classroom replace the church, we surmise, because a moral community is fortified, first, by the search for truth, one in which we build a scientific community that cares about such matters. The community is supported, second, by wanting to understand culture and society, thus extending a sense of moral community through studies of forgotten cultures and invisible relationships among social forces. Like Nietzsche, Rorty supports *a provisional hope,* a search for contingent truth to replace true belief, which used to bind communities together, sometimes to disastrous effect.[29]

Have we made too much of ontological questions of social hope and the meaning of life, so readily satirized? Perhaps, but teachers are guardians of hope and new learning, both process and content, and life purposes that slowly emerge in learners. Students in high school and college are trying on different meaning systems, sometimes in quick succession. In campus protests, students can be idealistic and passionate about religious or ideological questions, less inclined than their parents to apologize for an imperfect world and to temporize about how hard it is to affect change. Teachers and counselors should be ready to help students evaluate the content of competing meaning systems with which they are experimenting early in life, and out of which they will construct mature life purposes.

Today's bloody conflict in the Middle East, in particular, leads me to worry about fundamentalist movements both at home and abroad—political or religious, left or right—that are separatist, escapist, and dangerous reactions to modernity and all its contradictions. Surely, individual existence in modern, variegated society is never simple. And we have added that secular humanism brings with it uncertainty and new anxiety. But when religion becomes illiberal and zealots intrude on the rights and beliefs of others, the democratic prospect is put at risk.

So, educators are spiritual mentors who are there to help students in their own search for meaning in the life-project. If we do not recognize this work, students are left vulnerable to political and religious beliefs *du jour,* or a lifetime of civic disengagement. Being a mentor does not mean acting as ideologue or political recruiter, which sometimes happens. As examples of how to live fully, we want to keep our own minds alive, to cultivate that skeptical stance in learners, well captured in the definition of an intellectual attributed to Albert Camus, on the date of his death, January 4, 1960—a person "whose mind watches itself."[30]

New Questions

While writing this book my thinking about motivation and learning changed. I have noted the most important insights, for example, how intermediate range dynamics of attention and awareness are more important than those rare, peak experiences described so well by Maslow and Csikszentmihalyi. New questions, hopefully better questions, have evolved. It is too late in my narrative to do more than sketch a few topics, but I do so to stimulate new theory and research. I never anticipated one insight.

What marvelous information and learning creatures we are! Over many millions of years human beings have evolved to be magnificent, adaptive learners in most, but not all, respects. As I read neurobiology as well as studies of the human mind by Stephen Pinker and Daniel Dennett I came to a new appreciation of evolution and a new connection to other species with which we share so much basic biology. More than ever, I urge anyone close to education—teachers, counselors, administrators, trustees—to study applied behavioral physiology, to evaluate the curriculum from that understanding and to ask students to develop this understanding on their own.

How do we design curricula, keeping in mind the *immense variability* of attention, awareness, and, to a lesser extent, mood? Conventional curricula have been designed as if certain properties of attention, awareness, sleep, and mood systems either were unimportant or existed only to be overcome. Think about the processes, many unconscious and little understood, of the attention system—its potential, limits, and great variability—as it interacts with psychological mood and purposive behavior to give quality to life and work. What is constant is variability and change, not stability; but even so, somehow we learn how to function in that fluid world, probably by creating and interpreting patterns or sets. Empirical studies of what people understand of this variability and how they cope are needed. As educators do we understand the complexity of the information nexus in such situations? Then, too, educators should have working knowledge of neurotransmitters and hormones like testosterone as they affect mood, attention, and activity level, three variables so important in learning.[31]

Curriculum design set aside, we might help students develop a lifelong fascination with applied human physiology, the strengths and limits of the bodies and minds they inhabit. One can, within limits, learn to manage attention and mood, the two most important components of learning. Awareness or consciousness is more subtle than attention or mood but also possible to influence (but, like attention, impossible to control for long). But how one might apply this emerging knowledge of orienting systems is not straightforward. If bored, we cannot instruct—at least not yet—the adrenal gland to release five units of adrenaline to add exhilaration to one's day. But the brain-mind-body can be tricked to the same effect by riding a roller coaster or by putting oneself in danger on a speeding motorcycle.[32] If feeling depressed, we cannot tell ourselves to "feel better" and expect relief. But one can work out for thirty minutes to break a sweat, releasing endorphins and dopamine into the blood, improving mood, at least for a period. Many professionals do exactly this to maintain self-motivation.

My reading project led me to think anew about college as a human stage and the dramaturgic aspects of teaching and learning. I reread Erving Goffman's powerful concepts of role, team performances, and impression management.[33] Thinking about the subtle vagaries of human attention and awareness in class led me to ask about the *social adaptations* by which people feign paying attention, trying to look attentive, motivated to avoid being conspicuous. Young people, in particular, do not like being conspicuous in front of a peer group. Do we help learners understand how and why this works?

Another question surfaces, one I find more interesting than the small subterfuges to protect oneself or the group: Do schools and colleges cultivate *authentic individuality?* If we become hypersensitive to what is right and proper in school and corporate settings, to proper comportment in one or another circumscribed role, where is that independent mind to break through social conventions to challenge the routine? How do schools and colleges develop in students the authentic existence and independent spirit that could change modern society? Partial answers can be found in progressive schools that encourage wide participation in school and college governance, but this should not occur at the expense of other forms of learning, which is the special vulnerability of this type of institution. Can this insight be applied to large-scale educational institutions like universities? Ernest Pascarella and Patrick Terenzini's review of twenty years of research suggests that psychological scale can be achieved, at least partly, at the program or departmental level.[34]

One flawed mental model, in particular, has serious implications for education—the conception that human bodies are separate from the environs in which we move, work, and play. Human beings do not live "beneath the skin" in Dewey's evocative phrase. The ancient, dualistic conception of the body as separate from either the mind or the proximal environment is misleading. Why is this? The reason may be less a failure of logic than the misidentification of the corporal body as a separate thing apart from the stimulus conditions external to it, like the arrangement of the room and its conversations and ideas. We see the material body but not its connectedness. We see the built environment, but not its cues from which the learning organism samples endlessly, learns, and adapts. That is to say, like all living creatures we humans live in incessant, dynamic transactions with the near environment. With evolution of language, abstract thought, and cultural institutions like schools, libraries, and museums, Daniel Dennett reminds us, our species is able to interpret patterns, make meaning out of the information nexus and store these patterns. The remarkable human capacity to seek and learn from patterns has aided species survival and created modernity's rich, contradictory cultures.

Our mental models fail in another way—we underestimate the powerful effects of the built environment on behavior. Think instead about human beings from the "outside in" and the "inside out"—all the many connections between an interpreting, sentient creature managing transactions, half consciously at best, with its problem-posing environment. In these problem-posing environs the creature has to make judgments, to react and move according to changes in stimulus conditions.

The important part of that common term, "human being," is the second word, *being*. If the self is always transactional, both past and present, let us think about the ways we learn and develop while embedded in social networks, real and imagined.[35] What are the implications for personal change and organizational change? We want to reconceptualize how we think about attention, mood, and motivation, especially *the pivotal role that self-observation plays* in forming attitudes and attributions about self as learner. The most important transaction we observe is our ongoing evaluation of our own behavior. That is, social psychologists remind us that a counterintuitive order exists: We pay attention to some object, notice ourselves doing this (eventually), and call the activity fun, wanting to do it again. If we know more about how attention and self-justification work, we can be better learners.

In the same way, let us think about stress, learning, and energy transactions with the near environment. A popular conception of stress is that it is somehow harmful, which is only accurate in the extreme. Rather, moderate and varied stress stimulates and sustains human development because it occasions learning of many different kinds. But how might learning situations, broadly defined, be arranged to create optimal learning? We educators want to create moderately stressful situations in which to live and learn, environments that blend support and challenge in equal measure. Some evidence exists that people under moderate stress produce the hormones to help them become active, to learn better and adapt.[36]

Here is another challenge for new theory. Imagine learning as a developmental process between two or more people, not something that happens inside one person and is best measured there in a reductionist exercise. Individual behavior in teaching and learning could be viewed as a *conjoint construction of two actors, teacher and learner,* in contrast to a psychologically reductionist focus on separate actors and presumed characteristics like being "smart" or "dumb," "lazy" or "motivated." The focus should be the team performance and the "in betweens" in reciprocal human role sets.[37] Another theory challenge surfaces: Can we describe and study the optimal educational outcome where, in a given curriculum, both teacher and student are well motivated and learning? Educators might think of *reciprocal* learning rather than education as a zero-sum game.

Why does learning acquired under certain conditions endure whereas, under other conditions, what we learn seems quickly lost? Answers to this pivotal question will help us design better learning settings. A hint to one answer is found in the educational methods of progressive educators who look for multiple, interacting ways to engage learners. Work experience, personal experience, emotional experience, and cognitive learning in and out of class—all are used to explore a subject. Experience-based methods appear to motivate students better than those found along the narrow cognitive path, creating learning that seems to last longer than that acquired in a conventional, didactic venue. A skeptic might say our earnest educators do not understand why these methods work; but to be fair, many practitioners have effective methods for which their explanations are not valid.

The argument that experience-based learning endures makes intuitive sense, but exactly how or why is less certain. The causal connection between motivation and retained learning, which we have blithely assumed, is not likely to be straightforward, given the body systems involved with both motivation and learning. Does learning last because motivated students work harder? Longer? Do they work in different, more effective ways? Is it time on task, or something about the *quality* of that time, regardless of effort?

Deep learning is always holistic learning, and the reason why is less philosophic than physiologic. We want to make the brain-mind-body move and do work, and in doing so, to set in motion iterative, feedback cycles. Made to work in a certain environs, the brain-mind-body must cope with new information flows, both internal and external, of many sources and channels. By forcing the brain-mind-body to manage its information flows, learning in some degree happens, whether unconscious (at the cellular or muscular level), or highly formal (for example, the mastery of a specific theory). The brain-mind-body, awake or asleep, is always learning, having to adapt to changing information until the organism dies—what varies is direction, intensity, and the body system involved.

If one insight rises well above the rest, it is this: Make the brain-mind-body work! After all, human beings live, work, and, most important, learn in dynamic exchanges with the environment. We respond to what Martin Orne terms the *demand characteristics* of an environment and its social roles.[38] Learning uses the whole body—learning is not exclusively, or even primarily, cognitive, which sounds like heresy to higher educators. Cognitive events are only one of the mind's information sources. The brain-mind-body, so powerful as an all-purpose learning machine, must be made to do its work.

In contemporary education all the specializations work against holistic understanding. As psychologists and educators, we function as specialists called to work on one piece of human experience at a time: physical, cognitive, emotional, spiritual, not to mention the many specializations inside each profession. And few people are comfortable in the other specialist's waiting room. Ellen Langer would remind us that we are applying the wrong mind set to the problem and are not being mindful as learners. The challenge is to think whole, to take the many pieces of human experience and insights from reductionist disciplines and put them together in artful combination.

How we put the brain-mind-body to work makes a difference. We can make a general commitment to learning by enrolling for an advanced degree, joining a club, or trying out for a sport. Conversely, we cannot say, "Learn the concept of relativity now!" and expect a satisfactory outcome. The distinction is this: *General commitments are important in choosing one or another learning situation, but specific commandments to learn this or that concept or skill falsify the way the brain-mind-body works.* The human animal learns best, it seems, when many body systems beyond the merely cognitive are involved doing the work of learning. (I mean work, literally, in the sense of burning calories, forcing new events in the corporal brain and body.) Deep learning, Theodore Marchese and others say, is more likely when many spheres of learning are connected and that integration is active and repeated.[39] Physical, emotional, cognitive, and spiritual anchors—all are needed if we expect new learning to endure and to integrate new knowledge into existing knowledge and behavior.[40]

Another insight comes to mind, this one a cliché that nevertheless picks up an important insight. At so many levels of human existence, the maxim could well be: "Use it or lose it!" From cellular to muscular to character development, the brain-mind-body learns and grows only if stressed and stretched. Stop walking for a period because your leg is in a cast, and muscles atrophy. Even the elementary human action of walking only continues if we practice regularly. Muscles need to be worked, joints moved, fluids sent around the body. This insight will not be news to my middle-age readers who understand all too well how fast certain capacities like running degrade if not practiced. If we understand the intimate connection between person and environs, especially one that stresses us in reasonable measure, we appreciate underlying developmental principles that prolong quality of life. To develop oneself more fully, or to counter the effects of aging, choose environments that put the wondrous brain-mind-body to work.

Interesting implications follow. First, our speculation explains why psychomotor skills like riding a bike, swimming, throwing a ball, or playing the piano endure. Skills get rusty, we forget guiding concepts. But the neuronal network, acting like an old software program, is still resident in long-term memory and can, with practice, be strengthened and extended. We can also account for resistance to changing behaviors like alcohol and drug addiction, violent acting out, and child abuse, all criminal behaviors that involve much more than cognitive schema. Learning has been "burned in" more fully because powerful psychomotor and physiological systems are directly connected.

If this notion is valid, what does it suggest for designing optimal learning settings? First, we want to build rich connections to many facets of being. Learning new concepts is important but is only one source of information for the transducing, interpreting brain-mind-body. If we apply new concepts from work experience, or apply them in experiential exercises in classes that stimulate student emotions, that learning will last longer than learning acquired through one system. In contrast, concepts delivered only by lecture and test lack the full context and rich associations of experiential learning (objective tests also add anxiety). Other things being equal, the pattern has three parts: The more connections we develop, the more developed the neuronal network, the longer learning will last. So, experiential exercises help us in two ways: First, they stimulate intrinsic motivation by students, and second, being rich information feedback environments, they force the brain-mind-body to cope with more information, which will create a greater number of connections.

Coda

This book has explored two problems in living: the nature of human motivation, particularly self-motivation, and, from this understanding, the design of optimal learning settings. It has been both a scholarly and a personal project because my topic, constructing an engaged life in modern times, is not a casual choice. After all, the middle years are a rich period of life where the best use of time, measured in days more than months, and the moral imperative to use one's life fully and well, become paramount. As adults move through the middle years, unmistakable signs of physical decline appear even as we have more discipline and focus than earlier in life. How to use one's life fully in the time that remains becomes a daily concern.

Since beginning the project, I think about being engaged nearly every day, especially while writing or slowing down to read William James, John Dewey, Abraham Maslow, Maxine Greene, Ellen Langer, Mihaly Csikszentmihalyi, and many others we have reviewed who have pursued similar topics. The metaphor may seem odd, but I work the topic as if it were a small garden. I find myself wandering into it, sometimes unintentionally, almost every day, weeding and pruning old concepts to reveal a better form, cultivating the best to try to make them flower, and looking for new pieces to add (and being captured by the best of them), all the while worrying about if—and when—the whole will come together. Several of the examples and metaphors I use occurred to me while I was reflecting on a particular question while driving, or daydreaming while sitting in an interminable faculty meeting. Indeed, one of the most intriguing questions before us has been how attention and awareness work—that is, how the attention system copes with so many channels of incoming information, sorting out threats and opportunities, and how the mind becomes aware and stays aware of its actions. To understand human learning and motivation, we have to have an improved understanding of the ways that attention and mood seem to work. The possibility of achievement, increased learning, and an enhanced quality of life—all seem to connect to how we understand and try to use, if crudely, the attention system to direct awareness.

Somehow I feel caught up by a motive to create the larger work, which integrates personal and professional development (not unlike the hopes teachers in progressive schools have for students working on integrating papers). If only for a few minutes, I pick up the trowel to weed. A footnote is added, or a new sentence. Parts get moved around—I worry about finding the right word. There is always something new to read and I hold my breath, hoping not to find my book revealed to me under a different name. A critic offers advice and I try to bend the argument without breaking it. That is to say, thinking about what makes people become engaged with life has become a daily companion—and it has engaged me. Perhaps the value of writing a book is that it brings a diary to one's hurried life, a structure for awareness. It says to the hurried author, "Write in me. Today!"

Notes

Prologue

1. William James, *Principles of Psychology* (New York: Fawcett Publications, 1963), 208. Cited in David Bakan, *Attention* (Princeton: D. Van Nostrand, 1966), 16. *Compus sui* translates as "master of oneself."
2. Peter Kemp, *Théorie de L'engagement—Pathetique de L'engagement* [Theory of Engagement—Feeling of engagement] (Paris: Seuil, 1973). Consider all the variations in English: 1. To employ or hire; 2. To employ busily or occupy; 3. To hold fast, as in a person's attention; 4. To bind by contract; 5. To arrange beforehand; 6. To interlock two pieces of a mechanism; 7. To come into battle, as in rules of engagement; 8. To take part; 9. To pledge oneself, as in marriage. Julia Swannell, ed., *The Oxford Modern English Dictionary* (Oxford: Clarendon Press. 1993).
3. I am grateful to Maxine Greene for this powerful example, which she uses in her writing and lectures.
4. Psychologists distinguish between states and traits in terms of how long the psychological condition exists and how many facets of personality are implicated. Traits are assumed to be more constant forces in motivation than are temporary, psychological states.
5. Maxine Greene, *Landscapes of Learning* (New York: Teachers College Press, 1978). Greene developed this concept from the thinking of social philosopher Alfred Schutz, *On Phenomenology and Social Relations,* ed. Helmut Wagner (Chicago: University of Chicago Press, 1970); and Schutz with Thomas Luckmann, *The Structures of the Lifeworld* (Evanston, IL: Northwestern University Press, l973).
6. Arthur Chickering and Jackson Kytle, "The Collegiate Ideal in the Twenty-first Century," in *Reconceptualizing the Collegiate Ideal,* ed. J. Douglas Toma and Adrianna Kezar (San Francisco: Jossey-Bass, 1999), 109.
7. See Russell Jacoby's argument about the decline of public intellectuals in *The Last Intellectuals: American Culture in the Age of Academe* (New York: Basic Books, 1987). If educators were more active as public intellectuals outside their school or college walls, we might, in time, see more respect for the profession and less school bashing.
8. Mary C. Bateson, *Composing a Life* (New York: Atlantic Monthly Press, 1989).
9. For more on the Situationists, a small but influential movement of the late 1960s, see Guy Debord, *The Society of the Spectacle* (Detroit: Black and Red, 1977). Or use the web to find sources like the international site of the Situationist Internationale, http://www.nothingness.org/SI/.
10. Edmund V. O'Sullivan, *Transformative Learning: Building Educational Vision for the 21st Century* (London: Zed Press, 1999), 280.

Part I

1. Maxine Greene, *Landscapes of Learning* (New York: Teachers College Press, 1978), 46. (Emphasis added.)
2. Elizabeth Minnich, *Transforming Knowledge* (Philadelphia: Temple University Press, 1990).

Chapter 1

1. President Jimmy Carter quoted by Jim Wooten, "The Conciliator," *New York Times Magazine,* 29 January 1995, 28–54.
2. Of course, religious schools would argue that values are absolutely central to their mission. In that regard, many American independent colleges were started by a religious order. See George D. Kuh and Elizabeth J. Whitt, *The Invisible Tapestry* (Washington, DC: Association for the Study of Higher Education, 1988), 54–55. In the last fifty years or so, most of these have become secular institutions.
3. Gould's fascinating life and music have been studied. See a website in his name maintained by the National Library of Canada: http://www.gould.nic-bnc.ca/. Jonathan Cott, *Conversations with Glenn Gould* (Boston: Little, Brown & Company, 1984).
4. To expand the concept, think of the life-project as a personal construction site. Everyone builds a personal shelter for existence. Every day brings planning, hard work, mistakes, and new work orders. No sooner is the structure up than daily maintenance is required.
5. According to Helmut Wagner, life-world is Edmund Husserl's concept, which Alfred Schutz treated as the whole array of experiences in daily life in which people subjectively understand the world and act in it. It is a person's fundamental reality. Alfred Schutz, *On Phenomenology and Social Relations,* ed. Helmut Wagner (Chicago: University of Chicago Press, 1970), 14.
6. John Dewey, *Democracy and Education* (New York: Macmillan, 1961).
7. Benjamin Barber, *A Passion for Democracy* (Princeton: Princeton University Press, 1998), 185.
8. Paul L. Wachtel, *The Poverty of Affluence* (New York: Free Press, 1983).
9. Jurgen Habermas, *Legitimation Crisis* (Boston: Beacon Press, 1973), 75.
10. I am grateful to Professor Absher of Norwich Vermont College who made this point in a lecture on creative writing. Absher argued that the best writing reflects a Socratic search for truth, both in terms of breaking through the clichés we create around our experience that hide that experience from ourselves and others, and those clustered about the subject. He talked about *volte* in writing, turning the subject endlessly for a fresh look on both dimensions (the narrative and the subject). The reader demands something new and authentic, both in the narrative and the subject.
11. To cite a few, Fritz Heider, *The Psychology of Interpersonal Relations* (New York: Wiley and Sons, 1958); John Bowlby, *Attachment and Loss* (New York: Basic Books, 1969); Peter Senge, *The Fifth Discipline: The Art and Practice of the Learning Organization* (New York: Doubleday/Currency, 1990); Scott G. Paris and Richard S. Newman, "Developmental Aspects of Self-regulated Learning," *Educational Psychologist* 25, no. 1 (1990): 87–102.

12. While mental models are usually conceived as being cognitive representations, that might not be quite right because the brain-mind-body creates patterns that connect to emotional and motor systems.

13. Senge, *The Fifth Discipline.* Bowlby, in *Attachment and Loss,* prefers to say "working models," presumably to note the provisional nature of such representations.

14. Alexander Astin argues that many educators are not well prepared for teaching and they treat teaching as a black box, meaning internal events are obscure. Alexander Astin, *Achieving Educational Excellence* (San Francisco: Jossey-Bass, 1985), 135.

15. Frank Smith, *To Think* (New York: Teachers College Press, 1990).

16. Melvin Miller asserts a theory of the evolution of worldviews in "World Views, Ego Development, and Epistemological Changes from the Conventional to the Postformal: A Longitudinal Perspective," in *Transcendence and Mature Thought in Adulthood,* ed. Melvin E. Miller and Susanne R. Cook-Greuter (Lanham, MD: Rowman & Littlefield, 1994).

17. Theodore J. Marchese, "The New Conversations about Learning: Insights from Neuroscience and Anthropology, Cognitive Science and Work-Place Studies," *Assessing Impact: Evidence and Action* (Washington, DC: American Association for Higher Education, 1997).

18. Wendy Kohli observes that existential becoming is a central category in Greene's thinking in her essay "Philosopher of/for Freedom," in *A Light in Dark Times: Maxine Greene and the Unfinished Conversation,* ed. William Ayers and Janet L. Miller (New York: Teachers College Press, 1998).

19. Maxine Greene, "Revisioning John Dewey," lecture at the University of Vermont, 20 October 1997.

20. Maxine Greene, *Releasing the Imagination* (San Francisco: Jossey-Bass, 1995).

21. Ivan Illich, *Deschooling Society* (New York: Harper & Row, 1971).

22. Seymour Sarason, *Revisiting "The Culture of the School and the Problem of Change"* (New York: Teachers College Press, 1996), 386.

23. Donald Schön, *The Reflective Practitioner* (New York: Basic Books, 1983).

24. Robert Enright, "Michals the Archangel, an Interview with Duane Michals," *BorderCrossings* 17, no. 4 (1998): 14–28.

25. Richard Hofstatder, *Anti-intellectualism in American Life* (New York: Knopf, 1963).

26. One can see this in the difficulties that second-generation followers of counseling or teaching fads have achieving the success of charismatic founders who are not able to articulate their theories-in-use, or whose espoused theories are wrong because they misattribute the reasons for how their "system" works.

27. There are other literatures and perspectives to consider. Classic alienation theory: Richard Schacht, *The Future of Alienation* (Urbana, IL: University of Illinois Press, 1994). Dialectical learning: Paulo Freire, *Pedagogy of the Oppressed* (New York: Seabury, 1973). Self-directed learning: Stephen Brookfield, ed., *Self-directed Learning: From Theory to Practice* (San Francisco: Jossey-Bass, 1985).

28. Friedrich Nietzsche, *On the Genealogy of Morals and Ecce Homo,* trans. Walter Kaufman and R. J. Hollindale, ed. Walter Kaufman (New York: Vintage, 1967), 555.

29. Richard Rorty, "Method, Social Science, and Social Hope," in *The Postmodern Turn,* ed. Stephen Seidman (New York: Cambridge University Press, 1994), 105.

30. Sarason, *Revisiting "The Culture of the School and the Problem of Change."*

31. Greene, *Landscapes of Learning*.
32. Maurice Natanson, ed., *The Problem of Social Reality, Collected Papers 1* (The Hague: Martinus Nijhoff, 1967), 213.
33. Parker Palmer, *The Courage to Teach* (San Francisco: Jossey-Bass, 1998), 7.
34. Palmer, *The Courage to Teach,* 37. I admire Palmer's humanistic, spiritual perspective on education but worry about the extent to which the enlightened teacher's persona becomes yet another impediment to learning, if that soft authority dominates the group. Students can learn a great deal from autocrats and imperfect authorities who invest themselves fully in teaching.
35. Virginia Woolf, *Three Guineas* (New York: Harcourt Brace, 1938).
36. Elizabeth Minnich, *Transforming Knowledge* (Philadelphia: Temple University Press, 1990).
37. Bertell Ollman, *Alienation,* 2d. ed. (New York: Cambridge University Press, 1976).
38. Rorty, "Method, Social Science, and Social Hope."
39. Thanks to Richard J. Bernstein, Dean of the Graduate Faculty, New School University, for this idea, which is discussed in his *Hannah Arendt and the Jewish Question* (Cambridge, MA: MIT Press, 1996).
40. Frank Smith, *The Book of Learning and Forgetting* (New York: Teachers College Press, 1998).
41. Michel Foucault, *Power/Knowledge* (New York: Macmillan, 1980).
42. Astin, *Achieving Educational Excellence*.
43. Phenomenology is an important topic in philosophy and I draw upon only a few elements. For example, see Schutz, *Alfred Schutz: On Phenomenology and Social Relations*.

Chapter 2

1. Parker Palmer, *The Courage to Teach* (San Francisco: Jossey-Bass, 1998), 6. (Emphasis added.)
2. John Taylor Gatto, "Against School: How Public Education Cripples Our Kids, and Why," *Harper's Magazine,* September 2003, 33–38. Gatto, a sharp critic of contemporary education, faults compulsory public education. But what is the alternative, given the diversity of needs in modern society? The problem is less the compulsory part than what we do with the curriculum, its purposes, and design.
3. Arthur Chickering and Jackson Kytle, "The Collegiate Ideal in the Twenty-first Century," in *Reconceptualizing the Collegiate Ideal,* ed. J. Douglas Toma and Adrianna Kezar (San Francisco: Jossey-Bass, 1999).
4. Data taken from 1999 HERI survey of student attitudes. Survey responses of 261,217 freshmen who entered 462 two-year and four-year institutions in the fall. Adjusted data to represent population of 1.64 million, first-time, full-time freshmen. Available on the Internet at http://www.gseis.ucla.edu/heri or 3005 Moon Hall, UCLA, Box 951521 LA CA 90095–1521.
5. Arthur Levine and Jeanette S. Cureton, *When Hope and Fear Collide: A Portrait of Today's College Student* (San Francisco: Jossey-Bass, 1998).
6. Levine and Cureton, *When Hope and Fear Collide,* 157.
7. Palmer, *The Courage to Teach,* 17–21.

8. Academic Roundtable held by the New England Resource Center for Higher Education, sponsored by the University of Massachusetts at Boston.

9. Alan Guskin, personal communication with the author, 2000.

10. Robert B. Barr and John Tagg, "From Teaching to Learning: A New Paradigm for Undergraduate Education," *Change* 27, no. 6 (1995): 12–14.

11. Sarason argues that elementary and secondary schools have not adapted to social changes of the post–World War II era. Seymour Sarason, *Revisiting "The Culture of the School and the Problem of Change"* (New York: Teachers College Press, 1996).

12. Robert D. Putnam, *Bowling Alone: The Collapse and Revival of American Community* (New York: Simon & Schuster, 2000).

13. Deborah Meier, *In Schools We Trust: Creating Communities of Learning in an Era of Testing and Standardization* (Boston: Beacon Press, 2002).

14. Meier, *In Schools We Trust,* 5.

15. Edmund V. O'Sullivan, Amish Morrell, and Mary Ann O'Connor, eds., *Expanding the Boundaries of Transformative Learning* (New York: Palgrave, 2002), 4.

16. O'Sullivan, Morrell, and O'Connor, *Expanding the Boundaries of Transformative Learning,* 4–5.

17. See Benjamin Barber, *A Passion for Democracy* (Princeton: Princeton University Press, 1998), 214–224.

18. Sarason, *Revisiting "The Culture of the School and the Problem of Change,"* 379.

19. Ernest T. Pascarella and Patrick T. Terenzini, *How College Affects Students: Findings and Insights from Twenty Years of Research* (San Francisco: Jossey-Bass, 1991), 610.

20. Ernest Boyer, *College* (New York: Harper & Row, 1987), 2.

21. Arthur Chickering, personal communication with the author, 2000.

22. Deborah Meier, *The Power of Their Ideas* (Boston: Beacon Press, 1995).

23. Deborah Meier, "Educating a Democracy: Standards and the Future of Public Education," 2002, 5. Available on the Internet at http://www.bostonreview. mit.edu/BR24.6/ Originally published in the February/March 2000 issue of *Boston Review.*

24. Theodore Sizer, *Horace's Compromise* (Boston: Houghton Mifflin, 1984).

25. Theodore Sizer, *Horace's Hope: What Works for the American High School* (Boston: Houghton Mifflin, 1996). Long an advocate of alternative education, Sizer and his wife agreed to be co-principals of Parker, a new junior and senior high school founded on progressive principles such as employing individualized learning, empowering students and teachers in the school, and using exhibitions to demonstrate mastery rather than depend upon passing tests. See James Traub, "Sizer's Hope," *New York Times Educational Supplement,* 2 August 2 1998, 26.

26. A young woman I know works in a local deli on her off hours to supplement a rural teacher's salary. A social studies teacher, she has five classes a day of thirty students each, not counting administrative meetings. How much individual attention can her students get? What will happen to her enthusiasm and idealism for teaching under such a teaching load?

27. An anecdote related in *Shaping the Future,* a report on college math and science instruction by the National Research Council, 1996. Information on the National Research Council is available at http://www.nas.edu/nrc.

28. Barber, *A Passion for Democracy.*

29. Lewis Lapham, "Notebook: School Bells," *Harper's Magazine,* August 2000: 7–9.

Chapter 3

1. John Dewey, *Experience and Education* (New York: Macmillan, 1963), 49.
2. On alienation, see Richard Schacht, *The Future of Alienation* (Urbana, IL: University of Illinois Press, 1994). Carol S. Dweck, "Motivational Processes Affecting Learning," *American Psychologist* 41 (1986): 1040–1048.
3. William James, *The Varieties of Religious Experience* (New York: Modern Library, 1958).
4. James, *The Varieties of Religious Experience,* 243.
5. James, *The Varieties of Religious Experience,* 284.
6. See Stephen Rockefeller, *John Dewey: Religious Faith and Democratic Humanism* (New York: Columbia University Press, 1991); Robert B. Westbrook, *John Dewey and American Democracy* (Ithaca, NY: Cornell University Press, 1991); Louis Menand, *The Metaphysical Club* (New York: Farrar, Straus & Giroux, 2001); James Garrison, *Dewey and Eros* (New York: Teachers College Press, 1997); Stephen Fishman and Lucille McCarthy, *John Dewey and the Challenge of Classroom Practice* (New York: Teachers College Press, 1998).
7. Taken from Greene's 1997 lecture, "Revisioning John Dewey," on the occasion of John Dewey's birthday at the University of Vermont, Burlington, Dewey's birthplace, 20 October 1997.
8. Dewey, *Experience and Education,* 5. Later, on page 30, he puts the goal differently, writing of his search for "a coherent theory of experience, affording positive direction to selection and organization of appropriate educational methods and materials."
9. David Kolb makes the same point in *Experiential Learning* (Englewood Cliffs, NJ: Prentice-Hall, 1984).
10. Peter S. Hlebowitsh, *Radical Curriculum Theory Reconsidered: A Historical Approach* (New York: Teachers College Press, 1993). In addition to Dewey's endorsement of the scientific method and experimentation in education, Garrison comments on a intuitive, humanistic spirit of inquiry in Dewey's thinking in *Dewey and Eros.*
11. Dewey, *Experience and Education.*
12. Dewey, *Experience and Education,* 25.
13. Kolb extended Dewey's interest in experiential learning by developing a two-dimensional model of the learning *process,* leading to four learning modes: concrete experience, reflective observation, abstract conceptualization, and active experimentation, which are measured by the Learning Styles Inventory, widely used in adult education. Like Dewey and others we discuss, Kolb believes that learning is best conceived as a process—not in terms of fixed outcomes but as the result of continuous transactions between person and environment.
14. Dewey, *Experience and Education,* 27.
15. Dewey, *Experience and Education,* 27–28.
16. Dewey, *Experience and Education,* 37–38.
17. Jackson Kytle, "An Education Up Close and Personal," in *Progressive Education for the Nineties and Beyond,* ed. Wilfred Hamlin (Plainfield, VT: Goddard College, 1993).
18. Dewey, *Experience and Education,* 72.
19. Dewey, *Experience and Education,* 38.
20. John Dewey, *Art as Experience* (New York: Capricorn Books, 1958), 13. (Emphasis added.)

21. Dewey, *Experience and Education*, 39.
22. Dewey, *Experience and Education*, 43.
23. Dewey, *Experience and Education*, 45.
24. Until recently, accreditation associations and professional associations like the American Bar Association have weighed objective, input variables more heavily than process variables like motivation. The recent interest in moving away from input measures, like size of library, faculty credentials, and number of courses, to outcome measures allows more freedom in the way students and teachers construct learning situations.
25. Dewey, *Experience and Education*, 60.
26. Dewey, *Experience and Education*, 60.
27. Dewey, *Experience and Education*, 72.
28. For two applications of this idea, see Donald Schön, *The Reflective Practitioner* (New York: Basic Books, 1983); Laurent Daloz, *Effective Teaching and Mentoring* (San Francisco: Jossey-Bass, 1986).
29. All quotes from Dewey, *Experience and Education*, 18–19.
30. Attributed to Tim Pitkin. For more on Goddard and Pitkin, see Ann Benson and Frank Adams, *To Know for Real* (Adamant, VT: Adamant Press, 1987) and Wilfred Hamlin, ed., *Progressive Education for the Nineties and Beyond* (Plainfield, VT: Goddard College, 1993).
31. Dewey, *Experience and Education*, 67.
32. Hlebowitsh, *Radical Curriculum Theory Reconsidered*.
33. Dewey, *Experience and Education*, 48.
34. Dewey, *Experience and Education*, 22–23.
35. The first wave of progressive reform occurred in the 1930s, leading to the revitalization of Goddard, Bennington, and Sarah Lawrence, and the founding of Black Mountain. The second wave, thirty years later, created schools like Hampshire College, Evergreen State College, and New College (one in Florida and a separate one in San Francisco), and a host of progressive schools whose students were working adults, chiefly the off-campus Antioch units, Fielding Institute, Saybrook Institute, and the Union Institute, created at a conference organized by Goddard and Antioch. For more information on the history of progressive schools, see Lawrence Cremin, *The Transformation of the School* (New York: Vintage Books, 1964); Martin Duberman, *An Exploration in Community* (New York: Dutton, 1972); Gerald Grant and David Riesman, *The Perpetual Dream* (Chicago: University of Chicago Press, 1977); Forest Davis, *Things Were Different in Royce's Day* (Adamant, VT: Adamant Press, 1996).
36. Hlebowitsh, *Radical Curriculum Theory Reconsidered*, 66.
37. Hlebowitsh acknowledges the idealism of what he calls the progressive-experimentalist vision but is worried about excesses of the critical theory approach to curriculum theory because of its authoritarianism and unwillingness to adapt to the needs of real schools (see Hlebowitsh, *Radical Curriculum Theory Reconsidered*, 46) and the general threats that radical challenges pose to the democratic institution of the public school. Of critical theorists he says: "radical commentators have written much about how schools fail to abide by a visionary and enlightened ideal, but they have also left us with little in the way of solutions that might work within the social and political realities of our schools" (46).
38. See Dewey, *Experience and Education*, 89–90.
39. Abraham Maslow, *Religions, Values, and Peak Experiences* (New York: Penguin Books, 1977), 91–94.

40. Abraham Maslow, *Toward a Psychology of Being* (New York: Van Nostrand Reinhold Company, 1968), 114.

41. Maslow, *Religions, Values, and Peak Experiences,* 65.

42. For a comparable account of peak experience interpreted in religious terms, sometimes called the experience of the numinous, see Thomas Moore, *The Re-enchantment of Everyday Life* (New York: HarperCollins, 1996). We return to this topic in Part II.

43. Abraham Maslow, *The Farther Reaches of Human Nature* (New York: Penguin Arkana, 1993).

44. Abraham Maslow, "Deficiency Motivation and Growth Motivation," *Nebraska Symposium on Motivation* 3 (1955): 14.

45. Maslow, "Deficiency Motivation and Growth Motivation," 25.

46. Maslow, *Toward a Psychology of Being,* 115.

47. Maslow, *Toward a Psychology of Being,* 193.

48. Maslow, *Toward a Psychology of Being,* 210.

49. Maslow, *Toward a Psychology of Being,* 160.

50. Mihaly Csikszentmihalyi acknowledges the similarity of his work to Maslow's theory of peak experience in *The Evolving Self* (New York: HarperCollins, 1993).

51. Mihaly Csikszentmihalyi, *Flow* (New York: HarperPerennial, 1991), xi.

52. Mihaly Csikszentmihalyi, *Finding Flow* (New York: Basic Books, 1997), 28, 29, and 2.

53. Csikszentmihalyi, *Finding Flow,* 2.

54. Csikszentmihalyi, *Flow,* 31.

55. Csikszentmihalyi, *Finding Flow,* 26.

56. Csikszentmihalyi, *The Evolving Self,* 33.

57. Csikszentmihalyi, *Finding Flow,* 31.

58. Csikszentmihalyi, *Finding Flow,* 31.

59. Csikszentmihalyi, *Finding Flow,* 128.

60. Csikszentmihalyi, *Finding Flow,* 68.

61. Csikszentmihalyi, *Finding Flow,* 81.

62. Csikszentmihalyi, *Finding Flow,* 115.

63. Csikszentmihalyi, *Finding Flow,* 32, 131–132, 141.

64. Csikszentmihalyi also speculates about the transcendent self as an ideal self, referring to a person whose "psychic energy is joyfully invested in complex goals" in *The Evolving Self,* 208.

65. Ellen Langer, *Mindfulness* (Reading, PA: Addison-Wesley, 1998), 57.

66. See Ellen Langer, *The Power of Mindful Learning* (Reading, PA: Addison-Wesley, 1997), 63–64.

67. In Langer's most recent book, she makes no reference to the philosophy or practice of progressive education even though many of her insights and findings are relevant.

68. Langer, *The Power of Mindful Learning,* 13.

69. Langer, *The Power of Mindful Learning,* 137.

70. See William Kahn, "The Psychological Condition of Personal Engagement and Disengagement at Work," *Academy of Management Journal* 33, no. 4 (1990): 692–724 and "To Be Fully There: Psychological Presence at Work," *Human Relations* 45, no. 4 (1992): 321–345. It would be interesting to apply Tavistock concepts to how students learn and express themselves inside the formal role of student.

71. The extensive literature on alienated labor has been "forgotten" by contemporary management literature. The early Marx had powerful insights into the way

workers can be alienated from control of their labor with parallel separations from relations with fellow workers and the nature of language.

72. Charles Guignon and Dirk Pereboom are less convinced than I am about the implicit morality of existentialism. They note the argument that existentialism is a privileged discourse of the Western elite who focus on personal authenticity more than social justice. Charles Guignon and Dirk Pereboom, eds., *Existentialism: Basic Writings* (Indianapolis, IN: Hackett Publishing,1995), xxxvi-xxxvii. While there is no explicit morality, perhaps, social motives are important in Heidegger's theory, Nietzsche's protests on behalf of the common person, Camus's books, and Greene's request that we be awake in the world. That Heidegger once belonged to the Nazi party and that Nietzsche expressed anti-Semitic views complicates our evaluation of their theories and lives.

73. Blaise Pascal, *Thoughts,* trans. W. F. Trotter. (New York: P.F. Collier & Son Company, 1910), 78. Also cited in William Barrett, *What Is Existentialism?* (New York: Gross Press, 1964), 77.

74. A good starting point for reading Nietzsche is "Thus Spake Zarathustra," *The Portable Nietzsche,* ed. Walter Kaufmann (New York: Viking Penguin, 1982).

75. Albert Camus, *The Stranger* (New York: Alfred A. Knopf, 1942).

76. For a history of these changes, see Robert Nisbet, *The Social Philosophers* (New York: Thomas Y. Crowell Company, 1973).

77. Edmund O'Sullivan, Amish Morrell, and Mary Ann O'Connor discuss spiritual issues at length in *Expanding the Boundaries of Transformative Learning* (New York: Palgrave, 2002). For an example of a self-help approach to restoring a close relationship with life, see Thomas Moore, *The Re-enchantment of Everyday Life* (New York: HarperCollins, 1996).

78. Max Weber, *The Protestant Ethic and the Spirit of Capitalism* (New York: Charles Scribner's Sons, 1958).

79. See Friedrich Nietzsche, *The Gay Science* (New York: Vintage Books, 1974), 279.

80. Tony Judt calls Camus a model public intellectual. Camus had edited *Combat,* the French resistance paper in Word War II. "On 'The Plague,'" *The New York Review,* 29 November 2001, 6–9.

81. Maxine Greene, *Teacher as Stranger* (Belmont, CA: Wadsworth Publishing, 1973).

82. Albert Camus, *Albert Camus: Lyrical and Critical Essays,* edited by Philip Thody (New York: Vintage Books, 1970), 342. (Emphasis added.)

83. Guignon and Pereboom, *Existentialism: Basic Writings.* Compare their notion of predicament to Dewey's idea of the learning situation.

84. Jurgen Habermas, *Legitimation Crisis* (Boston: Beacon Press, 1973), 37.

85. Christopher Lasch, *The Culture of Narcissism* (New York: Norton, 1979); Paul L. Wachtel, *The Poverty of Affluence* (New York: Free Press, 1983); Michael Ignatieff, *The Needs of Strangers* (New York: Viking Penguin, 1985); Neil Postman, *Amusing Ourselves to Death: Public Discourse in the Age of Show Business* (New York: Penguin, 1985); Kenneth Gergen, *The Saturated Self* (New York: BasicBooks, 1991); Zygmunt Bauman, *Liquid Modernity* (Cambridge, MA: Polity Press, 2000).

86. See the underground anarchist text produced by the Situationist activist Guy Debord, *The Society of the Spectacle* (Detroit: Black and Red, 1977). For a broad collection of articles, see Ken Knabb, ed., *Situationist International Anthology* (Berkeley, CA: Bureau of Public Secrets, P.O. 1044, 1981).

87. For critiques of consumer society, see Debord, *The Society of the Spectacle*; Wachtel, *The Poverty of Affluence*; Andrew Schmookler, *Fool's Gold: The Fate*

of Values in a World of Goods (New York: HarperSanFrancisco, 1993); Benjamin Barber, *Jihad vs. McWorld* (New York: Ballantine Books, 1996). To read how retail stores study and manipulate consumers, see Paco Underhill, *Why We Buy: The Science of Shopping* (New York: Simon & Schuster, 1999).

88. Maxine Greene, *The Dialectic of Freedom* (New York: Teachers College Press, 1988), 3.

89. Jean-Paul Sartre, *Being and Nothingness* (New York: Gramercy Books, 1994). For an introduction to Martin Heidegger, see his *What Is Called Thinking?* (New York: Harper Torchbooks, 1968).

90. Albert Camus, *The Plague* (New York: Knopf, 1972), 6.

91. A reader has pointed out to me that my choice of authors, rather conveniently perhaps, leaves out religious existentialists like Soren Kierkegaard, Nicholas Berdyaev, Gabriel Marcel, Karl Jaspers, and others. These thinkers struggled with religious faith and meaning in life in ways that my summary does not acknowledge. My colleague also worries that in several places I discredit religious belief when, in fact, the existence of God is as much a faith statement as atheism. All this may be true, but religious belief systems still function psychologically in the same way that political belief systems do.

92. Maxine Greene, "Revisioning John Dewey," lecture at the University of Vermont, 20 October 1997.

93. Quotes from Greene, *The Dialectic of Freedom*, 2–3. Also, see Maxine Greene, *Releasing the Imagination* (San Francisco: Jossey-Bass, 1995); William Ayers and Janet Miller, eds., *A Light in Dark Times: Maxine Greene and the Unfinished Conversation* (New York: Teachers College Press, 1998).

94. Greene, "Revisioning John Dewey."

Part II

1. Lance Armstrong, *It's Not About the Bike* (New York: Putnam Publishing Group, 2000), 5. Armstrong's racing success has made him wealthy. The U.S. Postal Service "brand" has received widespread publicity and signed him to a four-year contract estimated at $25 million. Armstrong's hardcover book about his struggle with cancer spent forty weeks on *The New York Times* best-seller list, with 500,000 copies in print.

2. High altitude mountain climbing has attracted popular attention. Avoiding the possibility of death demands the highest concentration. For accounts, see Jon Krakauer, *Eiger Dreams: Ventures Among Men and Mountains* (New York: Anchor Books, 1990) and Jon Kaukauer, *Into Thin Air* (New York: Villard, 1997).

3. Armstrong, *It's Not About the Bike*, 5.

4. Armstrong, *It's Not About the Bike*, 49. (Emphasis added.)

5. Eliot Aronson, *The Social Animal*, 8th ed. (New York: Worth Publishers, 1999).

6. Candace Pert, *Molecules of Emotion* (New York: Scribner, 1997), 185.

7. Pert, *Molecules of Emotion*, 189.

8. Daniel Dennett, *Kinds of Minds* (New York: Basic Books, 1996), 74. My analysis here and elsewhere leans heavily on this thinking.

9. Dennett, *Kinds of Minds*, 72. He writes about the "Myth of Double Transduction"—that the brain somehow transduces neural signals into the "mysterious, nonphysical medium of the mind."

10. Also see Renate N. Caine and Geoffrey Caine, *Making Connections: Teaching and the Human Brain* (Reading, PA: Addison-Wesley, 1994).

11. The nature of the mind is a massive, difficult topic not considered here. For a representative collection of philosophical articles, see David M. Rosenthal, *The Nature of Mind* (New York: Oxford University Press, 1991).

12. Pert, *Molecules of Emotion,* 185. She speculates that "mind is the flow of information as it moves among the cells, organs, and systems of the body." Her explanation, while better than "the brain," does not tell us much about why or how this works. Kandel and colleagues suggest that studies of visual attention may provide ideas about conscious awareness. Evidence points away from a master area, or a grand synthesis, and more toward distributed, multistage processing about which little is known. Eric R. Kandel, James H. Schwartz, and Thomas M. Jessell, eds., *Essentials of Neural Science and Behavior* (Norwalk, CT: Appleton & Lange, 1995), 504.

13. Kandel, Schwartz, and Jessell, eds., *Essentials of Neural Science and Behavior,* 690. For a specialized discussion of anatomical structures, properties of neuronal pathways, and cell functions and chemistry, see this text and a more technical source, Kandel, Schwartz and Jessell, eds., *Principles of Neural Science,* 4th ed. (New York: McGraw-Hill, 2000).

14. See Dennett, *Kinds of Minds* and Rosenthal, *The Nature of Mind*; also John Searle, *The Mystery of Consciousness* (New York: New York Review Book, 1997); Stephen Pinker, *How the Mind Works* (New York: W.W. Norton, 1997); Richard Ornstein, *The Right Mind* (New York: Harcourt Brace & Co., 1997).

Chapter 4

1. Jerome Bruner, *In Search of Mind: Essays in Autobiography* (New York: Harper and Row, 1983), 66.

2. For an example, see Richard Ornstein, *The Right Mind* (New York: Harcourt Brace & Co., 1997).

3. My discussion borrows liberally from Dennett's theory of information transducing in human behavior and is informed by Pert's discussion of the role of neuropeptides in emotions. Daniel Dennett, *Kinds of Minds* (New York: Basic Books, 1996), and Candace Pert, *Molecules of Emotion* (New York: Scribner, 1997).

4. Pert, *Molecules of Emotion,* 194.

5. Eric R. Kandel, James H. Schwartz, and Thomas M. Jessell, eds., *Essentials of Neural Science and Behavior* (Norwalk, CT: Appleton & Lange, 1995).

6. Stephen Pinker observes that most of these systems have evolved because they help us learn and adapt. Also, current estimates are that life began in one form 3.5 billion years ago and through speciation, which requires millions of years and for which there is little direct evidence, 10 million species exist today (*World Book,* 1999).

7. Kandel, Schwartz, and Jessell, *Essentials of Neural Science and Behavior.*

8. Unless otherwise noted, my description depends upon Kandel, Schwartz and Jessell, *Essentials of Neural Science and Behavior,* and, to a lesser extent, on Eric R. Kandel, James H. Schwartz and Thomas M. Jessell, *Principles of Neural Science,* 4th ed. (New York: McGraw-Hill, 2000).

9. Bruner, *In Search of Mind,* 100.

10. Neuromuscular communication is not as complex as signaling among central neurons, which involves more varied transmitters, both excitatory and inhibitory functions, and different types of ion channels.

11. Dennett, *Kinds of Minds,* 72.

12. The molecular keys that unlock the gates that control transaction between nerve cells at the synaptic junctions are glutamate molecules, dopamine molecules, and norepinephrine molecules, among others.

13. Kandel, Schwartz, and Jessell, *Principles of Neural Science,* 251.

14. Kandel, Schwartz, and Jessell, *Essentials of Neural Science and Behavior,* 200.

15. Psychologists have studied individual differences in reactivity to external stimuli. See Herman Witkin's concept of field dependence. Herman A. Witkin and Philip K. Oltman, "Cognitive Style," *International Journal of Neurology* 6, (1967): 119–137, and Stanley Schachter, "The Interaction of Cognitive and Physiological Determinants of Emotional States," in *Advances in Experimental Social Psychology,* vol. 1, ed. Leonard Berkowitz (New York: Academic Press, 1964), 49–80.

16. In *Molecules of Emotion,* Pert describes contemporary research focuses on the nature of the neurotransmitter molecules—one type of information molecule called ligands—as they inhibit or accelerate the signal. Ligands are distributed though the brain and body where the main information channels are the nervous, blood, and cerebrospinal fluid systems.

17. Pert describes receptor molecules as made of strings of peptides made, in turn, of amino acids "strung together in crumpled chains, looking something like beaded necklaces that folded in on themselves." Pert, *Molecules of Emotion,* 22.

18. Pert's book *Molecules of Emotion* is fascinating for its mix of her work on peptides and emotional states, her struggle as a woman scientist, and her growing interest in holistic health.

19. Pert, *Molecules of Emotion,* 145.

20. From at least the time of Wundt, the properties of sensation have fascinated psychologists under the general topic of psychophysics.

21. Kandel, Schwartz, and Jessell, *Essentials of Neural Science and Behavior,* 656.

22. Thanks for this image to Professor William Hirst of New School University.

23. Kandel, Schwartz, and Jessell, *Essentials of Neural Science and Behavior,* 656.

24. See Renate N. Caine and Geoffrey Caine, *Making Connections: Teaching and the Human Brain* (Reading, PA: Addison-Wesley, 1994).

25. Kandel, Schwartz, and Jessell, *Essentials of Neural Science and Behavior,* 670.

26. Kandel, Schwartz, and Jessell, *Essentials of Neural Science and Behavior,* 664–665.

27. Kandel, Schwartz and Jessell, *Essentials of Neural Science and Behavior,* 665.

28. Kandel, Schwartz, and Jessell, *Essentials of Neural Science and Behavior,* 690.

29. J. Allan Hobson, *The Chemistry of Conscious States* (Boston: Little, Brown & Company, 1994). However, Kandel, Schwartz and Jessell, in *Essentials of Neural Science and Behavior,* would argue that no current theory of the functions of sleep receives unequivocal support. See page 945.

30. When evaluating theory *qua* theory, the principle of Ockham's razor asserts that parsimonious theories are preferred, other things being equal, because they carry fewer assumptions.

31. Scientific research has contributed little to uncovering hidden, Freudian meanings in dreams. Kandel, Schwartz and Jessell, *Principles of Neural Science,* 946.

32. Kandel, Schwartz, and Jessell, *Essentials of Neural Science and Behavior,* 671.

33. Bruner, *In Search of Mind,* 278.

34. Mihaly Csikszentmihalyi, *Flow* (New York: HarperPerennial, 1991).

35. Peter Milner, *Physiological Psychology* (New York: Holt, Rinehart and Winston, 1970).

36. Pain does not remain in long-term memory the way one might think. Mercifully, we seem to forget the full intensity and dimensions of pain like breaking a leg or childbirth although we remember *that* it was painful.

37. Hobson, *The Chemistry of Conscious States,* 167.

38. Bruner, *In Search of Mind,* 276.

39. Hobson, *The Chemistry of Conscious States,* 176.

40. Kandel, Schwartz, and Jessell, *Essentials of Neural Science and Behavior,* 656–661.

41. We cannot consider here an important relationship between genes, their expression and transcription and environmental influences that produce abnormal proteins, giving rise to disease and eventually cell transformation. For an introductory discussion, see Kandel, Schwartz, and Jessell, *Essentials of Neural Science and Behavior,* 693.

42. Dennett, *Kinds of Minds,* 55.

43. Dennett, *Kinds of Minds,* 157.

44. Kandell, Schwartz, and Jessell, *Principles of Neural Science,* 1318.

45. Although intentional behavior is observable in other species, Dennett notes that other species have remarkable gaps compared to humans, most notably the ability to test hypotheses about possible threats and to preserve higher representations of that experience.

46. Bruner, *In Search of Mind,* 278.

47. Dennett, *Kinds of Minds,* 134.

48. Dennett, *Kinds of Minds,* 139.

49. Kandel, Schwartz, and Jessell, *Essentials of Neural Science and Behavior,* 614.

50. Contemporary theory posits physiological servomechanisms that control homeostatic systems. A variable like thirst has a certain range, a feedback detector, a set point about a value, and an error detector (like a thermostat). See Kandel, Schwartz, and Jessell, *Essentials of Neural Science and Behavior,* 614–615.

51. Lesion studies support the theory that the hypothalamus and its substructures (the amygdala in the limbic system) are the coordinating center, processing organized inputs and well-organized response. The amygdala is required for effective place conditioning by which animals increase contact with safe zones and decrease contact with dangerous environments. Kandel, Schwartz, and Jessell, *Essentials of Neural Science and Behavior,* 607–610.

52. Caine and Caine, *Making Connections.*

53. Kandel, Schwartz, and Jessell, *Essentials of Neural Science and Behavior*; Antonio Damasio, *Descartes' Error: Emotion, Reason and the Human Brain* (New York: Plenum, 1994); Schachter, "The Interaction of Cognitive and Physiological Determinants of Emotional States," 49–80.

54. Kandel, Schwartz, and Jessell, *Essentials of Neural Science and Behavior,* 625.

55. Kandel, Schwartz, and Jessell, *Essentials of Neural Science and Behavior,* 626. Early in her career, Pert relates, funding was available for studying natural opiates because of federal mandates to understand and control drug abuse where substances like heroin introduce competing molecules of emotion to the blood stream. Understanding of neurology and communication systems has been advanced by research funded to reduce the considerable social costs of substance abuse.

56. In *Essentials of Neural Science and Behavior,* Kandel, Schwartz, and Jessell cite the work of Damasio. It would be a distraction here, but memory in my experience does not code the exact pleasure or pain of an event. We may recall *that* an event was painful or exquisitely pleasurable, but not the sensations of the moment, whereas form and color will be coded. Memory is highly selective with regard to features stored about an experience.

57. James M. Dabbs and Mary G. Dabbs, *Heroes, Rogues and Lovers: Testosterone and Behavior* (New York: McGraw-Hill, 2000).

58. I have not considered the possibility of sex differences in mood, attention, and hormonal influence.

Chapter 5

1. Abraham Maslow, *Religions, Values, and Peak Experiences* (New York: Penguin Books, 1977), 91–94.

2. Perhaps the positive mood changes teachers experience during a lecture reinforce the value they attach to the performance, making it hard for them to challenge the lecture as an educational medium.

3. Getting started is often the most difficult period because psychological experience is not yet elevated. If it is a cardiovascular activity like jogging, athletes know the first few minutes are likely to be uncomfortable.

4. Abraham Maslow, *The Farther Reaches of Human Nature* (New York: Penguin Arkana, 1993), 335.

5. Maslow, *The Farther Reaches of Human Nature,* 270–279.

6. Thomas Moore, *The Re-enchantment of Everyday Life* (New York: HarperCollins, 1996), p. xi.

7. Rudolf Otto, *The Idea of the Holy* (Chicago: University of Chicago Press, 1958). Cited by Moore, *The Re-enchantment of Everyday Life,* 299.

8. Phillip E. Hammond and David W. Machacek, *Soka Gakkai in America: Accommodation and Conversion* (New York: Oxford University Press, 1999).

9. Jim Castelli, *How I Pray* (New York: Ballantine Books, 1994).

10. See Harvey Cox, *The Rise of Pentecostal Spirituality and the Reshaping of Religion in the Twenty-first Century* (Reading, PA: Addison-Wesley, 1994) and Grant Wacker, *Heaven Below* (Cambridge, MA: Harvard University Press, 2003).

11. To illustrate the point, a friend whose mother had died told me about an awkward argument with an Episcopal priest. The priest insisted that only he, as an agent of Church and God, could speak at the funeral.

12. William James, *The Varieties of Religious Experience* (New York: Modern Library, 1958).

13. Thanks to Professor Margaret Blanchard for this observation. Personal communication with the author, 1996.

14. For a compendium of attention-getting devices used in carnivals, see Ricky Jay, *Learned Pigs & Fireproof Women* (New York: Farrar, Straus & Giroux, 1998).

15. Thich Nhat Hanh, *The Miracle of Mindfulness* (Boston: Beacon Press, 1987).

16. Mihaly Csikszentmihalyi, *Flow* (New York: HarperPerennial, 1991).

17. Steve Johnson, "Rocky Mountain High," *BMW ON Magazine* (February 1998): 40–41.

18. For colorful examples of people "going to the edge" in sports, hobbies, war, sex, and pursuits like running with the bulls in Pamplona, see Michael J. Apter, *The*

Dangerous Edge: The Psychology of Excitement (New York: The Free Press, 1992). Stephen Lyng, "Edgework: a Social Psychological Analysis of Voluntary Risk-taking," *American Journal of Sociology* 95, no. 4 (1990): 85–86.

19. Clifford Krauss, "Undercover Police Ride Wide Range of Emotion," *The New York Times,* 29 August 1994, B3.

20. Jack Katz, *Seductions of Crime: Moral and Sensual Attractions in Doing Evil* (New York: Basic Books, 1988).

21. Apter, *The Dangerous Edge,* 145.

22. A recent estimate is that yearly the American amusement-park industry books $9.6 billion and entertains 320 million people. American Coaster Enthusiasts, a voluntary association, has 8,500 members. "Coasting," *The Economist,* 28 June 2003, 30.

23. Marvin Zuckerman, *Sensation Seeking: Beyond the Optimal level of Arousal* (Hillsdale, NJ: Lawrence Erlbaum, 1979).

24. Edward Hallowell and John Ratey, *Driven to Distraction* (New York: Touchstone, 1994).

25. Eric Hoffer, *The True Believer* (New York: Harper and Row, 1951).

26. Margaret Singer et al., *Report of the APA Task Force on Deceptive and Indirect Techniques of Persuasion and Control,* 1986, available at http://www.rickross. com/reference/apologist/apologist23.html, also an online source for extreme groups by the Ross Institute for the Study of Cults, Controversial Groups and Movements. Their database has sources and information on more than 100 groups, including those discussed. Some scholars prefer the term "alternative religion" to "cult" because of the negative connotation attached.

27. Research on groups, social movements, and psychological identity began during World War II as social scientists, notably refugees from Germany and occupied Europe, sought to understand the rise of fascism in advanced countries like Germany and Italy.

28. Eugene Galanter, *Cults: Faith, Healing, and Coercion* (New York: Oxford University Press, 1989); Philip Zimbardo and Michael Leippe, *The Psychology of Attitude Change and Influence* (New York: McGraw-Hill, 1991); Neil Osherow, "Making Sense of the Nonsensical: An Analysis of Jonestown" in *Readings about the Social Animal,* ed. Eliot Aronson (New York: W. H. Freeman and Co., 1992), 68–86.

29. The final community meeting, which is hard to listen to, was recorded. Its documentation is not unlike the way that Palestinian suicide bombers use videotapes to convey the sincerity of their acts.

30. While not absolving leaders of their responsibility, let's admit that total groups evolve quickly and it is likely that the privations and intense demands of a total culture change or degrade the attitudes and dispositions of both leaders and followers.

31. Avishai Margalit, "The Suicide Bombers," *The New York Review* 50, no.1 (16 January 2003): 36–39.

32. Nasra Hassan, "Letter from Gaza: An Arsenal of Believers," *The New Yorker* (19 November 2001): 36–41.

33. Irving Janis, *Victims of Groupthink* (Boston: Houghton Mifflin, 1972), 9.

34. Groupthink might be thought of as an extreme form of Langer's mindlessness.

35. Zimbardo and Leippe, *The Psychology of Attitude Change and Influence*; Eliot Aronson, *The Social Animal,* 8th ed. (New York: Worth Publishers, 1999).

36. Leon Festinger, Stanley Schachter, and Kurt W. Back, *Social Pressure in Informal Groups* (New York: Harper, 1950).

37. Dissonance theory suggests a counterintuitive notion, namely, that it is easier to get behavior change in converts by getting them to proselytize even if they do not believe the message at first.

38. A related phenomenon is the Stockholm syndrome where captives form emotional bonds with their captors. One explanation is that human beings are social and adaptive animals whose attitudes, in the short term, can change. Attitude change is not necessarily a rational or conscious process.

39. Zimbardo and Leippe, *The Psychology of Attitude Change and Influence.*

40. Lee Ross, "The Intuitive Psychologist and His Shortcomings," in *Advances in Experimental Social Psychology,* vol. 10, ed. Leonard Berkowitz (New York: Academic Press, 1977), 173–220.

41. David Gutmann, "The Subjective Politics of Power: The Dilemma of Post-superego Man," *Social Research* 40, no. 4 (1973): 570–616.

42. While it seems easy enough to judge cults like Jonestown or social movements like National Socialism by looking at what these movements did, both to others as well as adherents, it is not simple to evaluate a group's morality by just looking at what they espouse. Almost without exception, total groups are remarkable for the clarity and dogmatic nature of group beliefs. Indeed, individual values like liberty or fraternity sound laudable and one can only judge their merits by looking to results.

43. Practical implications follow: to change a personal behavior, the good means is to affiliate with a group that carries the values and new behaviors. That is, rather than struggle against the habitual as a lone individual, join the right group and let it educate you!

44. Spatial metaphors like "higher" or "deeper" are misleading as are notions that consciousness or most complex human attributes are best denoted by a body organ like the brain. Instead of such reifications, we need to think in terms of information systems and networks of systems.

45. Special thanks go to Andrew Schmookler for redirecting my research early on. I was caught up with the psychological dynamics of peak experience and paid no attention to non-peak moments, or the all-important transitions.

46. By "correlated" I mean that they are not perfectly independent dimensions. Imagine a Venn diagram where the circle for each dimension shares some portion of the others' space.

47. Psychologists distinguish between states and traits in terms of how long the psychological condition exists and how many facets of personality are implicated. Traits are assumed to be more constant forces in motivation than are temporary psychological states.

48. Peter Milner, *Physiological Psychology* (New York: Holt, Rinehart and Winston, 1970).

49. David LaBerge, *Attentional Processing: The Brain's Art of Mindfulness* (Cambridge, MA: Harvard University Press, 1995).

50. J. Allan Hobson, *The Chemistry of Conscious States* (Boston: Little, Brown & Co., 1994), 83.

51. By aware I do not mean "conscious" in the Freudian sense, referring to the unconscious as a repository of repressed conflict and images, or the process through psychotherapy of making those motives available to consciousness. Nor is awareness a political category like political consciousness (as in consciousness raising), which refers to what people have learned about society or a political system. Awareness does not require the self-knowledge of either a

Freudian or political definition. It refers to an abstract and evanescent quality of human experience, not what one has learned.

52. Martha Nussbaum, *Upheavals of Thought: The Intelligence of Emotions* (New York: Cambridge University Press, 2001).

53. Daniel Dennett, *Kinds of Minds* (New York: Basic Books, 1996), 149 and 157.

54. Feeling self-conscious, in itself, is an interesting dimension, usually experienced by people as an uncomfortable feeling because one feels exposed, perhaps vulnerable. Made the butt of a practical joke, a person feels self-conscious, embarrassed; but this is not the same as being aware of what one is doing at a particular moment.

55. For example, see Robert W. White, "Competence and the Psychosexual Stages of Development," *Nebraska Symposium on Motivation* (Lincoln, NB: University of Nebraska Press, 1960); Richard DeCharms, *Personal Causation: The Internal Affective Determinants of Behavior* (New York: Academic Press, 1968); Edward Deci and Richard M. Ryan, *Intrinsic Motivation and Self-Determination in Human Behavior* (New York: Plenum, 1985); Julian Rotter, "Internal Versus External Control of Reinforcement: A Case History of a Variable," *American Psychologist* 45, no. 4 (1990): 489–493.

56. Charles Guignon and Dirk Pereboom, eds., *Existentialism: Basic Writings* (Indianapolis, IN: Hackett Publishing, 1995), 200.

57. Guignon and Pereboom, *Existentialism*, p. xxxv.

58. Jurgen Habermas, *Legitimation Crisis* (Boston: Beacon Press, 1973).

Part III

1. Donald Schön, *The Reflective Practitioner* (New York: Basic Books, 1983), 3. (Emphasis added.)

2. Jacques Ellul, *The Technological Society* (New York: Vintage Books, 1964).

Chapter 6

1. For examples, see Arthur Chickering and Zelda Gamson, eds., *Applying the Seven Principles for Good Practice in Undergraduate Education* (San Francisco: Jossey-Bass, 1991); Marcia Mentkowski et al., *Learning That Lasts* (San Francisco: Jossey-Bass, 1999); Deborah Meier, *In Schools We Trust: Creating Communities of Learning in an Era of Testing and Standardization* (Boston: Beacon Press, 2002); Theodore J. Marchese, "The New Conversations about Learning: Insights from Neuroscience and Anthropology, Cognitive Science and Work-Place Studies," *Assessing Impact: Evidence and Action* (Washington, DC: American Association for Higher Education, 1997).

2. For a lucid discussion of fabled Black Mountain College, now defunct, see Martin Duberman, *An Exploration in Community* (New York: Dutton, 1972); for detailed commentary on the second wave of progressive American colleges, see Gerald Grant and David Riesman, *The Perpetual Dream* (Chicago: University of Chicago Press, 1977).

3. Robert Putnam expresses his admiration for the public spiritedness of the Progressive Era in *Bowling Alone: The Collapse and Revival of American Community* (New York: Simon & Schuster, 2000).

4. Indeed, the more grand the promise, the more hidden the consequences. One has to expect a host of nontrivial, unanticipated consequences to purposive social action. The classic article is Robert K. Merton's "The Unanticipated Consequences of Purposive Social Action," *American Sociological Review* 1 (1936): 894.

5. Parker Palmer, "The Heart of a Teacher: Identity and Integrity in Teaching," *Change* 29, no. 6 (1997): 14–22.

6. Seymour Sarason, *Revisiting "The Culture of the School and the Problem of Change"* (New York: Teachers College Press, 1996), 379.

7. Renate N. Caine and Geoffrey Caine, *Making Connections: Teaching and the Human Brain* (Reading, PA: Addison-Wesley, 1994).

8. Marchese, "The New Conversations about Learning," 79–85.

9. Arthur Chickering, personal communication with author, 1999.

10. A college or university can also provide lifelong learning for one or more members of the same family who are active members of the college at different parts of their lives, earning different degrees and attending alumni colleges.

11. We have not always valued the contributions of small colleges to local communities. The new for-profit universities avoid the deferred maintenance of a built campus, which helps profitability. But they do not have enduring cultural commitments to the community.

12. For histories of The New School, see Peter Rutkoff and William Scott, *New School: A History of the New School for Social Research* (New York: The Free Press, 1986); Claus-Dieter Krohn, *Intellectuals in Exile*, trans. Rita and Robert Kimber (Amherst: The University of Massachusetts Press, 1993).

13. Davis chronicles the work of Royce ("Tim") Pitkin, President of Goddard College, who coined a phrase still alive in the community that students are not vessels to be filled nor lamps to be lighted. Only students light themselves.

14. William A. Kahn, "To be Fully There: Psychological Presence at Work," *Human Relations* 45, no. 4 (1992): 321–345.

15. Alfred N. Whitehead, *The Aims of Education and Other Essays* (New York: Macmillan, 1959).

16. The progressive school that wants to last has to find mechanisms for curbing narcissistic behavior and promoting genuine collaboration. The Quakers have a process call "eldering" by which difficult members of a group are pulled aside and encouraged to go along with the spirit of the group.

17. That is not to say that hazing that is demeaning or lacks safety supports is ever justifiable. But the psychological and group dynamics are the same, which partly explains why hazing has such appeal.

18. Roger C. Schank and Chip Cleary, *Engines for Education* (Hillsdale, NJ: Lawrence Erlbaum Associates, 1995).

19. Arthur Chickering, personal communication with author, 1997.

20. Distrust may be the byproduct of a difficult problem for universities: the packed nature of the curriculum that results from each discipline and student service fighting for its turf, leading to great pressure on students who then have to cut corners where they can. Too many means are used toward too many ends. The curriculum is out of control.

21. Maxine Greene, "Revisioning John Dewey," lecture at the University of Vermont, 20 October 1997.

22. Theodore Sizer, *Horace's Compromise* (Boston: Houghton Mifflin, 1984).

23. Paulo Freire and Ira Shor, *A Pedagogy for Liberation: Dialogues on Transforming Education* (Westport, CN: Bergin & Garvey/Greenwood Press, 1987); Stephen Brookfield, *Becoming a Critically Reflective Teacher* (San Francisco: Jossey-Bass, 1995); Pepi Leistnyna, Arlie Woodrum, and Stephen Sherblom, *Breaking Free: The Transformative Power of Critical Pedagogy* (Cambridge, MA: Harvard Educational Review, 1996).

24. Joe L. Kincheloe and Shirley R. Steinberg, *Unauthorized Methods: Strategies for Critical Thinking* (New York: Routledge, 1998).

25. Peter Senge, *The Fifth Discipline: The Art and Practice of the Learning Organization* (New York: Doubleday/Currency, 1990); Fred Kofman and Peter Senge, "Communities of Commitment," in *Learning Organizations,* ed. Sarita Chawla and John Renesch (Portland: Productivity Press, 1995).

26. Practices like block crediting lead to credit inflation because a teacher may be reluctant to fail a student for an entire semester if the work is marginal. If a student reaches too high and cannot finish parts of the learning plan, why should they get the same credit for the term as a student who chooses more realistic goals and meets each of them? Having standards for the partial award of academic credit gives teachers a more flexible tool than all or nothing crediting.

27. Laurent A. Daloz, *Effective Teaching and Mentoring* (San Francisco: Jossey-Bass, 1986).

28. Carl Rogers, *Freedom to Learn for the '80s* (Columbus, OH: Charles E. Merrill Publishing Co., 1983).

29. Friedrich Nietzsche, *Human, All Too Human* (Cambridge: Cambridge University Press, 1986).

30. Parker Palmer, "The Heart of a Teacher: Identity and Integrity in Teaching," *Change* 29, no. 6 (1997): 14–22.

31. Sizer, *Horace's Compromise,* 163.

32. See Sizer, *Horace's Compromise*; Deborah Meier, *The Power of Their Ideas* (Boston: Beacon Press, 1995); Stanley Aronowitz, *The Knowledge Factory: Dismantling the Corporate University and Creating True Higher Learning* (New York: Beacon, 2000).

33. Robert Kegan, *In Over Our Heads* (Cambridge: Harvard University Press, 1994).

34. Peter D. Kramer, *Moments of Engagement: Intimate Psychotherapy in a Technological Age* (New York: W. W. Norton, 1989).

35. For example, see Robert B. Barr and John Tagg, "From Teaching to Learning: A New Paradigm for Undergraduate Education," *Change* 27, no. 6 (1995): 12–14.

36. Perhaps we do not understand how power works in the archetypal role set of learner and master learner, either from the perspective of a conventional discipline like social psychology or as seen by a radical philosopher like Michel Foucault in his *Power/Knowledge* (New York: Macmillan, 1980).

37. Certain extreme views in progressive education hold that no difference in power should exist. How the difference in power is used and explained, and whether teachers are able to let go, as they should when students move in a different direction, makes all the difference.

38. Robert Tremmel, "Zen and the Art of Reflective Practice in Teacher Education," *Harvard Educational Review* 63, no. 4 (1993): 438. (Emphasis added.)

39. Tremmel, "Zen and the Art of Reflective Practice in Teacher Education," 456.

40. I am not arguing against technology, either electronic or in the form of group dynamics, seen as a technical intervention in human relations. Rather, we should begin with clear purposes, being alert to misuse of powerful tools.

41. George Kuh et al., *Involving Colleges: Successful Approaches to Fostering Student Learning and Development Outside the Classroom* (San Francisco: Jossey-Bass, 1991), 111.

42. Meier, *The Power of Their Ideas,* 107.

43. Meier, *The Power of Their Ideas,* 111–112.

44. Meier, *The Power of Their Ideas,* 113. (Emphasis added.)

45. Meier, *The Power of Their Ideas,* 113.

46. Sizer, *Horace's Compromise,* 40. (Emphasis added.)

47. Guy Debord, *The Society of the Spectacle* (Detroit: Black and Red, 1977). For other critiques, see Neil Postman, *Amusing Ourselves to Death: Public Discourse in the Age of Show Business* (New York: Penguin, 1985) and Benjamin Barber, *A Passion for Democracy* (Princeton: Princeton University Press, 1998), 214–224.

48. Kuh, *Involving Colleges*; Ernest T. Pascarella and Patrick T. Terenzini, *How College Affects Students: Findings and Insights from Twenty Years of Research* (San Francisco: Jossey-Bass, 1991).

49. Students who attend commuter colleges and adults attending low-residency programs face special problems because their experience on campus is limited. There also may not be intentional programming of out-of-class experience, which could reinforce and extend learning and development. Pascarella and Terenzini say one-third of American colleges do not have student residences.

50. Craig Howley and Robert Bickel, "Research about School Size and School Performance in Impoverished Communities," in *ERIC Digest* (December 2000), ERIC, ED 448968.

51. The argument for having large schools and consolidated schools has been economies of scale and access to specialized academic subjects. But lower completion and achievement rates attached to large size reduce real savings. Cost per graduate is a better measure than cost per student.

52. Too little distance between student and teacher is also problematic. Classic psychoanalytic theory, for example, holds that a degree of distance and objectivity enhances the therapeutic process because defense mechanisms like projection and displacement are visible to both therapist and client. Transference relations are central to the treatment. Humanistic psychology argues for less distance, but this may be confusing because the client may not welcome the closeness and may be disturbed by irrational projections.

53. See Martin Heidegger, *What Is Called Thinking?* (New York: Harper Torchbooks, 1968), 75. (Emphasis added.)

54. John Dewey, *Experience and Education* (New York: Macmillan, 1963), 48.

55. Maxine Greene, *Releasing the Imagination* (San Francisco: Jossey-Bass, 1995).

56. See Menkowski et al., *Learning that Lasts.*

57. Where the content to be studied, however, is an advanced skill that affects the lives of others, like psychological testing, bridge construction, or flying a plane, learning content must be given more weight. Even for my counterexamples, however, curricular ideas that increase student motivation and improve quality of learning are better.

58. Greene, *Releasing the Imagination,* 52.

59. Greene, *Releasing the Imagination,* 52.

60. I borrow this term, retroduction, from Selltiz et al., who say this is the actual logic used in social research. Claire Selltiz, Lawrence S. Wrightsman, and Stuart W. Cook, *Research Methods in Social Relations,* 3rd edition (New York: Holt, Rinehart and Winston, 1976).

61. See www.wanttolearn.org, my website, for most recent sources and discussion.

62. For more information, access www.compact.org/aboutcc/

63. This small group of colleges has recently formed a consortium, Work Colleges, funded by a federal grant. For connection to the consortium, go to www.berea. edu/WCC/WCC.html. Also see Donald Asher, *Cool Colleges* (Berkeley, CA: Ten Speed Press, 2000). I am not thinking about federal work-study, which has less substance in most colleges than envisioned because student work is poorly supervised.

64. See Brian Harward and Louis Albert, "Service and Service-learning: a Guide for Newcomers," *AAHE Bulletin* 46, no. 6 (1994): 10–12; Robert A. Rhoads and Jeffrey P. Howard, eds., *Academic Service Learning: A Pedagogy of Action and Reflection* (San Francisco: Jossey-Bass, 1997).

65. As defining as Antioch's co-op program has been to the college, later extended in the 1970s to its adult centers nationwide, the potential of the co-op experience was never met at the Antioch College because the co-op experience receives only perfunctory reflection. Some members of the academic faculty pay lip service to co-op. To provide supervision, the institution relies on a separate co-op faculty who are treated as second-class educators with different requirements and status. Antioch's adult centers do better and make intentional use of work experience by asking learners to incorporate concurrent work experience in their studies. Formal integration papers are required in Professional Development Seminars intended as formal supervision of work practice. For more about Antioch, see Burton Clark, *The Distinctive Colleges: Antioch, Reed, and Swarthmore* (Chicago: Aldine Press, 1990); Dan Hotaling and Dorothy Scott, *An Antioch Career* (Yellow Springs, OH: Antioch University, 1995); Alan E. Guskin, *Notes for a Pragmatic Idealist* (Yellow Springs, OH: Antioch University, 1997).

66. For reviews of motivation methods, see Raymond J. Wlodkowski, *Enhancing Adult Motivation to Learn* (San Francisco: Jossey-Bass, 1988) and Raymond J. Wlodkowski and Margery B. Ginsberg, *Diversity and Motivation: Culturally Responsive Teaching* (San Francisco: Jossey-Bass, 1995). For a more-or-less technical comparison of contemporary approaches to motivation, see Michael Theall, ed., *Motivation from Within: Approaches for Encouraging Faculty and Students to Excel* (San Francisco: Jossey-Bass, 2000).

67. Thomas A. Angelo and Patricia K. Cross, *Classroom Assessment Techniques: A Handbook for College Teachers*, 2d. ed. (San Francisco: Jossey-Bass, 1994).

68. Alfie Kohn, *Punished by Rewards* (Boston: Houghton Mifflin, 1993).

69. Laurent A. Daloz, *Effective Teaching and Mentoring* (San Francisco: Jossey-Bass, 1986).

70. G. Wiggins, *Educative Assessment: Designing Assessments to Inform and Improve Student Performance* (San Francisco: Jossey-Bass, 1998).

71. Students applying to a traditional school, especially in science or business, may have problems getting their transcript accepted. Personal intervention by the faculty member or the dean usually gets around this problem. Some institutions like Antioch allow grade equivalents, but this erodes institutional and consumer confidence in the legitimacy of narrative feedback.

72. Kegan, *In Over Our Heads*, 42.

73. The same argument can be extended to using certain forms of testing, especially where a technical vocabulary must be learned. Here, it is helpful to check on what is really being understood (or taught), using a pop quiz. Nodding heads in class cannot be trusted. But having said this, we may mistake the appearance of

learning in skillful test taking for its substance, how well new concepts are integrated into existing knowledge structures.

74. Peter Elbow, *Everyone Can Write: Essays Toward a Hopeful Theory of Writing and Teaching Writing* (New York: Oxford University, 2000); John C. Bean, *Engaging Ideas: The Professor's Guide to Integrating Writing, Critical Thinking and Active Learning in the Classroom* (San Francisco: Jossey-Bass, 1996).

75. Much the same point could be made for building formal public speaking into most classes (not just as a specialized course). Goddard and Vermont College ask their adult students to present their own work to peers and the faculty twice a semester, which helps them identify with it and, in time, helps them become self-confident as artists and intellectuals. Although not intended as a formal learning outcome, graduates become public speakers, which helps them become leaders.

Chapter 7

1. Alexander Astin, *Achieving Educational Excellence* (San Francisco: Jossey-Bass, 1985), 133.

2. George D. Kuh and Elizabeth J. Whitt, *The Invisible Tapestry: Culture in American Colleges and Universities* (Washington, DC: Association for the Study of Higher Education, 1988), 13.

3. See Alexander Astin, *What Matters in College?* (San Francisco: Jossey-Bass, 1993); George Kuh et al., *Involving Colleges: Successful Approaches to Fostering Student Learning and Development Outside the Classroom* (San Francisco: Jossey-Bass, 1991).

4. Astin, *Achieving Educational Excellence*, 143.

5. Kuh et al., *Involving Colleges*.

6. Astin, *Achieving Educational Excellence*.

7. Cited by Kuh and Whitt, *The Invisible Tapestry*, 71–72.

8. Arthur Chickering, personal communication with author, 1999.

9. Astin, *Achieving Educational* Excellence; Astin, What *Matters in College?*

10. Arthur Chickering and Linda Reisser, *Education and Identity* (San Francisco: Jossey-Bass, 1993).

11. As a college student, I did better academically when I had to balance the demands of classes with sports and being involved in student government.

12. Fred Kofman and Peter Senge, "Communities of Commitment," in *Learning Organizations*, ed. Sarita Chawla and John Renesch (Portland, OR: Productivity Press, 1995).

Epilogue

1. Zencey, personal communication with author, 1996.

2. Too late for this book I began to think about one rare but frightening form of adaptation to modernity that deserves serious study: the alienation of males who do not have relationships and meaningful work, may not know how to process their feelings about being alone or angry, and take it out on others whether as rape, murder, serial killing, or work and school violence.

3. Marx's theory of alienation and Durkheim's and Merton's conceptions of anomie have been out of favor for some time as worthy topics in American academic circles. For a contemporary review of alienation theory, see Richard Schacht, *The Future of Alienation* (Urbana, IL: University of Illinois Press, 1994) and Brian Baxter, *Alienation and Authenticity* (London: Tavistock Publications, 1982). For earlier reviews, see Bertell Ollman, *Alienation* (New York: Cambridge University Press, 1976); Joachim Israel, *Alienation from Marx to Current Sociology* (Boston: Allyn and Bacon, 1971). A large companion literature exists for the twin topics of anomie (external social forces) and anomia (the psychological consequences of anomic environs), and here, the focus is less on quality of work life than on integration into society.

4. Thanks to Professor Ann Stanton for her observation that the social role of mother and wife puts special demands on the attention system.

5. See William A. Kahn, "To be Fully There: Psychological Presence at Work," *Human Relations* 45, no. 4 (1992): 321–345.

6. Martha Nussbaum argues for a cognitive-evaluative view of emotion in which appraisal, cognition, emotion, and sense of identity interact in *Upheavals of Thought: The Intelligence of Emotions* (New York: Cambridge University Press, 2001).

7. Michael Apter and others make a similar point in asking why people pursue excitement, especially when bored. Apter, *The Dangerous Edge: The Psychology of Excitement* (New York: The Free Press, 1992). But my observation is more general than the pursuit of excitement, or peak experience per se. What fascinates me is the human propensity to manipulate lived experience, that motive being daily, unceasing, and mostly unconscious.

8. Edward J. Khantzian, *Addiction and the Vulnerable Self* (New York: Guilford Press, 1990).

9. Athletes use "mind exercises" and aerobic workouts to tune their physiology, especially to increase alertness and elevate mood as a function of changes in neurotransmitters, hormones in the blood stream, and the release of dopamine when the body is made to work hard. See Steven Ungerleider, *Mental Training for Peak Performance* (Emmaus, PA: Rodale Press, 1996).

10. Mihaly Csikszentmihalyi, *Finding Flow* (New York: Basic Books, 1997), 26.

11. Erving Goffman, *The Presentation of Self in Everyday Life* (Garden City, NY: Doubleday Anchor, 1959).

12. Professor Ann Stanton of Vermont College talks about the dirty secret of education, that getting an education costs money, time, and brings an inevitable discomfort because learning introduces doubt and cognitive tension. Personal communication with author, 1999.

13. Isaiah Berlin, *The Crooked Timber of Humanity* (New York: Princeton University Press, 1991), 13–14; last Berlin quote cited by Alan Ryan, "Wise Man," *New York Review,* December 17, 1998, 36.

14. I am grateful to Professor Tom Abshire of Vermont College for pointing out that influential clergy of the day also adopted existentialist views and saw no contradiction with articles of faith.

15. Emmy van Deurzen-Smith, *Existential Counseling in Practice* (London: Sage Publications, 1988).

16. Something of this exists in the widespread use of group dynamics in schools and corporate training to elevate mood and motivation, independent of the nature of the goals being discussed.

17. For two examples, see Phillip Candy, *Self-direction for Lifelong Learning* (San Francisco: Jossey-Bass, 1991), and Gary Confessore and Sharon Confessore, *Guideposts to Self-Directed Learning* (King of Prussia, PA: Organizational Design and Development, Inc, 1992).
18. Jacques Ellul wrote a searching critique of modernity in *The Technological Society* (New York: Vintage Books, 1964) in which, like Max Weber, he critiques the ways that technique and rational control have penetrated so many parts of modern life that were once subjective, whole, and human.
19. Jack Mezirow, "A Critical Theory of Self-directed Learning," in *Self-directed Learning: From Theory to Practice,* ed. Stephen Brookfield (San Francisco: Jossey-Bass, 1985).
20. Richard Rorty, "Method, Social Science, and Social Hope," in *The Postmodern Turn,* ed. Stephen Seidman (New York: Cambridge University Press, 1994), 63.
21. Morton Deutsch, my advisor at Columbia, was a student of Kurt Lewin's when the latter taught at MIT.
22. Csikszentmihalyi, *Finding Flow,* 131.
23. Thich Nhat Hanh, *The Miracle of Mindfulness* (Boston: Beacon Press, 1987).
24. Teachers know that the mood of young people can be quite intense and volatile, positive and negative, sometimes leading to self-destructive acts. They also bring great idealism so important to learning.
25. Quotes from Rorty, "Method, Social Science, and Social Hope," 57. He cautions that neither the lean, analytical language of natural science nor the objective-appearing language of behaviorese, which apes the natural sciences, is "Nature's Own Language" and neither can gain intellectual legitimacy with such language.
26. See Andrew Delbanco for a historical perspective on the origins of hope in the American experiment in democracy. *The Real American Dream: A Meditation on Hope* (Cambridge, MA: Harvard University Press, 1990); also James W. Frazer, *A History of Hope* (New York: Palgrave Macmillan, 2003).
27. Rorty, "Method, Social Science, and Social Hope," 62.
28. Rorty, "Method, Social Science, and Social Hope," 64.
29. Rorty's cautious, optimistic tone is quite apparent in his comment that Dewey's vocabulary "allows room for unjustifiable hope, and an ungroundable but vital sense of human solidarity." "Method, Social Science, and Social Hope," 64.
30. James B. Simpson, *Simpson's Contemporary Quotations* (New York: Houghton Mifflin, 1988).
31. We would be better teachers and counselors if we thought more about adequate rest as it affects motivation and learning. Fatigue is common in modern organizations, including schools, where it affects the performance of both students and teachers.
32. Technology for direct manipulation of body systems and accompanying mood states is available today and improving, a fact that is surfacing ethical-political debates, as Herman Kahn predicted in the 1960s. To use his provocative example from a lecture at Columbia in 1969, will I be allowed to hardwire my hypothalamus for pleasure, or will the state or corporation lock me out for so many hours a day to work?
33. Erving Goffman, *The Presentation of Self in Everyday Life.*
34. Ernest T. Pascarella and Patrick T. Terenzini, *How College Affects Students: Findings and Insights from Twenty Years of Research* (San Francisco: Jossey-Bass, 1991).

35. What are the images we use to imagine the exchanges between person and environment, and the human experience? After many tries, I do not have the right metaphor to describe how connected to information flows human beings really are. I do know that the notion of a discrete, corporal body misleads. If the information flows could be made visible and the body invisible, we would be suspended in space, Gulliver-like, by hundreds of pieces of string.

36. James M. Dabbs and Mary G. Dabbs, *Heroes, Rogues and Lovers: Testosterone and Behavior* (New York: McGraw-Hill, 2000).

37. See Goffman, *The Presentation of Self in Everyday Life*; Elizabeth Ellsworth, *Teaching Positions: Difference, Pedagogy, and the Power of Address* (New York: Teachers College Press, 1997).

38. Martin Orne wrote about demand characteristics in experiments, an idea extended to therapy and other settings. See his "On the Social Psychology of the Psychological Experiment: With Particular Reference to Demand Characteristics and their Implications," *American Psychologist* 17 (1962): 776–783.

39. Theodore J. Marchese, "The New Conversations about Learning: Insights from Neuroscience and Anthropology, Cognitive Science and Work-Place Studies," *Assessing Impact: Evidence and Action* (Washington, DC: American Association for Higher Education, 1997). Enduring learning benefits from reworking memory and connecting it to new experience, not unlike developing character. Mary Bateson likens character formation to making baklava, where we constantly fold-in our work and rework the dough of human experience. In her book, *Composing a Life* (New York: Atlantic Monthly Press, 1989).

40. I have not considered the idea that neuronal networks are in competition with one another, or the way that new networks are activated when we sleep, checking the networks.

Bibliography

Ainley, Mary. "Styles of Engagement with Learning: Multidimensional Assessment of Their Relationship with Strategy Use and School Achievement." *Journal of Educational Psychology* 85, no. 3 (1993): 395–405.

Angelo, Thomas, and Patricia K. Cross. *Classroom Assessment Techniques: A Handbook for College Teachers.* 2d. ed. San Francisco: Jossey-Bass, 1994.

Apter, Michael J. *Reversal Theory: Motivation, Emotion and Personality.* London: Routledge, 1989.

———. *The Dangerous Edge: The Psychology of Excitement.* New York: The Free Press, 1992.

Armstrong, Lance. *It's Not About the Bike.* New York: Putnam Publishing Group, 2000.

Aronowitz, Stanley. *The Knowledge Factory: Dismantling the Corporate University and Creating True Higher Learning.* New York: Beacon, 2001.

Aronson, Eliot, ed. *Readings about the Social Animal.* New York: W.H. Freeman and Co., 1992.

———. *The Social Animal.* 8th ed. New York: Worth Publishers, 1999.

———, Timothy D. Wilson, and Robin M. Akert. *Social Psychology.* New York: Longman, 1999.

Asher, Donald. *Cool Colleges.* Berkeley, CA: Ten Speed Press, 2001.

Astin, Alexander, et al. *Involvement in Learning.* Washington, DC: National Institute of Education, 1984.

———. *Achieving Educational Excellence.* San Francisco: Jossey-Bass, 1985.

———. *What Matters in College?* San Francisco: Jossey-Bass, 1993.

Ayers, William. *To Teach: The Journey of a Teacher.* New York: Teachers College Press, 1993.

———, and Janet Miller, eds. *A Light in Dark Times: Maxine Greene and the Unfinished Conversation.* New York: Teachers College Press, 1998.

Bakan, David. *Attention.* Princeton, NJ: D. Van Nostrand, 1966.

Barber, Benjamin. *Jihad vs. McWorld.* New York: Ballantine Books, 1996.

———. *A Passion for Democracy.* Princeton, NJ: Princeton University Press, 1998.

Barr, Robert B. and John Tagg. "From Teaching to Learning: A New Paradigm for Undergraduate Education." *Change* 27, no. 6 (1995): 12–14.

Barrett, William. *What Is Existentialism?* New York: Gross Press, 1964.

Bateson, Mary C. *Composing a Life.* New York: Atlantic Monthly Press, 1989.

Bauman, Zygmunt. "Is There a Postmodern Sociology?" In *The Postmodern Turn: New Perspectives on Social Theory*. Edited by Steven Seidman. New York: Cambridge University Press, 1994.

————. *Liquid Modernity*. Cambridge, MA: Polity Press, 2000.

Baxter, Brian. *Alienation and Authenticity*. London: Tavistock Publications, 1982.

Bean, John C. *Engaging Ideas: The Professor's Guide to Integrating Writing, Critical Thinking and Active Learning in the Classroom*. San Francisco: Jossey-Bass, 1996.

Belenky, Mary, et al. *Women's Ways of Knowing*. New York: Basic Books, 1986.

Bellah, Robert, et al. *Habits of the Heart*. Berkeley, CA: University of California Press, 1985.

Benasayag, Miguel. *Cette Douce Certitude du Pire: Pour une Theorie Critique du L'engagement* [Assuming the worst: towards a theoretical critique of engagement]. Paris: La Decouverte, 1991.

Benson, Ann G., and Frank Adams. *To Know for Real: Royce S. Pitkin and Goddard College*. Adamant, VT: Adamant Press, 1987.

Berlin, Isaiah. *The Crooked Timber of Humanity*. New York: Princeton University, 1991.

Bernstein, Richard J. *Hannah Arendt and the Jewish Question*. Cambridge, MA: MIT Press, 1996.

Blackburn, Simon. *Being Good: A Short Introduction to Ethics*. New York: Oxford University Press, 2001.

Bosworth, Kris, and Sharon J. Hamilton, eds. *Collaborative Learning: Underlying Processes and Effective Techniques*. San Francisco: Jossey-Bass, 2000.

Bowlby, John. *Attachment and Loss*. New York: Basic Books, 1969.

Boyer, Ernest. *College*. New York: Harper & Row, 1987.

————. *Scholarship Reconsidered*. San Francisco: Jossey-Bass, 1990.

Brookfield, Stephen, ed. *Self-directed Learning: From Theory to Practice*. San Francisco: Jossey-Bass, 1985.

————. *The Skillful Teacher*. San Francisco: Jossey-Bass, 1990.

————. *Discussion as a Way of Teaching*. San Francisco: Jossey-Bass, 1990.

————. *Becoming a Critically Reflective Teacher*. San Francisco: Jossey-Bass, 1995.

Brown, Lyn, and Carol Gilligan. *Meeting at the Crossroads*. Cambridge, MA: Harvard University Press, 1972.

Bruffee, Kenneth. *Collaborative Learning*. Baltimore: Johns Hopkins University Press, 1993.

————. "Sharing our Toys: Cooperative Learning Versus Collaborative Learning." *Change* 27, no. 1 (1995): 12–18.

Bruner, Jerome. *In Search of Mind: Essays in Autobiography*. New York: Harper and Row, 1983.

Caine, Renate N., and Geoffrey Caine. *Making Connections: Teaching and the Human Brain*. Reading, PA: Addison-Wesley, 1994.

Camus, Albert. *The Stranger*. New York: Alfred A. Knopf, 1942.

―――. *Lyrical and Critical Essays*. New York: Vintage Books, 1970.

―――. *The Plague*. New York: Knopf, 1972. (Original work published 1948.)

Candy, Phillip C. *Self-direction for Lifelong Learning*. San Francisco: Jossey-Bass, 1991.

Castelli, Jim. *How I Pray*. New York: Ballantine Books, 1994.

Chickering, Arthur. *Commuting Versus Residential Students: Overcoming Educational Inequities of Living Off Campus*. San Francisco: Jossey-Bass, 1974.

―――. *Experience and Learning: An Introduction to Experiential Learning*. New Rochelle, NY: Change Magazine Press, 1977.

―――, and Zelda Gamson, eds. *Applying the Seven Principles for Good Practice in Undergraduate Education*. San Francisco: Jossey-Bass, 1991.

―――, and Jackson Kytle. "The Collegiate Ideal in the Twenty-first Century." In *Reconceptualizing the Collegiate Ideal*. Edited by J. Douglas Toma and Adrianna Kezar. San Francisco: Jossey-Bass, 1999.

―――, and Linda Reisser. *Education and Identity*. San Francisco: Jossey-Bass, 1993.

―――, and Nancy Schlossberg. *How to Get the Most Out of College*. Needham Heights, MA: Allyn and Bacon, 1995.

Clark, Burton. *The Distinctive Colleges: Antioch, Reed, and Swarthmore*. Chicago: Aldine Press, 1990.

"Coasting: Seasonal Excitement." *The Economist*, 28 June 2003, 64.

Confessore, Gary J., and Sharon J. Confessore, eds. *Guideposts to Self-Directed Learning*. King of Prussia, PA: Organizational Design and Development, Inc., 1992.

Cott, Jonathan. *Conversations with Glenn Gould*. Boston: Little, Brown & Company, 1984.

Cox, Harvey. *The Rise of Pentecostal Spirituality and the Reshaping of Religion in the Twenty-first Century*. Reading, PA: Addison-Wesley, 1994.

Cremin, Lawrence. *The Transformation of the School*. New York: Vintage Books, 1964.

Csikszentmihalyi, Mihaly. *Flow*. New York: HarperPerennial, 1991.

―――. *The Evolving Self*. New York: HarperCollins, 1993.

―――. *Finding Flow*. New York: Basic Books, 1997.

―――, and Isabella S. Csikszentmihalyi, eds. *Optimal Experience: Psychological Studies of Flow in Consciousness*. New York: Cambridge University Press, 1988.

Dabbs, James M., and Mary G. Dabbs. *Heroes, Rogues and Lovers: Testosterone and Behavior*. New York: McGraw-Hill, 2000.

Daloz, Laurent A. *Effective Teaching and Mentoring*. San Francisco: Jossey-Bass, 1986.

Damasio, Antonio R. *Descartes' Error: Emotion, Reason and the Human Brain*. New York: Plenum, 1994.

Davis, Forest. *Things Were Different in Royce's Day*. Adamant, VT: Adamant Press, 1996.

Debord, Guy. *The Society of the Spectacle*. Detroit: Black and Red, 1977.

DeCharms, Richard. *Personal Causation: The Internal Affective Determinants of Behavior*. New York: Academic Press, 1968.

Deci, Edward, and Richard M. Ryan. *Intrinsic Motivation and Self-Determination in Human Behavior*. New York: Plenum, 1985.

Delbanco, Andrew. *The Real American Dream: A Meditation on Hope*. Cambridge, MA: Harvard University Press, 1990.

Dennett, Daniel C. *Kinds of Minds*. New York: Basic Books, 1996.

Dewey, John. *Reconstruction in Philosophy*. Boston: Beacon Press, 1957. (Original work published 1920.)

———. *Art as Experience*. New York: Capricorn Books, 1958. (Original work published 1934.)

———. *Democracy and Education*. New York: Macmillan, 1961. (Original work published 1916.)

———. *Experience and Education*. New York: Macmillan, 1963. (Original work published 1938.)

Diggins, John P. *The Rise and Fall of the American Left*. New York: W.W. Norton & Co., 1992.

Duberman, Martin. *An Exploration in Community*. New York: Dutton, 1972.

Dweck, Carol S. "Motivational Processes Affecting Learning." *American Psychologist* 41 (1986): 1040–1048.

Elbow, Peter. *Everyone Can Write: Essays Toward a Hopeful Theory of Writing and Teaching Writing*. New York: Oxford University, 2000.

Ellsworth, Elizabeth. *Teaching Positions: Difference, Pedagogy, and the Power of Address*. New York: Teachers College Press, 1997.

Ellul, Jacques. *The Technological Society*. New York: Vintage Books, 1964.

Enright, Robert. "Michals the Archangel, an Interview with Duane Michals." *BorderCrossings* 17, no. 4 (1998): 14–28.

Evans, Phil. *Motivation and Emotion*. New York: Routledge, 1989.

Festinger, Leon, Albert Pepitone, and Theodore Newcomb. "Some Consequences of Deindividuation in a Group." *Journal of Abnormal and Social Psychology* 47 (1952): 382–389.

———, Stanley Schachter, and Kurt W. Back. *Social Pressure in Informal Groups*. New York: Harper, 1950.

Finger, Matthias, and José M. Asun. *Adult Education at the Crossroads: Learning Our Way Out*. New York: Zed Books, 2000.

Fishman, Stephen, and Lucille McCarthy. *John Dewey and the Challenge of Classroom Practice*. New York: Teachers College Press, 1998.

Foucault, Michel. *The Order of Things*. New York: Pantheon, 1972.

———. *Power/Knowledge*. New York: Macmillan, 1980.

Foster, Nelson, and Jack Shoemaker, eds. *The Roaring Stream, a New Zen Reader*. Hopewell, NJ: Ecco, 1996.

Frazer, James W. *A History of Hope*. New York: Palgrave Macmillan, 2003.

Freire, Paulo. *Pedagogy of the Oppressed*. New York: Seabury, 1973.

———, and Ira Shor. *A Pedagogy for Liberation: Dialogues on Transforming Education.* Westport, CT: Bergin & Garvey/Greenwood Press, 1987.

Friedlander, Myrna, et al. "Sustaining Engagement: A Change Event in Family Therapy." *Journal of Counseling Psychology* 41, no. 4 (1994): 438–448.

Fuller, John. *Motivation: A Biological Perspective.* New York: Random House, 1962.

Galanter, Marc. *Cults: Faith, Healing, and Coercion.* New York: Oxford University Press, 1989.

Gamson, Zelda. "Collaborative Learning Comes of Age." *Change* 26, no. 5 (1994): 44–49.

Gardner, Howard. *Multiple Intelligences.* New York: Basic Books, 1993.

Garrison, James. *Dewey and Eros.* New York: Teachers College Press, 1997.

Gatto, John Taylor. "Against School: How Public Education Cripples Our Kids, and Why." *Harper's Magazine,* September 2003, 33–38.

Gendlin, Eugene T. *Focusing.* New York: Bantam, 1981.

Gergen, Kenneth J. *The Saturated Self.* New York: Basic Books, 1991.

Giroux, Henry. *Schooling and the Struggle for Public Life: Critical Pedagogy in the Modern Age.* Minneapolis: University of Minnesota Press, 1988.

Goffman, Erving. *The Presentation of Self in Everyday Life.* Garden City, NY: Doubleday Anchor, 1959.

Grant, Gerald. *The World We Created at Hamilton High.* Cambridge, MA: Harvard University Press, 1988.

———, and David Riesman. *The Perpetual Dream.* Chicago: University of Chicago Press, 1977.

Greene, Maxine, ed. *Existential Encounters for Teachers.* New York: Random House, 1967.

———. *Teacher as Stranger.* Belmont, CA: Wadsworth Publishing, 1973.

———. *Landscapes of Learning.* New York: Teachers College Press, 1978.

———. *The Dialectic of Freedom.* New York: Teachers College Press, 1988.

———. *Releasing the Imagination.* San Francisco: Jossey-Bass, 1995.

———. "What Counts as a Philosophy of Education." In *Critical Conversations in Philosophy of Education.* Edited by Wendy Kohli. New York: Routledge, 1995.

———. "Revisioning John Dewey." Lecture at the University of Vermont, 20 October 1997.

Guignon, Charles, and Dirk Pereboom, eds. *Existentialism: Basic Writings.* Indianapolis, IN: Hackett Publishing, 1995.

Guskin, Alan. "Reducing Student Costs and Enhancing Student Learning." *Change* 26, no. 4 (1994): 23–29.

———. "Restructuring the Role of Faculty." *Change* 26, no. 5 (1994): 16–25.

———. "Facing the Future: The Change Process in Restructuring Universities." *Change* 28, no. 4 (1996): 27–37.

————. *Notes for a Pragmatic Idealist.* Yellow Springs, OH: Antioch University, 1997.

Gutmann, David. "The Subjective Politics of Power: The Dilemma of Post-superego Man." *Social Research* 40, no. 4 (1973): 570–616.

Habermas, Jurgen. *Legitimation Crisis.* Boston: Beacon Press, 1973.

Hallowell, Edward M., and John Ratey. *Driven to Distraction.* New York: Touchstone, 1994.

Hamlin, Wilfred, ed. *Progressive Education for the Nineties and Beyond.* Plainfield, VT: Goddard College, 1993.

Hammond, Phillip E., and David W. Machacek. *Soka Gakkai in America: Accommodation and Conversion.* New York: Oxford University Press, 1999.

Hanh, Thich Nhat. *The Miracle of Mindfulness.* Boston: Beacon Press, 1987.

Harward, Brian, and Louis Albert. "Service and Service-learning: A Guide for Newcomers." *AAHE Bulletin* 46, no. 6 (1994): 10–12.

Hassan, Nasra. "Letter from Gaza: An Arsenal of Believers." *The New Yorker* (19 November 2001): 36–41.

Heidegger, Martin. *What Is Called Thinking?* New York: Harper & Row, 1968.

Heider, Fritz. *The Psychology of Interpersonal Relations.* New York: Wiley and Sons, 1958.

Hlebowitsh, Peter S. *Radical Curriculum Theory Reconsidered: A Historical Approach.* New York: Teachers College Press, 1993.

Hobson, J. Allan. *The Chemistry of Conscious States.* Boston: Little, Brown & Company, 1994.

Hoffer, Eric. *The True Believer.* New York: Harper and Row, 1951.

Hofstatder, Richard. *Anti-intellectualism in American Life.* New York: Knopf, 1963.

Horton, John. "The Dehumanization of Anomie and Alienation: A Problem in the Ideology of Sociology." *British Journal of Sociology* 15 (1964): 283–300.

Hotaling, Dan, and Dorothy Scott. *An Antioch Career.* Yellow Springs, OH: Antioch University, 1995.

Howley, Craig and Robert Bickel. "Research about School Size and School Performance in Impoverished Communities." In *ERIC Digest,* December 2000, ERIC, ED 448968.

Ignatieff, Michael. *The Needs of Strangers.* New York: Viking Penguin, 1985.

Illich, Ivan. *Deschooling Society.* New York: Harper & Row, 1971.

Israel, Joachim. *Alienation from Marx to Current Sociology.* Boston: Allyn and Bacon, 1971.

Jacoby, Russell. *The Last Intellectuals: American Culture in the Age of Academe.* New York: Basic Books, 1987.

James, William. *The Varieties of Religious Experience.* New York: Modern Library, 1958. (Original published 1902.)

————. *Principles of Psychology, Vol. 1.* Excerpted in David Bakan, *Attention.* Princeton: D. Van Nostrand, 1966, 3–22.

Janis, Irving L. *Victims of Groupthink.* Boston: Houghton Mifflin, 1972.

Jarvis, Peter. *Paradoxes of Learning.* San Francisco: Jossey-Bass, 1992.

Jay, Ricky. *Learned Pigs & Fireproof Women.* New York: Farrar, Straus & Giroux, 1998.

Jervis, Kathe, and Carol Montag, eds. *Progressive Education for the 1990s.* New York: Teachers College Press, 1991.

Johnson, David W., Roger T. Johnson, and Karl Smith. *Cooperative Learning.* Washington, DC: School of Education and Human Development, George Washington University, 1991.

Johnson, Steve. "Rocky Mountain High." *BMW ON Magazine* (February 1998).

Judt, Tony. "On 'The Plague.'" *The New York Review,* 29 November 2001, 6–9.

Juvonen, Jaana, and Kathryn R. Wentzel. *Social Motivation.* New York: Cambridge University Press, 1996.

Kabat-Zinn, Jon. *Wherever You Go There You Are: Mindfulness Meditation in Everyday Life.* New York: Hyperion, 1994.

Kahn, William A. "The Psychological Condition of Personal Engagement and Disengagement at Work." *Academy of Management Journal* 33, no. 4 (1990): 692–724.

————. "To Be Fully There: Psychological Presence at Work." *Human Relations* 45, no. 4 (1992): 321–345.

Kandel, Eric R., James Schwartz, and Thomas Jessell, eds. *Essentials of Neural Science and Behavior.* Norwalk, CT: Appleton & Lange, 1995.

————, James Schwartz, and Thomas Jessell, eds. *Principles of Neural Science.* 4th ed. New York: McGraw-Hill, 2000.

Kaplan, David E., and Andrew Marshall. *The Cult at the End of the World.* New York: Crown Publishers, 1996.

Katz, Jack. *Seductions of Crime: Moral and Sensual Attractions in Doing Evil.* New York: Basic Books, 1988.

Kaufmann, Walter. *Existentialism from Dostoevsky to Sartre.* New York: Meridian Books, 1957.

————. *Basic Writings of Nietzsche.* New York: Penguin Books, 1982.

Kegan, Robert. *The Evolving Self.* Cambridge: Harvard University Press, 1982.

————. *In Over Our Heads.* Cambridge: Harvard University Press, 1994.

Kemp, Peter. *Théorie de L'engagement—Pathetique de L'engagement* [Theory of Engagement—Feeling of Engagement]. Paris: Seuil, 1973.

Khantzian, Edward J. *Addiction and the Vulnerable Self.* New York: Guilford Press, 1990.

Kincheloe, Joe L., and Shirley R. Steinberg. *Unauthorized Methods: Strategies for Critical Thinking.* New York: Routledge, 1998.

Knabb, Ken, ed. *Situationist International Anthology.* Berkeley, CA: Bureau of Public Secrets, P.O. Box 1044, 1981.

Knowles, Malcom. *Self-directed Learning.* Chicago: Follett, 1975.

Kofman, Fred, and Peter Senge, "Communities of Commitment." In *Learning Organizations.* Edited by Sarita Chawla and John Renesch. Portland: Productivity Press, 1995.

Kohli, Wendy, ed. *Critical Conversations in the Philosophy of Education.* New York: Routledge, Chapman, & Hall, 1995.

————. "Philosopher of/for Freedom." In *A Light in Dark Times: Maxine Greene and the Unfinished Conversation.* Edited by William Ayers and Janet L. Miller. New York: Teachers College Press, 1998.

Kohn, Alfie. *Punished By Rewards.* Boston: Houghton Mifflin, 1993.

Kolakowski, Leszek. *Modernity on Endless Trial.* Chicago: University of Chicago Press, 1990.

Kolb, David. *Experiential Learning.* Englewood Cliffs, NJ: Prentice-Hall, 1984.

Krakauer, Jon. *Eiger Dreams: Ventures Among Men and Mountains.* New York: Anchor Books, 1990.

————. *Into Thin Air.* New York: Villard, 1997.

Kramer, Peter D. *Moments of Engagement: Intimate Psychotherapy in a Technological Age.* New York: W. W. Norton, 1989.

————. *Listening to Prozac.* New York: Penguin, 1993.

Krauss, Clifford. "Undercover Police Ride Wide Range of Emotion." *The New York Times,* 29 August 1994, B3.

Krohn, Claus-Dieter. *Intellectuals in Exile.* Trans. Rita and Robert Kimber. Amherst, MA: The University of Massachusetts Press, 1993.

Kuh, George D., and Elizabeth J. Whitt. *The Invisible Tapestry: Culture in American Colleges and Universities.* ASHE-ERIC Higher Education Report No. 1, Washington, DC: Association for the Study of Higher Education, 1988.

Kuh, George D. et al. *Involving Colleges: Successful Approaches to Fostering Student Learning and Development Outside the Classroom.* San Francisco: Jossey-Bass, 1991.

Kytle, Jackson. "The Power and Problematics of Experience-based Curriculum Methods." In *Roads to the Learning Society.* Edited by Lois Lamdin. Chicago: CAEL Publications, 1991.

————. "An Education Up Close and Personal." In *Progressive Education for the Nineties and Beyond.* Edited by Wilfred Hamlin. Plainfield, VT: Goddard College, 1993.

————. "On Constructing an Engaged Life." In *Spirituality, Ethics and Relationship in Adulthood: Clinical and Theoretical Explorations.* Edited by Melvin Miller and Alan West. Madison, WI: Psychosocial Press, 2000.

LaBerge, David. *Attentional Processing: The Brain's Art of Mindfulness.* Cambridge, MA: Harvard University Press, 1995.

Lambert, Nadine M., and Barbara L. McCombs, eds. *How Students Learn: Reforming Schools through Learner-Centered Education.* Washington: American Psychological Association, 1998.

Langer, Ellen J. *Mindfulness.* Reading, PA: Addison-Wesley, 1998.

————. *The Power of Mindful Learning.* Reading, PA: Addison-Wesley, 1997.

Lapham, Lewis. "Notebook: School Bells." *Harper's Magazine* (August 2000): 7–9.

Lasch, Christopher. *The Culture of Narcissism.* New York: Norton, 1979.

Leistnyna, Pepi, Arlie Woodrum, and Stephen Sherblom. *Breaking Free: The Transformative Power of Critical Pedagogy.* Cambridge, MA: Harvard Educational Review, 1996.

Levine, Arthur, and Jeanette S. Cureton. *When Hope and Fear Collide: A Portrait of Today's College Student.* San Francisco: Jossey-Bass, 1998.

Lewin, Kurt. *Field Theory in the Social Sciences.* New York: Harper & Row, 1951.

Lieberman, Ann, ed. *The Work of Restructuring Schools.* New York: Teachers College Press, 1995.

Lifton, Robert J. *Thought Reform and the Psychology of Totalism.* Chapel Hill, NC: University of North Carolina Press, 1989.

Limon, John. *Stand-up Comedy in Theory, or Abjection in America.* Durham, NC: Duke University Press, 2000.

Love, Patrick. G., and Ann G. Love. *Enhancing Student Learning.* ASHE-ERIC Higher Education Report No. 4., Washington, DC: The George Washington University, Graduate School of Education and Human Development, 1995.

Luke, Carmen, Suzanne de Castell, and Allan Luke. "Beyond Criticism: The Authority of the School Text." *Curriculum Inquiry* 13, no. 2 (1983): 111–127.

Lyng, Stephen. "Edgework: A Social Psychological Analysis of Voluntary Risk-Taking." *American Journal of Sociology* 95, no. 4 (1990): 85–86.

MacGregor, Jean, James L. Cooper, and Karl A. Smith, eds. *Strategies for Energizing Large Classes: From Small Groups to Learning Communities.* San Francisco: Jossey-Bass, 2000.

MacGregor, Jean, ed. *Student Self-evaluation: Fostering Reflective Learning.* San Francisco: Jossey-Bass, 2000.

Marchese, Theodore J. "The New Conversations about Learning: Insights from Neuroscience and Anthropology, Cognitive Science and Work-Place Studies." In *Assessing Impact: Evidence and Action.* Washington, DC: American Association for Higher Education, 1997.

Margalit, Avishai. "The Suicide Bombers." *The New York Review* 50, no. 1 (16 January 2003): 36–39.

Maslow, Abraham. "Deficiency Motivation and Growth Motivation." *Nebraska Symposium on Motivation* 3 (1955): 1–30.

————. *Toward a Psychology of Being.* New York: Van Nostrand Reinhold Company, 1968.

————. *Motivation and Personality.* New York: HarperCollins, 1970.

————. *Religions, Values, and Peak Experiences.* New York: Penguin Books, 1977.

————. *Motivation and Personality.* 3rd ed. Edited by Robert Frager and James Fadiman. New York: Harper & Row, 1987.

———. *The Farther Reaches of Human Nature*. New York: Penguin Arkana, 1993. (Original work published 1971.)

McLaughlin, Barry, ed. *Studies in Social Movements*. New York: Free Press, 1969.

Meier, Deborah. *The Power of Their Ideas*. Boston: Beacon Press, 1995.

———. "Educating a Democracy: Standards and the Future of Public Education." 2002. Available at http://www.bostonreview.mit.edu/BR24.6/. Originally published in the February/March 2000 issue of *Boston Review*.

———. *In Schools We Trust: Creating Communities of Learning in an Era of Testing and Standardization*. Boston: Beacon Press, 2002.

Menand, Louis. *The Metaphysical Club*. New York: Farrar, Straus & Giroux, 2001.

Mentkowski, Marcia, et al. *Learning That Lasts*. San Francisco: Jossey-Bass, 1999.

Merton, Robert K. "The Unanticipated Consequences of Purposive Social Action." *American Sociological Review* 1, (1936): 894–904.

———. "Anomie, Anomia, and Social Interaction: Contexts of Deviant Behavior." In *Anomie and Deviant Behavior*. Edited by Marshall Clinard. New York: Free Press, 1964.

Mezirow, Jack. "A Critical Theory of Self-directed Learning." In *Self-directed Learning: From Theory to Practice*. Edited by Stephen Brookfield. San Francisco: Jossey-Bass, 1985.

Miller, Jack. *Education and the Soul*. Albany, NY: SUNY Press, 2000.

Miller, Melvin E. "World Views, Ego Development, and Epistemological Changes from the Conventional to the Postformal: A Longitudinal Perspective." In *Transcendence and Mature Thought in Adulthood*. Edited by Melvin E. Miller and Susanne R. Cook-Greuter. Lanham, MD: Rowman & Littlefield, 1994.

Milner, Peter. *Physiological Psychology*. New York: Holt, Rinehart and Winston, 1970.

Minnich, Elizabeth. *Transforming Knowledge*. Philadelphia: Temple University Press, 1990.

Mook, Douglas G. *Motivation*. New York: W.W. Norton & Company, 1987.

Moore, Thomas. *The Re-enchantment of Everyday Life*. New York: HarperCollins, 1996.

Munro, Donald, John F. Schumaker, and Stuart Carr, eds. *Motivation and Culture*. New York: Routledge, 1997.

Natanson, Maurice, ed. *The Problem of Social Reality, Collected Papers I*. The Hague: Martinus Nijhoff, 1967.

Newton, Friedrich. "The Stressed Student." *About Campus* 3, no. 2 (1998): 4–10.

Nietzsche, Friedrich. *On the Genealogy of Morals and Ecce Homo*. Translated by Walter Kaufmann and R. J. Hollingdale. Edited by Walter Kaufmann. New York: Vintage, 1967.

———. *The Gay Science*. New York: Vintage Books, 1974. (Original work published 1887.)

———. "Thus Spake Zarathrustra." In *The Portable Nietzsche*. Edited by Walter Kaufmann. New York: Penguin Books, 1982. (Original work published 1892.)

———. *Human, All Too Human*. Cambridge: Cambridge University Press, 1986. (Original work published 1878.)

Nisbet, Robert. *The Social Philosophers*. New York: Thomas Y. Crowell Company, 1973.

Noddings, Nel. *The Challenge to Care in Schools*. New York: Teachers College Press, 1982.

———. *Caring: a Feminist Approach to Ethics and Moral Education*. Berkeley, CA: University of California Press, 1984.

Norman, Donald. *Things That Make Us Smart*. Reading, PA: Addison-Wesley, 1993.

Nussbaum, Martha. *Upheavals of Thought: The Intelligence of Emotions*. New York: Cambridge University Press, 2001.

Ollman, Bertell. *Alienation*. 2d. ed. New York: Cambridge University Press, 1976.

Orne, Martin. "On the Social Psychology of the Psychological Experiment: With Particular Reference to Demand Characteristics and Their Implications." *American Psychologist* 17 (1962): 776–783.

Ornstein, Richard. *The Right Mind*. New York: Harcourt Brace & Co., 1997.

Osherow, Neil. "Making Sense of the Nonsensical: An Analysis of Jonestown." In *Readings about the Social Animal*. Edited by Eliot Aronson. New York: W. H. Freeman and Co., 1992.

O'Sullivan, Edmund V. *Transformative Learning: Building Educational Vision for the 21st Century*. London: Zed Press, 1999.

———, Amish Morrell, and Mary Ann O'Connor, eds. *Expanding the Boundaries of Transformative Learning*. New York: Palgrave Macmillan, 2002.

———, and Marilyn Taylor. *Learning Toward and Ecological Consciousness*. New York: Palgrave Macmillan, 2003.

Otto, Rudolf. *The Idea of the Holy*. Chicago: University of Chicago Press, 1958.

Palmer, Parker. *To Know as We Are Known: A Spirituality of Education*. San Francisco: Harper, 1983.

———. "Community, Conflict and Ways of Knowing." *Change* 19, no. 5 (1987): 20–25.

———. *The Active life: A Spirituality of Work, Creativity, and Caring*. San Francisco: Harper, 1992.

———. "The Heart of a Teacher: Identity and Integrity in Teaching. *Change* 29, no. 6 (1997): 14–22.

———. *The Courage to Teach*. San Francisco: Jossey-Bass, 1998.

Paris, Scott G., and Richard S. Newman. "Developmental Aspects of Self-regulated Learning." *Educational Psychologist* 25, no. 1 (1990): 87–102.

Pascal, Blaise. *Thoughts*. Translated by W. F. Trotter. New York: P. F. Collier & Son Company, 1910.

Pascarella, Ernest T., and Patrick T. Terenzini. *How College Affects Students: Findings and Insights from Twenty Years of Research.* San Francisco: Jossey-Bass, 1991.

Pert, Candace B. *Molecules of Emotion.* New York: Scribner, 1997.

Piet, Susanne. "What Motivates Stunt Men?" *Motivation and Emotion* 11, no. 2 (1987): 195–213.

Pinker, Stephen. *How the Mind Works.* New York: W.W. Norton, 1997.

Postman, Neil. *Teaching as a Subversive Activity.* New York: Delacorte Press, 1969.

———. *Amusing Ourselves to Death: Public Discourse in the Age of Show Business.* New York: Penguin, 1985.

Putnam, Robert D. *Bowling Alone: The Collapse and Revival of American Community.* New York: Simon & Schuster, 2000.

Rappaport, Richard L. *Motivating Clients in Therapy.* New York: Routledge, 1997.

Rhoads, Robert A., and Howard, Jeffrey P., eds. *Academic Service Learning: A Pedagogy of Action and Reflection.* San Francisco: Jossey-Bass, 1997.

Rockefeller, Stephen. *John Dewey: Religious Faith and Democratic Humanism.* New York: Columbia University Press, 1991.

Rogers, Carl. *Freedom to Learn for the '80s.* Columbus, OH: Charles E. Merrill Publishing Co., 1983.

Rosenthal, David M. *The Nature of Mind.* New York: Oxford University Press, 1991.

Ross, Lee. "The Intuitive Psychologist and His Shortcomings." In *Advances in Experimental Social Psychology.* Vol. 10. Edited by Leonard Berkowitz. New York: Academic Press, 1977.

Rorty, Richard. *Philosophy and the Mirror of Nature.* Princeton, NJ: Princeton University Press, 1979.

———. *Contingency, Irony, and Solidarity.* New York: Cambridge University Press, 1989.

———. "Method, Social Science, and Social Hope." In *The Postmodern Turn.* Edited by Stephen Seidman. New York: Cambridge University Press, 1994.

———. *Achieving Our Country.* Cambridge, MA: Harvard University Press, 1998.

Rotter, Julian. "Internal Versus External Control of Reinforcement: A Case History of a Variable." *American Psychologist* 45, no. 4 (1990): 489–493.

Rutkoff, Peter, and William Scott. *New School: A History of the New School for Social Research.* New York: The Free Press, 1986.

Ryan, Alan. "Wise Man." *New York Review,* 17 December 1998, 29–37.

Sarason, Seymour. *Revisiting "The Culture of the School and the Problem of Change."* New York: Teachers College Press, 1996.

Sartre, Jean-Paul. *Being and Nothingness.* New York: Gramercy Books, 1994. (Original work published 1956.)

Schacht, Richard. *The Future of Alienation.* Urbana, IL: University of Illinois Press, 1994.

Schachter, Stanley. "The Interaction of Cognitive and Physiological Determinants of Emotional States." In *Advances in Experimental Social Psychology*. Vol. 1. Edited by Leonard Berkowitz. New York: Academic Press, 1964.

Schanck, Richard L. "Study of a Community and Its Groups and Institutions Conceived of as Behaviors of Individuals." *Psychological Monographs* 43, no. 2 (1932): 195.

Schank, Roger C., and Chip Cleary. *Engines for Education*. Hillsdale, NJ: Lawrence Erlbaum Associates, 1995.

Schechner, Richard. *Performance Theory*. London: Routledge, 1994.

Schmookler, Andrew. *Fool's Gold: The Fate of Values in a World of Goods*. New York: HarperSanFrancisco, 1993.

Schön, Donald. *The Reflective Practitioner*. New York: Basic Books, 1983.

Schutz, Alfred. *The Phenomenology of the Social World*. Evanston, IL: Northwestern University Press, 1967.

———. *On Phenomenology and Social Relations*. Edited by Helmut Wagner. Chicago: University of Chicago Press, 1970.

———, and Thomas Luckmann. *The Structures of the Lifeworld*. Evanston, IL: Northwestern University Press, 1973.

Searle, John. *The Mystery of Consciousness*. New York: New York Review Book, 1997.

Seeman, Melvin. "Alienation and Engagement." In *The Human Meaning of Social Change*. Edited by Angus Campbell and Philip Converse. New York: Russell Sage, 1972.

Selltiz, Claire, Lawrence S. Wrightsman, and Stuart W. Cook. *Research Methods in Social Relations*. 3rd ed. New York: Holt, Rinehart and Winston, 1976.

Senge, Peter. *The Fifth Discipline: The Art and Practice of the Learning Organization*. New York: Doubleday/Currency, 1990.

Singer, Margaret et al. *Report of the APA Task Force on Deceptive and Indirect Techniques of Persuasion and Control*, 1986. Available at http://www.rickross.com/reference/apologist/apologist23.html.

Sizer, Theodore. *Horace's Compromise*. Boston: Houghton Mifflin, 1984.

———. *Horace's School*. Boston: Houghton Mifflin, 1992.

———. *Horace's Hope: What Works for the American High School*. Boston: Houghton Mifflin, 1996.

Skinner, Ellen A. *Perceived Control, Motivation and Coping*. Thousand Oaks, CA: Sage Publications. 1995.

Smith, Frank. *To Think*. New York: Teachers College Press, 1990.

———. *The Book of Learning and Forgetting*. New York: Teachers College Press, 1998.

Solomon, Robert, ed. *Existentialism*. New York: Modern Library, 1974.

———. *No Excuses: Existentialism and the Meaning of Life*. Springfield, VA: The Teaching Company, 1995 (recorded audio tapes). Available at: http://www.teachco.com.

Srole, Leo. "Social Integration and Certain Corollaries: An Exploratory Study." *American Sociological Review* 21 (1956): 709–716.

Sutherland, Tracey E., and Charles B. Bonwell, eds. *Using Active Learning in College Classes: A Range of Options for Faculty*. San Francisco: Jossey-Bass, 2000.

Taylor, Charles. *The Ethics of Authenticity*. Cambridge, MA: Harvard University Press, 1991.

Teitelbaum, Kenneth. *Schooling for "Good Rebels."* New York: Teachers College Press, 1995.

Tharp, Roland, and Ronald Gallimore. *Rousing Minds to Life*. New York: Cambridge University Press, 1988.

Theall, Michael, ed. *Motivation from Within: Approaches for Encouraging Faculty and Students to Excel*. San Francisco: Jossey-Bass, 2000.

Thody, Philip, ed. *Albert Camus: Lyrical and Critical Essays*. New York: Vintage Books, 1970.

Traub, James. "Sizer's Hope." *New York Times Education Life Supplement*, 2 August 1998, 26.

Tremmel, Robert. "Zen and the Art of Reflective Practice in Teacher Education." *Harvard Educational Review* 63, no. 4 (1993): 434–458.

Underhill, Paco. *Why We Buy: The Science of Shopping*. New York: Simon & Schuster, 1999.

Ungerleider, Steven. *Mental Training for Peak Performance*. Emmaus, PA: Rodale Press, 1996.

van Deurzen-Smith, Emmy. *Existential Counseling in Practice*. London: Sage Publications, 1988.

Wachtel, Paul L. *The Poverty of Affluence*. New York: Free Press, 1983.

Wacker, Grant. *Heaven Below*. Cambridge, MA: Harvard University Press, 2003.

Walsh, Roger. "Phenomenological Mapping: A Method for Describing and Comparing States of Consciousness." *Journal of Transpersonal Psychology* 27, no. 1 (1995): 25–56.

Wane, Njoki, "African Women and Spirituality." In *Expanding the Boundaries of Transformative Learning*. Edited by Edmund O'Sullivan, Amish Morrell, and Mary O'Connor. New York: Palgrave Macmillan, 2002.

Watson, Justin. *The Martyrs of Columbine*. New York: Palgrave Macmillan, 2002.

Weber, Max. *The Protestant Ethic and the Spirit of Capitalism*. New York: Charles Scribner's Sons, 1958.

Westbrook, Robert B. *John Dewey and American Democracy*. Ithaca, NY: Cornell University Press, 1991.

White, Robert W. "Competence and the Psychosexual Stages of Development." *Nebraska Symposium on Motivation*. Lincoln, NB: University of Nebraska Press, 1960.

Whitehead, Alfred N. *The Aims of Education and Other Essays*. New York: Macmillan, 1959.

———. *Modes of Thought*. New York: Free Press, 1968. (Original work published 1938.)

Wiggins, G. *Educative Assessment: Designing Assessments to Inform and Improve Student Performance*. San Francisco: Jossey-Bass, 1998.

Wilkerson, Luann, and Wim H. Gijselaers, eds. *Bringing Problem-based Learning to Higher Education: Theory and Practice.* San Francisco: Jossey-Bass, 2000.

Witkin, Herman A., and Philip K. Oltman. "Cognitive Style." *International Journal of Neurology* 6, (1967): 119–137.

Wlodkowski, Raymond J. *Enhancing Adult Motivation to Learn.* San Francisco: Jossey-Bass, 1988.

———, and Margery B. Ginsberg. *Diversity and Motivation: Culturally Responsive Teaching.* San Francisco: Jossey-Bass, 1995.

Woolf, Virginia. *Three Guineas.* New York: Harcourt Brace, 1938.

Wooten, Jim. "The Conciliator." *The New York Times Magazine,* 29 January 1995, 28–54.

Zablocki, Benjamin, and Thomas Robbins. *Misunderstanding Cults.* Toronto, CN: University of Toronto Press, 2001.

Zimbardo, Philip, and Michael Leippe. *The Psychology of Attitude Change and Influence.* New York: McGraw-Hill, 1991.

Zuckerman, Marvin. *Sensation Seeking: Beyond the Optimal Level of Arousal.* Hillsdale, NJ: Lawrence Erlbaum, 1979.

Index

230 *Index*